EDITING THE BIBLE

Society of Biblical Literature

Resources for Biblical Study

Susan Ackerman, Hebrew Bible/Old Testament Editor
Tom Thatcher, New Testament Editor

Number 69

EDITING THE BIBLE

Assessing the Task Past and Present

EDITING THE BIBLE

ASSESSING THE TASK PAST AND PRESENT

Edited by
John S. Kloppenborg
and
Judith H. Newman

Society of Biblical Literature
Atlanta

EDITING THE BIBLE
Assessing the Task Past and Present

Library of Congress Cataloging-in-Publication Data

Editing the Bible : assessing the task past and present / edited by John S. Kloppenborg
and Judith H. Newman.
      p. cm. — (Society of Biblical Literature resources for biblical study ; no. 69)
    Includes bibliographical references and index.
    ISBN 978-1-58983-648-8 (paper binding : alk. paper) — ISBN 978-1-58983-649-5
    (electronic format)
    1. Bible—Criticism, Redaction—History. 2. Bible—Criticism, interpretation, etc.—
History. I. Kloppenborg, John S., 1951–. II. Newman, Judith H. (Judith Hood), 1961–.
III. Title.
    BS500.E35 2012
    220.6'6—dc23   2012006318

Contents

Acknowledgements vii

Abbreviations ix

Editing the Bible: Assessing the Task Past and Present
John S. Kloppenborg and Judith H. Newman 1

The Genealogy of the Biblical Editor
John Van Seters 9

The Evolutionary Composition of the Hebrew Bible
Eugene Ulrich 23

Editing the Hebrew Bible: An Overview of Some Problems
Eibert Tigchelaar 41

Evidence from the Qumran Scrolls for the Scribal Transmission
of Leviticus
Sarianna Metso 67

Greek Papyri and the Texts of the Hebrew Bible
Kristin De Troyer 81

What Text Is Being Edited? The Editing of the New Testament
Michael W. Holmes 91

The Coherence-Based Genealogical Method: A New Way to
Reconstruct the Text of the Greek New Testament
Klaus Wachtel 123

Scribal Practices and the Transmission of Biblical Texts: New
    Insights from the Coherence-Based Genealogical Method
    Holger Strutwolf 139

The New Testament in the Light of Book Publishing in Antiquity
    David Trobisch 161

Unseen Variants: Conjectural Emendation and the New Testament
    Ryan Wettlaufer 171

Bibliography 195

Contributors 213

Index of Primary Sources 215

Index of Modern Authors 221

Acknowledgements

Most of the essays in this volume had their start in Toronto at the forty-third Conference on Editorial Problems, a longstanding colloquium held yearly at the University of Toronto to discuss problems associated with the editing of numerous corpora of literature, ancient and modern. Perhaps surprisingly, the 2007 conference, organized and convened by John Kloppenborg, was the first to focus on the Bible, which may be the most edited of any set of books. Moreover, the conference offered what to our knowledge was a rare opportunity for text-critical scholars addressing both the Hebrew Bible and the New Testament to discuss jointly issues in their respective corpora. The confluence allows scholars to assess both the similarities and the marked differences involved in these two parts of the Bible. The volume thus gathers together a unique collection of essays that illuminate issues related to critical editions of the Hebrew Bible, Septuagint, and New Testament. We are grateful to Fred Unwalla, Director of CEP, for his initial invitation to organize the conference and for his gracious support throughout. We thank the University of St. Michael's College for hosting the conference, the Department for the Study of Religion for financial and logistical support, and many graduate students from the Department and Emmanuel College for assisting in various ways. The editors would also like to express special gratitude to the Social Sciences and Humanities Research Council of Canada, which provided generous financial support both for the conference and for the editorial and production work connected with this volume. Three of the papers offered at the conference, by Peter Head, Robert Kraft, and Hindy Najman, are not included here. Robert Kraft's illustrated presentation can be found online at http://ccat.sas.upenn.edu/rak//temp/toronto3/report-frame.html.

We are honored that the volume is included in the SBL's Resources for Biblical Study series. We are grateful to its editors, Susan Ackerman and Tom Thatcher, for accepting the volume in the series and for their valuable suggestions for improving its contents. Thanks are due as well to the excellent SBL professionals responsible for overseeing the production and marketing of this volume: Leigh Andersen, Bob Buller, Billie Jean Collins, and Kathie Klein. Last but not least, we would like to thank our dedicated graduate students who ably assisted in crucial tasks of formatting, proofreading, and indexing: Sherry Coman, Lelia Fry, Gabriel Holt, David Kaden, Nathalie LaCoste, Carmen Palmer, and Ryan Stoner.

Abbreviations

AB	Anchor Bible
ABD	*Anchor Bible Dictionary.* Edited by David Noel Freedman. 6 vols. New York: Doubleday, 1992.
ANTF	Arbeiten zur neutestamentlichen Textforschung
ASOR	American Schools of Oriental Research
ATD	Das Alte Testament Deutsch
BASOR	*Bulletin of the American Schools of Oriental Research*
BHK	*Biblia Hebraica.* Edited by Rudolf Kittel.
BHQ	*Biblia Hebraica Quinta*
BHS	*Biblica Hebraica Stuttgartensia.* Edited by Karl Elliger and Wilhelm Rudolph.
BHT	Beträge zur historichen Theologie
Bib	*Biblica*
BIOSCS	*Bulletin of the International Organization for Septuagint and Cognate Studies*
BWANT	Beiträge zur Wissenschaft vom Alten (und Neuen) Testament
CBET	Contributions to Biblical Exegesis and Theology
CBGM	Coherence-Based Genealogical Method
CBQ	*Catholic Biblical Quarterly*
CJA	Christianity and Judaism in Antiquity
CSCO	Corpus scriptorum christianorum orientalium
DJD	Discoveries in the Judaean Desert
DSD	*Dead Sea Discoveries*
ECM	*Editio Critica Maior*
ExpTim	*Expository Times*
GRM	Graeco-Roman Memoirs
HB	Hebrew Bible
HG	Harclensis Group
HSM	Harvard Semitic Monographs

HTB	Histoire du texte biblique
HTCNT	Herders theological commentary on the New Testament
HTKNT	Herders theologischer Kommentar zum Neuen Testament
HTR	*Harvard Theological Review*
HUB	*Hebrew University Bible*
HUBP	Hebrew University Bible Project
IGNTP	The International Greek New Testament Project
INTF	Institut für Neutestamentliche Textforshung
JBL	*Journal of Biblical Literature*
JSJ	*Journal for the Study of Judaism in the Persian, Hellenistic, and Roman Periods*
JSNT	*Journal for the Study of the New Testament*
JSNTSup	Journal for the Study of the New Testament Supplement Series
JSPSup	Journal for the Study of the Pseudepigrapha Supplement Series
JTS	*Journal of Theological Studies*
LCL	Loeb Classical Library
LDAB	Leuven Database of Ancient Books
LXX	Septuagint
MBE	*Monumenta biblica et ecclesiastica*
MSU	Mitteilungen des Septuaginta-Unternehmens
MT	Masoretic Text
NA	*Novum Testamentum Graece.* Edited by Eberhard Nestle and Kurt Aland.
NIGTC	New International Greek Testament Commentary
NovT	*Novum Testamentum*
NovTSup	Supplements to Novum Testamentum
NRSV	New Revised Standard Version
NT	New Testament
NTS	*New Testament Studies*
NTTS	New Testament Tools and Studies
NTTSD	New Testament Tools, Studies and Documents
OBO	Orbis biblicus et orientalis
OG	Old Greek
OHB	*Oxford Hebrew Bible*
OL	Old Latin
OTL	Old Testament Library
OtSt	Oudtestamentische Studiën

RB	*Revue biblique*
RevQ	*Revue de Qumran*
SBLRBS	Society of Biblical Literature Resources for Biblical Study
SCS	Septuagint and Cognate Studies
SD	Studies and Documents
SJT	*Scottish Journal of Theology*
SNTS	Society for New Testament Studies
SNTSMS	Society for New Testament Studies Monograph Series
SP	Samaritan Pentateuch
SSEJC	Studies in Early Judaism and Christianity
STDJ	Studies on the Texts of the Desert of Judah
TCHB	*Textual Criticism of the Hebrew Bible.* Emanuel Tov. 2nd ed. Minneapolis: Fortress, 2001. 3rd ed. 2011.
TENT	Texts and Editions for New Testament Study
Text	*Textus*
TSAJ	Texte und Studien zum antiken Judentum
UBS	*The Greek New Testament,* United Bible Societies, 4th ed.
VC	*Vigiliae christianae*
VT	*Vetus Testamentum*
VTSup	Vetus Testamentum Supplements
WBC	Word Biblical Commentary
WUNT	Wissenschaftliche Untersuchungen zum Neuen Testament
ZAH	*Zeitschrift für Althebräistik*
ZAW	*Zeitschrift für die alttestamentliche Wissenschaft*
ZNW	*Zeitschrift für die neutestamentliche Wissenschaft und die Kunde der älteren Kirche*

Editing the Bible:
Assessing the Task Past and Present

John S. Kloppenborg and Judith H. Newman

1. Introduction

The Bible may be the most edited document of Western civilization, or even of world literature. The famous New Testament editions of Cardinal Ximines in 1512 and Erasmus in 1516 were only among the most prominent—due to the invention of movable type—in a much longer process of copyists making what we might think of as editorial, or even authorial, decisions as they decided how to render their exemplars. The singular term *Bible* belies the complex nature of this compilation and masks the complicated processes by which it took shape. During the span of more than two and a half millennia in which the Bible has come into being, the cultural contexts for producing and copying those texts have changed dramatically. We move from a period of low literacy with a limited number of scribes serving as textual tradents to the current era of widespread access not only to education but to digital media and hypertext biblical editions. While we are familiar with the contemporary context for editing the Bible in the computer age, the historical reconstruction of scribal activities in antiquity continues to come into focus. In addition to the purely technical aspects of producing a critical edition of the Bible, understanding the theoretical dimension of editing biblical texts requires disciplined scholarly imagination, involving many implicit and explicit presuppositions.

Today the Hebrew Bible and the New Testament present distinctively different sets of problems for the editor. This volume offers a collection of essays that treat some of the major editorial and reconstructive challenges involved in making editions of the Bible, with attention both to the artifactual evidence and the methods used to construct such editions. The aim of the two major critical editions discussed most fully in this volume, the *Oxford Hebrew Bible* and the *Novum Testamentum Graecum, Editio Critico Maior* is to reconstruct the archetypes of biblical manuscripts, that is, the earliest inferable state of the biblical text by means of an eclectic edition, drawing from many different manuscripts. What is implicit in this endeavor? The projects reify as entities a "Hebrew Bible" and a "New Testament" that in fact conceptually postdate the archetypes. Such abstract, theoretical modeling focuses on hypothetical earliest layers. Critical editions also necessitate a choice concerning relevant books to be included in such a reconstructed Bible. The current projects represent books related to the Protestant canon and Jewish Tanakh. Yet it is important to bear in mind that a second-century B.C.E. collection of Hebrew Scriptures might well have included the books of Jubilees, 1 Enoch, and Ben Sira. A first-century collection of Christian Scripture might have included the Wisdom of Solomon or the Apocalypse of Peter. Moreover, the resulting critical editions bracket social contexts and diachronic change related to the texts that are included. The essays in this volume address such issues in order to offer a fuller picture of the processes involved in editing the Bible and understanding the nature of the texts that it comprises.

2. Scribes and Editors

In the case of both the Hebrew Bible and the New Testament, the concept of the Bible cannot be fully disentangled from early modern practices of print and production and, indeed, the idea of a critical edition of a Bible itself. In the first essay of this volume, John Van Seters offers cautionary words about anachronism in biblical studies. He argues that scribes and other literary compilers of antiquity cannot be understood as serving the same functions as the editor of the early Modern period. To use the same term for both is potentially misleading. In the study of the Bible and classical texts, scribes and Renaissance editors worked with very different tools, almost completely different assumptions about the nature of their texts, and rather different purposes in mind. Moreover, the Textus Receptus used as the basis for the first critical editions of the New Testament does not reflect a standard "canonical" text from antiquity, but rather represents later manuscripts adopted for expedience en route to publication. With these qualifications in mind we can better contextualize the modern text-critical projects that are underway.

3. Editing the Hebrew Bible

The modern editor of the Hebrew Bible confronts a manuscript situation radically transformed from sixty years ago. The discovery and publication of the Dead Sea Scrolls have had a major impact on understanding the composition and textual evolution of the Hebrew Bible. The implications of the textual finds have not yet been fully disseminated and digested among biblical scholars, not to mention scholars from related fields and among the general public. Prior to their discovery, the earliest Hebrew manuscript of the Bible was the Aleppo codex (ca. 920 C.E.). Owing to its near destruction in a synagogue fire in 1947, only two-thirds of this manuscript is extant. The Leningrad codex B19A (1008/9 C.E.) remains the earliest complete manuscript of the Tanakh and still must form the basis of critical editions of the Hebrew Bible. The Dead Sea Scrolls offer no such single manuscript, but have yielded fragmentary texts of portions of all books found in the Tanakh except the book of Esther. Of these Hebrew texts, some stand closer to books in the Masoretic textual tradition, some to the Old Greek, others to the Samaritan Pentateuch, and many other seemingly "biblical" manuscripts do not align themselves to any of these three manuscript traditions. No single textual tradition shows dominance.

Given the relatively few manuscripts available on which to base text-critical analysis, qualitative work on the texts is necessitated because quantitative work such as is being done in New Testament text criticism is not possible. The Dead Sea Scrolls with their pluriform scriptural texts have made apparent how important the Old Greek and Samaritan Pentateuch are as witnesses to the early development of the Hebrew Bible. In the second essay, Eugene Ulrich argues for a paradigm shift in de-centering the Masoretic Text from its current privileged place in textual reconstruction in favor of taking the pluriform Hebrew textual forms into account as reflecting the earliest stages of the Hebrew Bible. In reviewing the history of the composition of the Hebrew Bible from its compositional stages onward, Ulrich argues that the MT is not a single text, but a collection of different books each with its own textual history, albeit the only collection that has been preserved in the original language since the second century C.E.

Eibert Tigchelaar's essay provides a detailed assessment of three major Hebrew Bible critical editions that are underway (the *Hebrew University Bible*, *Biblia Hebraica Quinta*, and the *Oxford Hebrew Bible*). His essay raises two issues arising from the textual record. The first regards what some have termed variant "literary editions" in light of the nature of the

Qumran texts. How does one assess so-called "para-biblical" literature, that is, pluriform texts that contain material very much like that found in later biblical texts, but with significant variations, such as 4QpaleoExod^m or 4QRP (Reworked Pentateuch)? Are they to be considered "scriptural" and thus to be factored into a critical apparatus of the Bible, or should they be understood as nonscriptural because they do not accord with the MT? A second issue is the use of Walter Greg's theory of "copy texts" appropriated from the study of Renaissance literature. The editor of the *Oxford Hebrew Bible* project proposes to use the orthographics, vocalization, and accents of the Masoretic Text in order to reconstruct the biblical archetype. This raises the theoretical issue of whether the tradition should be included as a normative part of the text even at its incipient stages. In discussing the future of how the Hebrew Bible might be edited, Tigchelaar also envisions electronic publication and hypertexts as the inevitable evolution of the future. Such publication might easily provide the necessary flexibility to present various archetypes of the biblical manuscripts.

In light of such considerations, two essays offer case studies in text-critical work. Sarianna Metso focuses on the process by which the book of Leviticus took shape, from a body of cultic instructions to priests to a gradually stabilizing text. Like the book of Isaiah, the Leviticus textual tradition at Qumran shows more textual stability than is the case with such books as Exodus, Numbers, and Jeremiah. What becomes clear from her analysis is that the Old Greek preserves an alternative Hebrew version of Leviticus.

Whereas Metso focuses on the implications of the Hebrew texts of Leviticus found at Qumran to illuminate the development of the book, Kristin De Troyer focuses on Greek witnesses to Joshua and Leviticus. They reflect two tendencies, both variant from and with corrections toward the MT. Like the MT, the Septuagint must be understood as a collection of discrete books, not a seamless, uniform whole. By describing the scribal work evident in the Schøyen Papyri she points to their pluriform character and illuminates important aspects of both the history of the Old Greek text and the Hebrew texts.

4. A Critical Edition of the New Testament

Issues relating to the editing of the New Testament contrast considerably with those relating to the Hebrew Bible. The Hebrew Bible presents comparatively few manuscripts. But for the New Testament, the sheer volume and complexity of manuscript witnesses create a problem for editors: 5,300

Greek manuscripts from the late second to fourteenth centuries c.e., along with a large number of manuscripts of early versions in Coptic, Syriac, Latin, Armenian, Georgian, Ethiopic, and Gothic. These offer daunting problems that require special techniques for sorting and collating manuscripts, classifying variant readings, and reconstructing an archetype that accounts for subsequent textual transformation. Not only are there thousands of points where the available manuscripts differ from one another—it has been estimated that there are 250,000 to 350,000 variation points—but the complex relationships among manuscripts and cross-fertilizations have made it impossible to establish simple stemma diagrams to establish genealogical relationships. The situation is comparable in complexity to that of the Human Genome Project, in which any individual can share characteristics with multiple identity groups. Indeed, mathematical modeling developed for the genome project has now been employed in the analysis of New Testament manuscripts.

In the case of the New Testament, there has been no hesitation to reconstruct an eclectic archetype from the available manuscripts. But the problems in constructing such an archetype derive from several factors: (1) The earliest attestations of New Testament writings are from the late second century or early third, but are in the form of highly fragmentary papyri. These already show considerable variation from later fourth-century parchment codices (Codex Vaticanus and Codex Sinaiticus) and evidence a stage in the transmission of the text that was less "supervised" than later copying. (2) The sheer volume of New Testament manuscripts presents a problem for editors, a problem that is only now being addressed at a practical and theoretical level. At a practical level, the digitization of all available manuscripts has been undertaken by the Institut für neutestamentliche Textforschung (Münster), which has allowed for electronic collation through sampling of pre-selected variant locations. At a theoretical level sorting and classification methods developed in the sciences for large-scale multi-variant sorting have been applied to New Testament manuscripts. Klaus Wachtel and Holger Strutwolf provide thorough accounts of this new project.

5. What New Testament Text is Being Edited?

Another set of problems that has not been addressed in a consistent way derives from the fact that many of the individual books of the New Testament putatively belong to the first century c.e. but in fact represent early collections from the early second century. 2 Corinthians is almost universally regarded as a letter collection; 1 Corinthians and Philippians may be collections, and in any event, the earliest Pauline canon (P46) has already associated Hebrews, a non-Pauline writing, with ten Pauline letters (excluding the Pastoral Epistles). This raises the question, what text is actually being edited and presented in a critical edition of the New Testament: the putative first-century letter of Paul or a second-century compilation? Is the text of Mark that is edited in a Bible a putative text circa 70 C.E. or a mid-second century archetype that accounts for all later manuscripts?

In other books of the New Testament there are a large number of recognized interpolations and modifications—the longer ending of Mark, the Johannine "comma" (1 John 5:7–8), the Johannine story of the woman caught in adultery (John 7:53–8:11), and possibly Luke 22:43–44—interpolations that might represent the state of the New Testament text in the mid- to late second century. Should these be included or excluded? How early can we imagine the idea of a collection of Christian Scriptures being formulated, *how* was such a collection imagined, and what belonged to it? David Trobisch argues that the New Testament is the product of a careful and deliberate editorial process and was complete as early as the middle of the second century C.E.

6. Conjectural Emendation

Although accepted in the editing of classical texts as a valid principle, and accepted at least in theory in the editing of the Bible, conjectural emendation is employed very rarely by biblical text critics. Yet in the case of books of the Bible where we lack a continuous or complete set of witnesses and where there are intractable grammatical or lexicographic problems, conjectural emendation seems a viable option. Erasmus engaged in some emendations of letters such as James where the received text is nonsensical or highly problematic. Yet more recent critics usually prefer elaborate exegetical solutions to what may be a matter of textual corruption. The reticence to employ emendation might be a function of the canonical status of the writings involved, or the result of the disconnection of the editing of the Bible from the practice of editing of ancient manuscripts more generally (or both). In any event, this is an issue that deserves investigation. Ryan Wettlaufer's paper is on this topic.

One common element is reflected in the material evidence underlying both Hebrew Bible and New Testament editions. The critical text, that is, the earliest layer of text that can be reconstructed, is at some historical remove from the beginning of the text's existence, that is, its composition. The gap would seem to be a matter of centuries in the case of the Hebrew Bible; in the New Testament, this might for some books be a matter of decades. The textual situation in the case of both the Hebrew Bible and the New Testament reflect a mixture of both fluidity and stability at early stages of textual transmission, though how this might be characterized differs markedly even among the Hebrew texts or Greek texts themselves. In his overview essay, Michael Holmes thus characterizes the New Testament situation as suggesting "a combination of what might be termed macro-level stability (from the paragraph level on up) and micro-level fluidity (from the sentence level on down)."

The collection of essays in this volume point in balance to a consensus that the editorial task of biblical criticism is to reconstruct, where possible, the history of the text without privileging as normative any particular stage in its development. In any case, laying bare what "text" is being edited and articulating the presuppositions entailed in that commitment are imperative to sound biblical scholarship. To the degree that the essays of this volume have contributed to that endeavor, they have succeeded.

THE GENEALOGY OF THE BIBLICAL EDITOR

John Van Seters

As the starting point for discussing what is problematic in the task of editing the Bible, I want to begin with some comments on the notion of the Textus Receptus as both the result of earlier editing of the biblical text and as the supposed object or goal of present editorial endeavors. The term refers in the first instance, of course, to the edition of the New Testament produced by Erasmus in 1516 for the printer Froben, made in haste in order to be the first in print, using manuscripts that were not the best ones available. This *editio princeps* subsequently went through a number of editions, the fourth being the definitive one. It was this form of the text that was used for many translations of the Bible as a standard text, and thus the reprint of the text by the Elzevir brothers in 1633 was advertised as "the text which is now received by all"—hence the term *Textus Receptus*. In the first instance, therefore, Textus Receptus simply means a consensus text, recognizing the fact that Erasmus's New Testament text won out over the competition to become the standard text used by New Testament scholars and by so many churches in the production of their vernacular versions.[1] This standardization of a particular Greek text by the book trade created for it a quasi-canonical status that persisted for centuries. A parallel development took place in the case of the Hebrew Bible: the Christian publisher Daniel Bomberg employed the Jewish scholar Jacob ben Chayim to produce an edition of the Masoretic Bible in 1524–1526 that likewise became for centuries the standard or Textus Receptus of the Hebrew Bible.[2] In both cases, the manu-

---

1. Bruce M. Metzger, *The Text of the New Testament* (2nd ed.; Oxford: Clarendon, 1968), 95–118; Edward J. Kenney, *The Classical Text: Aspects of Editing in the Age of the Printed Book* (Berkeley: University of California Press, 1974), 49–51.

2. Christian D. Ginsburg, *Introduction to the Masoretico-Critical Edition of the Hebrew Bible* (1897; reprinted with a prolegomenon by Harry M. Orlinsky; New York:

scripts used were not the most superior ones of that time but merely those that were available to a particular publisher. Nevertheless, recognition of that fact did not change the "canonical" status of the editions within the faith communities that made use of them, at least not for a long time.

In spite of the fact that both forms of the Textus Receptus, the one in the Greek New Testament and the other in the Hebrew Bible, have been contested in academia, the term *Textus Receptus* with all its connotations of a standard edited text, a canonically received text, and a definitive form of the text, has been read back into antiquity. This is especially the case with respect to the Hebrew Bible, and I will restrict myself primarily to this corpus. The fact that the Masoretic Text of this sixteenth-century Hebrew Bible had a biblical text tradition that went back to a proto-MT text family of the first century C.E. suggested a standardization, at least within the rabbinic tradition of Judaism, and this encouraged anachronistically reading back into this period the notion of such a text as a Textus Receptus with all the connotations of a consciously edited text under the control of a religious authority, a text that was given canonical status. In spite of objections against such notions of a Masoretic Textus Receptus by Harry Orlinsky, among others, there is a strong impulse to think in terms of an archetypal text of this kind within the Masoretic Text tradition with all the characteristics attributed to a Textus Receptus.[3] A variation on this scheme has been to identify three basic text families corresponding to three distinct religious traditions: rabbinic Judaism, the Samaritans, and the Christians, each with their own canonical text traditions.[4]

However, the Qumran scrolls with their great diversity of texts have made all such schemes problematic.[5] The Essenes of Qumran could tolerate a wide range of textual diversity without showing any great preference for a particular family of texts.[6] Nor is there any evidence, so far as I can

---

Ktav, 1966), 956–76; Paul E. Kahle, *The Cairo Geniza* (2nd ed.; Oxford: Blackwell, 1959), 119–31.

3. Harry M. Orlinsky, "Prolegomenon: The Masoretic Text: A Critical Evaluation," in Ginsburg, *Introduction to the Masoretico-Critical Edition of the Hebrew Bible*, i–xlv.

4. Shemaryahu Talmon, "The Textual Study of the Bible—A New Outlook," in *Qumran and the History of the Biblical Text* (ed. F. M. Cross and S. Talmon; Cambridge: Harvard University Press, 1975), 321–400.

5. See the review in John Van Seters, *The Edited Bible: The Curious History of the "Editor" in Biblical Criticism* (Winona Lake, Ind.: Eisenbrauns, 2006), 298–350.

6. See in particular the remarks by Eugene Ulrich, "Our Sharper Focus on the Bible and Theology Thanks to the Dead Sea Scrolls," *CBQ* 66 (2004): 1–24.

see, that they ever attempted to create an edited version in the sense of producing an eclectic critical text that could be considered as a standard. It is also clear that the various methods of biblical interpretation practiced by the Essenes of Qumran, the Hellenistic Jews of Alexandria, the rabbis, and the Christians, could make just about any text say what they wanted it to say, with little concern for a correct text. If there was a particular verse of the Bible that created a problem in the course of religious controversy between sects, it could sometimes be adjusted by means of a simple scribal "emendation." In exceptional cases, a scholar such as Origen became concerned with the problem of textual diversity between the Septuagint and the Hebrew Bible.[7] Origen's massive Hexapla did not result in a standard text edition, but merely led to even more diversity. Origen himself, in his homilies, could sometimes prefer a reading from the Hebrew Bible, sometimes one from the Seventy, depending entirely on what suited his theological interests at the time.[8] Jerome's various attempts to create a more correct version of the Old Testament based upon the Hebrew text did not receive widespread recognition in his own lifetime and only became the recognized standard at the Council of Trent.[9]

Thus it is fair to say that a Textus Receptus in the sense of a standard text produced by means of an editorial process under the aegis of book publishers to be widely distributed and recognized as "canonical" for a particular religious community is a complete anachronism for antiquity. It is an erroneous application of an analogy of a text that is based upon the results of a highly competitive book trade eager to produce standard editions of classical and sacred texts for obvious financial reasons in the early modern period. It is entirely understandable that those scholars who were expert in the study of ancient manuscripts that could be turned into printed editions were used by publishers for this purpose. These scholars became known as "editors" or "redactors." Thus, "editors" came into being with the rise of the printing press and the publishing trade at the very time that there was a revival in classical scholarship, along with the recovery of a great quantity of ancient manuscripts. These manuscripts provided the thriving book trade with classical and sacred texts that could be turned

---

7. Van Seters, *Edited Bible*, 83–97.

8. William McKane, *Selected Christian Hebraists* (Cambridge: Cambridge University Press, 1989), 22–31.

9. Ibid., 31–41. On editing the Bible among the church fathers, see Van Seters, *Edited Bible*, 83–109, with literature cited there.

into "first editions." Thus scholarly editors produced in printed form from manuscripts, by means of recension and emendation, the first editions of the classics, various medieval religious texts, and the Bible. Such editors, in collaboration with book publishers, became the indispensable means for the transmission and proliferation of the cultural and religious heritage.[10]

With this understanding of *editor* in mind and the role of the editor within the development of the standard text or Textus Receptus, let us turn to consider the notion of editor as it was used in the history of biblical scholarship, especially as it has to do with the origin of biblical books. At the very outset of historical criticism in the seventeenth century, it was suggested by the great Catholic scholar Richard Simon that the Pentateuch and the historical books were compiled by inspired scholarly editors who brought together ancient texts and historical sources that were preserved in the temple or the court archives to produce the editions that now make up the Bible. These anonymous editors added nothing of their own; they were only the collectors and faithful transmitters of the older traditions. This theory was put forward to counter the "minimalist" rationalists who suggested that one must consider many of the stories in the biblical texts to be fiction, merely myths and legends. Simon's understanding of this ancient editorial practice was clearly modeled on the scholarly activity that was typical of his own time, when scholars were collecting and editing classical and biblical manuscripts recovered from monastic and church archives. For Simon, the clearest biblical example of such scholarly activity was that of Ezra the scribe, who became known as the editor of the Pentateuch.[11]

Consequently, the notion of ancient editors responsible for the final form (the *editio princeps*) of the classics and the Bible became widely accepted in both biblical and classical scholarship. However, in addition to the scholarly editors of texts, another kind of editor came into great prominence during the Romantic era of the late eighteenth and the nineteenth centuries. This was an era in which much attention was given to the collecting and editing of *oral* folklore as the invaluable repository of a people's past, the embodiment of their spirit or *Volksgeist*. Thus the editor became the vital means by which this oral past—the collective memory of the people—was preserved and transmitted in written form. Some of

---

10. See especially Kenney, *Classical Text*, 3–25.
11. McKane, *Selected Christian Hebraists*, 111–50.

these editors, such as the Grimm brothers, became famous in their own right. In classical studies Friedrich Wolf, in his *Prolegomena to Homer* (1795), undertook to map out a critical text history of the *Iliad*, in which he applied the analogy of just such an editor to the oral tradition of Homer.[12] Thus he saw Homer as a collection of originally independent, orally composed songs that were brought together by a group of anonymous editors to form the two poems, the *Iliad* and the *Odyssey*, under the patronage of Peisistratus, tyrant of Athens, in the mid-sixth century B.C.E. This transition from oral songs to the first written form of Homer was followed by a period of textual diversity and corruption until a succession of Alexandrian scholars, particularly the last one, Aristarchus, edited the diverse extant manuscripts of the Homeric poems to create the definitive recension, which in Wolf's view became the Textus Receptus or vulgate that is used today. Variations of this general hypothesis continued throughout the nineteenth century in Homeric studies, giving prominence to the role of the editor as the one responsible for both the initial literary unity from disparate oral sources and for the final textual form of the poems restored from the conflicting manuscript tradition.[13] Please note, however, that these are two different kinds of editors, the one who gives written form, shape, and arrangement to his collection of anonymous traditional materials, and the one who attempts to faithfully recover and transmit the written texts of specific authors. In the Romantic era of Wolf, however, both types of editors were connected to the publishing trade and none were anonymous.

I draw attention here to this example from Homeric studies because all biblical scholars in the nineteenth century were trained in the classics. The fields of classical and biblical studies were very closely associated with each other, with influence going in *both* directions, so that literary theories developed in the one disciple would have their counterpart in the other. This is particularly the case with Wolf's studies concerning the text history of Homer, its *Überlieferungsgeschichte*, and its impact upon pentateuchal studies. Thus it is not hard to see how Simon's editors

---

12. Frederick A. Wolf, *Prolegomena to Homer* (1795; trans. with introduction and notes by A. Grafton, G. W. Most, and J. E. G. Zetzel; Princeton: Princeton University Press, 1985); Anthony Grafton, *Defenders of the Text: The Traditions of Scholarship in an Age of Science, 1450-1800* (Cambridge: Harvard University Press, 1991), 214–43; Van Seters, *Edited Bible*, 133–51.

13. Ibid., 151–63.

of historical documents, combined with Wolf's editors of oral tradition, could come to play such a significant role in biblical studies regarding notions about an editor combining independent written sources, which were themselves collections of oral materials, as well as the subsequent role of editors in the transmission of these texts into their final form. All of this comes to flower in the classical Documentary Hypothesis and in Wellhausen's *Prolegomena,* which is an *Überlieferungsgeschichte* of the Pentateuch and historical books of the Hebrew Bible.[14] Most of the literary theories regarding the composition of the Pentateuch fluctuate between an emphasis upon the editing of written documents as authors (J, E, D, P) and the editing of collections of oral tradition (in the works of Hermann Gunkel and Martin Noth), in which the authors tend to fade or even disappear.[15]

There is, in addition, another problem with the notion of ancient editors of texts, and that is how to distinguish between the "editorial" transmission of texts and the evidence of numerous interpolations and expansions that appear in the texts over the course of time. In order to distinguish between editors who combined sources, as in the Documentary Hypothesis, and subsequent revisions in the text, pentateuchal studies made use of Greek terms derived from Homeric studies: the one, *diorthōtēs,* meaning an editor (like Aristarchus of Alexandria) whose intent was to preserve the text and to eliminate errors, that is, to create a recension, but not to make any additions of his own to the text; the other, *diaskeuastēs,* was someone who made additions and interpolations into the text for any number of different reasons.[16] It is clear that the second category hardly represents an editor in either sense that we have described above, but instead is used for a scribe who corrupts or glosses a text with additions for his own personal use. Yet both categories are lumped together by biblical scholars under

---

14. Julius Wellhausen, *Prolegomena to the History of Ancient Israel* (New York: Meridian Books, 1957); repr. of *Prolegomena to the History of Israel* (trans. J. Sutherland Black and A. Enzies, with preface by W. Robertson Smith; Edinburgh: Adam & Charles Black, 1885).

15. See Van Seters, *Edited Bible,* 223–69.

16. The distinction may be found in Abraham Kuenen, *An Historico-critical Inquiry into the Origin and Composition of the Hexateuch* (London: Macmillan, 1886), 341 n. 14; see also Alexander Rofé, "Abraham Kuenen's Contribution to the Study of the Pentateuch: A View from Israel," in *Abraham Kuenen (1828-1891): His Major Contributions to the Study of the Old Testament* (ed. P. B. Dirksen and A. van der Kooij; OtSt 29; Leiden: Brill, 1993), 105–12; Van Seters, *Edited Bible,* 235–38.

the general rubric of redactor (R), leading to great confusion in the role of the "editor" in literary criticism. Indeed, it is now suggested that this kind of editor is to be understood on the analogy of a rabbinic exegete, such that the additions are construed as interpretive midrash or explanatory notations. The increasingly popular study of biblical intertextuality has pushed this new understanding of redactor to the forefront. Any text that has an "intertextual" relationship with another text is construed as a "redactional" interpretation of the other text.[17] The editor has thus become both the canonizer of the biblical text—the one responsible for its final form—and its authoritative interpreter.

There was yet a further development in biblical studies that has added to the hopeless confusion that surrounds the figure of the ancient editor. Julius Wellhausen, during his third academic career as a New Testament scholar, introduced into the study of the Gospels the notion of the evangelists as redactors. On the analogy of the redactor's role in the Pentateuch as the combiner of sources, he viewed Matthew and Luke as editors who combined Mark and Q along with some other sources of their own.[18] Even Mark, who assembled early Christian oral tradition, could be understood as an editor in the romantic understanding of this term. Form critics such as Bultmann emphasized the process of the growth of the small oral units of tradition into the larger composites.[19] They seized upon Wellhausen's understanding of the evangelists as editors, so that the Synoptic Gospels became primarily the repositories of Christian tradition. This strongly resembled the view of Hermann Gunkel and Hugo Gressmann toward the pentateuchal sources J and E within form criticism of the Pentateuch. Yet a strong protest against such a treatment of the pentateuchal sources, especially J, was raised by Gerhard von Rad, who sought to restore the Yahwist to the status of author and historian, as Martin Noth also did for the Deuteronomistic Historian.[20] The biblical writers were not merely

---

17. See in particular Michael Fishbane, *Biblical Interpretation in Ancient Israel* (Oxford: Clarendon, 1985).

18. Nils A. Dahl, "Wellhausen on the New Testament," *Semeia* 25 (1982): 89–110.

19. Rudolf Bultmann, *The History of the Synoptic Tradition* (trans. J. Marsh; New York: Harper & Row, 1963).

20. Gerhard von Rad, "The Form-Critical Problem of the Hexateuch," in *The Problem of the Hexateuch and Other Essays* (Edinburgh: Oliver & Boyd, 1966), 1–78; trans. of *Das formgeschichtliche Problem des Hexateuch* (BWANT 4; Stuttgart: Kohlhammer, 1938); Martin Noth, "Überlieferungsgeschichtliche Studien," *Schriften der Königsberger Gelehrten Gesellschaft. Geisteswissenschaftliche Klasse* 18 (1943): 43–266.

compilers of tradition or editors of archival documents. The examples of von Rad and Noth were taken up in New Testament studies by Hans Conzelmann, Willi Marxsen, and others who sought to restore to the evangelists their status as writers and theologians in their own right.[21]

However, within this new direction in New Testament studies, Marxsen made a grave mistake that has caused no end of trouble on the subject of the editor. Although he argued for Mark as an author and not just a collector of church tradition, he was nevertheless willing to retain the older terminology and refer to this new compositional study of the Gospels as "redaction history," even though the evangelists were certainly more than "mere redactors."[22] In spite of some protest against this obvious abuse of language, in which author and redactor are treated as synonymous for the sake of convenience and continuity with the older form criticism, redaction criticism has established a firm hold within New Testament studies. Furthermore, this redaction criticism has also been read back into Old Testament studies by Klaus Koch and Odil Steck, turning both von Rad and Noth into redaction critics, quite against their clearly expressed views.[23] The biblical authors that von Rad and Noth so strongly championed against the form critics have now become mere editors. In this strange way, everything in compositional analysis has become *Redactionsgeschichte*.

In this curious history of the *editor* in biblical studies we have gone from the very limited notion of the editor as one who merely combined and arranged earlier written documents that make up the Pentateuch and historical books (Simon), to include: (1) one who collected, arranged, and edited the oral traditions of the community (Wolf's romantic editor of folklore); (2) one who gave to the textual tradition its final recensional form (like Aristarchus); (3) one who inserted interpretive additions and interpolations into the text (the *diaskeuastai* of Kuenen); and (4) one who is a hybrid author/editor (modeled on Marxsen's Gospel writers). The *editor* is now responsible for the whole literary process and the final form

---

21. Hans Conzelmann, *The Theology of St. Luke* (London: Faber & Faber, 1960); Willi Marxsen, *Mark the Evangelist: Studies on the Redaction History of the Gospel* (Nashville: Abingdon, 1969). See also Van Seters, *Edited Bible*, 283–96.

22. Marxsen, *Mark the Evangelist*, 21 n. 17.

23. Klaus Koch, *The Growth of the Biblical Tradition: The Form-Critical Method* (New York: Charles Scribner's Sons, 1969), 57–67; Odil Hannes Steck, *Old Testament Exegesis: A Guide to the Methodology* (SBLRBS 33; Atlanta: Scholars Press, 1995), 79–94.

of the biblical text. The sheer absurdity of this editorial history should give us pause for reflection.

The fact of the matter is that any literary theory or text history of the Bible that relies upon the notion of "editors" or fixed and authorized "editions" in the ancient period is highly problematic and guilty of serious anachronism. The best possible examples that we have of ancient editors are the scholars of Alexandria, and we know that their scholarly editions did not have any significant impact on the standard edition of Homer. They were "ivory tower" scholars who had no direct connection with the book trade and their critical editions, imbedded in huge learned commentaries, were not reproduced, except in very abbreviated form in the scholia of Homer. The text of Homer was entirely dependent upon the dynamics of the book trade, which popularized a medium-sized text that became the standard text, certainly not Aristarchus's recension. There is nothing that is comparable to the Alexandrian scholars for the Hebrew Bible; all attempts to find traces of critical editing in the time of the *sopherim* are unconvincing. Furthermore, it is likely that the *sopherim* had little to do with the creation of a standard text, which was simply the result of the book trade. As in the case of the modern Textus Receptus, the text that survived to become the standard, as reflected in MT, was not always the best text, from a text-critical point of view, so that it should not be privileged any more than Erasmus's Textus Receptus for the New Testament or Ben Chayim's Masoretic Text for the Hebrew Bible.

This leaves the modern biblical editor with the problem of how to understand or define the *Urtext* that in theory at least is the critic's goal. The rich textual diversity of the Qumran scrolls has created something of a dilemma in trying to understand exactly what text should be reconstructed as the standard and consensus text for scholarly study and the creation of new vernacular versions. *There was never an authorized, edited, canonical* Urtext *in antiquity.* Recently, there has been a new emphasis on an old way of attacking this problem and that is to see an *editorial* continuity from the earliest creation of the biblical text by editors through all the subsequent stages of its revisions and changes to its later exemplars.[24] This is what Friedrich Wolf thought he could do for the text of Homer in the *Prolegomena* prior to his attempt to produce a critical edition of

---

24. See Emanuel Tov, *Textual Criticism of the Hebrew Bible* (Minneapolis: Fortress, 1992), 177–80.

the *Iliad*. It was his *Überlieferungsgeschichte* of Homer, his history of the transmission of the text, which scholars now call *Redaktionsgeschichte*, from the first edition to its final vernacular form. It is this scheme that Wellhausen emulated in his *Prolegomena*, at least for the Pentateuch and historical books, which he also referred to as their *Überlieferungsgeschichten*. This *editorial process* has become identified by Brevard Childs and James Sanders with the *canonical process*, which can accommodate every type of compositional process as well as every variation and deviation in the textual witnesses, and make it into an organic unity from beginning to end.[25] The grand scheme, which is extolled by so many leading figures in textual criticism, in literary criticism, in canonical exegesis and in the innerbiblical exegesis school, tends to envelop the whole of biblical studies. But it still leaves this critical scholar with a sense of unease about such an editorial process.

The whole elaborate structure of this editorial history is a house of cards. There never was an editor or group of editors who created texts or standardized texts in antiquity. The famous scholarly editors who created the "canonical" texts of the New Testament and the Hebrew Bible for their respective publishers in the modern era have no counterpart in antiquity. It was a completely unhistorical analogy that Wolf used to understand Aristarchus's editing of Homer, which, as I said, never became the basis for the vulgate text. *There never was an ancient edited recension of Homer that became an archetype of a later text tradition!* Consequently, Saul Lieberman is wrong when he appeals to the analogy of Aristarchus and his editing of Homer to suggest that the *sopherim* did the same thing for the standardization of the MT in the Hellenistic or Roman period.[26] Likewise, when Wolf used an anachronistic analogy to reconstruct the earliest edition of Homer in the time of Peisistratus, biblical scholars employed the same analogy from Homeric studies for Gunkel's collections of oral tradition in the Pentateuch, corresponding to the J and E sources, combined by a redactor, R[JE]. Both of Wolf's foundation blocks have been thoroughly demolished in classical studies,[27] but not before they were used as

---

25. Van Seters, *Edited Bible*, 351–76.

26. Saul Lieberman, *Hellenism in Jewish Palestine: Studies in the Literary Transmission, Beliefs and Manners of Palestine in the I Century B.C.E.—IV Century C.E.* (2nd ed.; New York: Jewish Theological Seminary of New York, 1962); cf. Van Seters, *Edited Bible*, 63–81.

27. Thomas W. Allen, *Homer: The Origins and Transmission* (Oxford: Clarendon,

corresponding models for the Bible's supposed editorial history, and they persist there still. This editorial process is a myth built on anachronistic analogies—the unforgivable sin in historical criticism—and we are left to pick up the pieces.

In a recent monograph, Karel van der Toorn has attempted to bolster the existence of ancient editors of the Bible by proposing to identify them as an elite class of scholarly scribes who belonged to the priesthood of the Second Temple community and whose task it was to write down, edit and copy the sacred "stream of tradition" during the second half of the first millennium B.C.E.[28] For him, such scribes were both authors and editors of the original books, as well as copyists and the guardians of what became the final canonical form of the text. The primary support for this view in the biblical tradition he finds in redaction criticism as currently practiced by biblical scholars, which points to "editorial expansions, scribal annotations, seams and incongruities in the text."[29] Such an argument is, of course, completely circular. There is nothing "editorial" about scribal expansions, annotations, and the like. Furthermore, one can clearly discern in this model of learned scribes all of the dubious notions about the role of the *sopherim* and their editing of the authoritative biblical texts of the temple, which is then read back into the Persian period. Van der Toorn's model likewise resembles closely the notions about the origins of Homer's epics by learned scribes of Athens in the sixth century B.C.E. and the subsequent establishment of the standard text by the scholars of Alexandria, all of which has been thoroughly discredited.

I will not spell out in detail a critique of van der Toorn's book, since I have done that elsewhere.[30] Instead, I will briefly take up one example of how he views his scholarly scribes as redactors. Van der Toorn uses the book of Deuteronomy as representative of the process of composition, redaction and transmission of the Mosaic stream of tradition.[31] For this

---

1924); Cedric H. Whitman, *Homer and the Homeric Tradition* (Cambridge: Harvard University Press, 1958), 65–86; Richard Janko, *Books 13–16* (vol. 4 of *The Iliad: A Commentary*; Cambridge: Cambridge University Press, 1992), 20–32.

28. Karel van der Toorn, *Scribal Culture and the Making of the Hebrew Bible* (Cambridge: Harvard University Press, 2007).

29. Ibid., 3.

30. John Van Seters, "The Role of the Scribe in the Making of the Hebrew Bible," *JANER* 8 (2008): 99–129.

31. Van der Toorn, *Scribal Culture*, 143–72.

purpose he takes over for convenience the long-outdated redaction criticism of Robert H. Pfeiffer[32] with its simplified scheme of four editions, and with modifications he makes it fit his own ideas. While discussing Deuteronomy he ignores the competing Mosaic tradition in the rest of the Pentateuch and only in a brief dismissive remark suggests that the quite different Priestly tradition in Leviticus may represent a split within the priestly ranks resulting in two competing scribal authorities in the same temple community.[33] He says nothing at all about the quite non-Priestly corpus of the Yahwist, which is also in competition with Deuteronomy at many points. Ezra, the priestly scribe, who for him is the final editor of Deuteronomy, also becomes the editor of the whole Torah. Yet Ezra's role as the "editor" of the Torah and then of the whole corpus of twenty-two books of the Bible is based upon very late Jewish tradition, and van der Toorn has nothing to say about the *sopherim*, who in the same rabbinic tradition provide the "editorial" continuity between Ezra and the first century C.E. rabbis, the period in which textual diversity actually proliferated. The scribal and editorial scheme he imposes upon Deuteronomy adds nothing to clarifying the problems of pentateuchal criticism and hardly supports the notion of a unified editorial process. Consequently, in spite of this recent effort by van der Toorn, no one has ever successfully demonstrated that ancient editors produced, transmitted, and controlled the reproduction of a particular form or "edition" of a biblical text.

Does this mean that we give up the task of editing the Bible if we have no hope of recovering a "canonical" or *Urtext* of the Hebrew Scriptures? Of course not! As modern critical scholars we have no option but to understand critically the history of the text and to base our exegesis and interpretation on such an understanding. However, for the present-day editing of the Bible, we must still ponder the question: What does it matter if there are no ancient editors, no ancient *editio princeps* and no ancient *recensions*? We have found that we can give up Erasmus's Textus Receptus for the New Testament or Ben Chayim's MT for the Hebrew Bible, but where will we look for the standard texts, the *Urtexten*? The aim of text-critical studies has been to get behind these faulty modern standards to the more primitive *texti recepti*. For Richard Bentley that meant the supposed "canonical" text of the Council of Nicaea. He never found it in his lifetime,

---

32. Robert H. Pfeiffer, *Introduction to the Old Testament* (New York: Harper & Brothers, 1941), 182–87.

33. Van der Toorn, *Scribal Culture*, 160.

but Karl Lachmann took up the cause and used the critical method he developed to discredit the Textus Receptus of Erasmus. Yet he still did not find that elusive canonical text. What he found instead was the fact that the task of editing the text is a historical undertaking, which means that the goal of an ancient *edited* Bible—Hebrew or Greek—is a chimera that must be abandoned. In the case of the Hebrew Bible, there are many texts and text families belonging to so many different religious communities at so many different periods of time, none of which can claim indisputable primacy or "first edition" status.

Furthermore, once we give up the notion that the task of textual criticism—editing the Bible—is the recovery of a "canonical" text, one that is the result of an editorial process, then we are left with identifying Bibles, or parts thereof, and their usage within various communities and within their historical and social settings. This means that there never was a single MT for rabbinic Judaism, or an original LXX for Greek Jews and for Christians, let alone a single text of the Torah or collection of prophetic books for the Essenes. Why did Rabbi Meir, in his capacity as a professional scribe, make elegant copies of the Torah for use in synagogues, using an exemplar that did not correspond with the MT text as we understand it? Why did Philo think he was using the inspired text of the Seventy, when his text appears to correspond to a quite different "recension"? Why did the Qumran scribes tolerate so many variant texts without any indication that they attempted to produce a final edition of their canon, if they had one? Jerome recognized that there were three different Greek text traditions in use in the church of his day, but then he decided to create a Latin version based on none of these but upon what he erroneously thought was the *Hebraica veritas*, no doubt some version of the proto-MT family. But Augustine felt quite free to reject his effort because it was not based upon the Textus Receptus, namely, the Greek text that had long been accepted for use in the church. The rabbis demonstrated time and time again in the Talmud that their midrashic and halakic interpretations were not based upon a single text tradition, but whatever text suited their purpose at the time. One could multiply these examples many times over.[34]

In my view, and it is only a rather timid suggestion, an edited Bible must always be a practical compromise between the historical reality of

---

34. See Bertil Albrektson, "Reflections on the Emergence of a Standard Text of the Hebrew Bible," in *Congress Volume Göttingen* (VTSup 29; Leiden: Brill, 1978), 49–65; Ulrich, "Our Sharper Focus."

great textual diversity and the need to create a text that will be useful for the scholarly community, as well as a base text for the production of modern versions. This paper is not the place to begin a detailed discussion of what those edited texts should look like, both for the Hebrew Bible and the New Testament—they would almost certainly be quite different kinds of texts.[35] I leave that to the text critics among us to debate.[36] However, an edited Bible, no matter how diligently reconstructed, can never claim to be a new Textus Receptus, a canonical text, a reflection of an ancient final form that may be used to justify those popular forms of academic exegesis and interpretation that so lightly dismiss the need for historical-critical reflection. Literary criticism and textual criticism have been a part of historical criticism since the seventeenth century (whether or not one calls them "higher" and "lower" criticism). When there is a radical adjustment in our understanding within the one, it must inevitably have implications for the other. It is just such a joint discussion that I am trying to stimulate with my remarks in this paper.

---

35. In the case of the Hebrew Bible, one should probably use a fairly conservative text as a base, well-annotated with probable textual alternatives and critical evaluation. The diversity of texts makes a common stemma for most parts of the Hebrew Bible impossible. The great importance of the versions, particularly the Septuagint, makes the creation of an eclectic text problematic. Yet the critical exegete invariably works with an eclectic text, and any edited Bible must give him or her the appropriate tools to do so.

36. See the essay in this volume by Eibert Tigchelaar, "Editing the Hebrew Bible: An Overview of Some Problems."

THE EVOLUTIONARY COMPOSITION
OF THE HEBREW BIBLE

Eugene Ulrich

One normally encounters the Hebrew Bible—that is, the Jewish Tanak, the Christian Old Testament—in a single clearly printed form. That apparent simplicity, however, is the result of editorial judgment by scholarly or ecclesiastical committees. The diverse manuscripts bearing the text of the Hebrew Bible, as they have traversed the centuries and arrive in the twenty-first century, form a puzzling web of witnesses. Thus, scholarly or ecclesiastical committees have chosen a single form from among the many variant and possible forms on the basis of editorial or religious criteria at the macro and micro levels.

I would like to explore how the Hebrew Bible textual tradition became so diverse and how contemporary scholars are attempting to produce editions of the Bible according to various principles. This presentation will be in three parts: (1) the authors and editors who contributed to the developmental composition of the biblical books; (2) the "editors" visible behind the variant editions we see in the biblical Dead Sea Scrolls; and (3) a brief report on five different types of editions of the Hebrew Bible currently in progress.

I think it is important to make two statements at the start. First, a paradigm shift is needed in the textual criticism and editing of the Hebrew Bible. The traditional view of the text of the Hebrew Bible is that it is basically a "purified" Masoretic Text (MT). That is, once the obvious errors are removed, the single text form that the rabbis and the Masoretes handed on, the traditional Textus Receptus, is considered to present the "original text." Accordingly, most Bible translations translate "the MT except where there is a problem," at which point they look to the Samaritan Pentateuch (SP), the Septuagint (LXX), the versions, or emendation. But the Qumran scrolls show that the MT is not the central text of the Hebrew Bible, but simply one of several forms that existed in antiquity. Therefore, we must reassess how we approach the text of the Hebrew Bible.

Second, the biblical scrolls from Qumran are not "sectarian" but display the Scriptures of general Judaism. They are the oldest, most valuable, and most authentic evidence for the shape of the Scriptures as they circulated in Palestine at the time of the origins of rabbinic Judaism and Christianity. They demonstrate that the text was pluriform: that many of the books circulated in variant literary editions simultaneously, each of which apparently enjoyed equal status. Thus the Scrolls offer unforeseen new riches, but also a formidable challenge for new editions of the Hebrew Bible.

We can begin by recalling how the biblical books were put together from their beginnings up to their final stage.

1. The Authors and Editors of the Biblical Books

The authors as well as the transmitters of the Hebrew Scriptures were the community of Israel (בני ישראל) spanning the course of a millennium. The composition of the various religious works that form the Hebrew Bible anthology was sporadic in one sense, gradual and continual in another. The popular imagination formed long ago envisioned a few holy men (e.g., Moses, Samuel, Isaiah, Daniel) as the authors of the books that bear their names, similar to classical or modern authors who individually compose and publish books under their own name. Prior to the Enlightenment, however, a few attentive readers raised suspicions about those views of authorship, and with the Enlightenment those suspicions gained momentum. Ever since the Enlightenment, sustained critical analysis of the biblical books has overwhelmingly concluded that most of the books of the biblical anthology were composed in stages, usually with earlier source materials being brought together into a unified work by an anonymous person who is usually labeled an editor or redactor. Textual critics detected further minor developments within the major stages of the compositions, noting additions to, losses from, and errors in the text of each book after it had been composed and as it continued to be recited or copied from generation to generation. Thus the Scriptures were seen to be composed over the course of approximately a millennium, from premonarchic times to within a generation or so of the fall of the Second Temple in 70 C.E.

Due both to the complexity of the processes of composition for the various books, which differed from book to book, and to the lack of solid evidence in the form of preserved manuscripts, the terminology that different scholars used to describe the processes they were uncovering can now, in retrospect, be seen as in need of examination and possible revision.

John Van Seters has recently produced a serious monograph attempting to clarify the terminology and the realities behind the terminology.[1] He has proposed definitions and careful descriptions of various instances of editorial activity. I will try to describe as precisely as possible what the various handlers of the texts were doing, to see what terminology best fits their activity, and thus what terminology we should adopt in order both to think clearly and to teach others to think clearly about these matters.

For simplicity, in this paper I will make use of Julius Wellhausen's Documentary Hypothesis, Hermann Gunkel's form criticism of units, Martin Noth's tradition history of pentateuchal traditions, and Norman Gottwald's socio-literary approach to the origins of Israel. I will make use of these theories for the sake of simplicity, not necessarily endorsing them in all their details, since they are widely known and thus require little discussion. Though, for example, the Documentary Hypothesis is under siege both generally and in many of its details (e.g., only four authors, written documents, dating, etc.), most of its fundamental understandings of how Israel's literature came to be are correct and will not be so much proved false as shown to be much more complex.

1.1. THE COMPOSITION OF THE TORAH

In all likelihood, early Israel had oral accounts of its formation as a people. It seems inconceivable that they lacked any oral-tradition accounts of their origins. Noth posited five themes of oral traditions that were eventually woven together to form what became the Tetrateuch or Pentateuch: the promise to the patriarchs, the guidance out of Egypt, the wandering through the wilderness, the revelation at Sinai, and the occupation of the land. Historically it is unlikely that any single group experienced the events behind all five of these traditions. Rather, different groups experienced different events which eventually were memorialized in these themes, and someone—whom Van Seters would term a historiographer—

---

1. John Van Seters, *The Edited Bible: The Curious History of the "Editor" in Biblical Criticism* (Winona Lake, Ind.: Eisenbrauns, 2006). See also his essay in this volume (9–22).

wove the themes together, probably adding some of his own insights and commentary.

The Yahwist is usually credited with many of the stories in Genesis, and it will be instructive to watch how he, or a predecessor, worked. Most of the stories were isolated, unconnected oral traditions. Here is a sample from Gen 12–22.

Genesis 12:1–3, the call and blessing of Abraham, was probably taken from the liturgy, or was possibly a creation by the Yahwist.

Genesis 12:10–19 was an old Canaanite chieftain hero tale about someone (whose name may or may not have been Abraham or Isaac) taking his wife down to Egypt, being afraid, and having her say she is his sister, plus the resulting complications.

Genesis 14 was simply an isolated old war tale, which included a blessing of a victorious chieftain by the Canaanite god, El Elyon.

Genesis 15 appears to be a Mesopotamian or Canaanite story of an inheritance-adoption problem, including a promise of land and descendants by the personal god to a tribal chieftain.

Genesis 16 is a personal conflict story about the favorite but barren wife versus the fertile concubine.[2]

Genesis 18 + 21 was a nomadic aetiological story about the name Isaac (which means "Let [El] laugh"), in combination with a hospitality-exhortation story, since they did not have motels in those days.

Genesis 22, the celebrated story of Abraham's sacrifice of Isaac, was an evolving story that may have originally favored child sacrifice, then was developed into a polemic against child sacrifice, and was also used as an aetiology for a sacred site.

---

2. Mesopotamian legal documents have been found that illustrate the underlying social and legal situations of both Gen 15 and Gen 16.

These and other originally unconnected stories were assembled by either the Yahwist or a predecessor, who lined them up in the following order:[3]

Gen 12:1–3	Call of Abraham, promise, blessing
Gen 12:10–19	Promise immediately in jeopardy
Gen 15	Need for a son: adopted son is heir
Gen 16	– son by concubine
Gen 21	– son is finally born
Gen 22	– son must be sacrificed
Gen 24:3	– son must not marry a Canaanite
Gen 26:3–4, 24	Promise passed to Isaac
Gen 27:28–29	Isaac blesses Jacob
Gen 28:13–16	Promise passed to Jacob
Gen 30:27	Laban receives blessing through Jacob
Gen 39:5	Joseph brings blessing to Egyptian's house
Exod 3:16–18; (3:6); 4:5	Promise passed to Moses
Exod 12:32	Pharaoh begs blessing from Moses!
Exod 32:7–14	Jeopardy again immediately after covenant, but Moses saves promise
Num 14:1–19	Moses mediates again
Num 24	Balaam is brought to curse Israel, but blesses
Deut 34:1b–5a, 6, 10	Promise fulfilled: "This is the land...."

Thus these originally unconnected stories were presumably placed in their present order to produce a masterful plot with artistic suspense and to proclaim a basic theme: that Abraham and his descendants (the Davidic monarchy) are blessed by God and are in turn to be a blessing to the

---

3. In his *History of Pentateuchal Traditions,* Martin Noth would argue that the main lines of this story would have been put together already in the tribal, premonarchic period. It does not seem possible to divide exactly between the tribal epic narrative and the monarchic revision (J) of it.

nations. This creative ordering of traditional materials in effect produces a whole new pattern of what can be termed Salvation History: God has a master plan and a purpose behind all these seemingly random events. Whereas biblical critics might well call this creative artist a redactor, Van Seters is probably correct to insist that the role is more properly that of an author or historiographer. That is, the composer of this pattern created a new composition, both at the macro level as illustrated above, and frequently at the micro level.[4]

Yet another major advance in the composition of the Pentateuch was the joining of the traditional J and P material. The monarchic J narrative had been triumphant, announcing the ancient promises of old and the experienced fulfillment of those promises in land and kingship. But after the national disasters of the Babylonian war, destruction, and exile, there was a desperate need for a restorative account of God's favor that did not rely on autonomous kingship, war, or trust in the historical process. The P materials answered that need, with emphasis on a cosmic creation, an eternal covenant, and a theocracy. Scholars are divided on whether the pentateuchal material traditionally assigned to P was a full narrative strand or separate fragments interspersed into the monarchic epic narrative, but that need not concern us. Some major figure joined the J and P material in the creation account, the flood narrative, the genealogical schema from Adam to Abraham, and the Moses story. That person is often labeled the "redactor" (R^{J+P}). Due to the uncertainties regarding the character of the P material and how much creativity the compiler of J+P is responsible for producing, it is difficult to know what the precise term should be for the person who combined J and P.

There is insufficient space here to discuss the Deuteronomistic Historian, though the books of Deuteronomy to Kings are a parade example. I think I would agree with Van Seters that the Dtr fully merits the title of historiographer.[5]

---

4. An example would be the naming of Yahweh in Gen 18:1 as the "editorial" introduction to the narrative which continues with the (original) "three men." The identification of Yahweh as the visitor who announces the future birth of Abraham's heir is a skillful literary and theological move, incorporating this originally separate story neatly into the ongoing major plot of the promise and its fulfillment.

5. Van Seters, *Edited Bible*, 260–69.

1.2. The Composition of the Prophetic Books

The prophetic books also offer a wide variety of examples of literary activity, the terminology for which should be investigated. For example, there are at least three major layers discernible in the composition of the book of Amos. Similarly, the book of Isaiah is generally acknowledged as consisting of the work of three major figures who should be called authors: the persons responsible for First Isaiah, Second Isaiah, and Third Isaiah. In addition, there were countless people who added material in small and large amounts to the developing Isaiah corpus. For example, the apocalyptic section in chapters 24–27 is a late addition. Parts of the oracles against the nations in chapters 13–23 are supplements to the earlier text. Comparison of the 1QIsaᵃ scroll with the MT and the LXX highlight at least nine secondary insertions of one to three verses into the MT that are not in 1QIsaᵃ or not in the LXX; most of them could be called supplements or commentary.[6] The numerous insertions introduced by ביום ההוא are *ad hoc* reflections or commentary added to the already-existing text.[7]

We do not have time to examine all the books. The compilation of each differs from others, but the process is analogous for all. The composition of the Scriptures was dynamic, organic. It was even evolutionary, insofar as the traditions remained static for a period and then were transformed through a burst of literary creativity to a new literary edition, due to the creative work which some religious leader produced, often in response to a new historical, political, social, or religious situation.

---

6. See Eugene Ulrich, "The Developmental Composition of the Book of Isaiah: Light from 1QIsaᵃ on Additions in the MT," *DSD* 8/3 (2001): 288–305. Similarly, there are insertions into the text of Jeremiah of four verses in Jer 10 and eight verses between chs. 7 and 8: see idem, "Qumran Witness to the Developmental Growth of the Prophetic Books," in *With Wisdom as a Robe: Qumran and Other Jewish Studies in Honour of Ida Fröhlich* (ed. K. Daniel Dobos and M. Köszeghy; Hebrew Bible Monographs 21; Sheffield: Sheffield Phoenix, 2009), 263–74.

7. Regarding ch. 2, Joseph Blenkinsopp (*Isaiah 1–39: A New Translation with Introduction and Commentary* [AB 19; New York: Doubleday, 2000], 194) speaks of "picking our way through the editorial debris that has gradually accumulated in this passage." He also notes (72) that throughout the book "there are numerous notes or addenda in prose, many of them introduced with the future-looking or eschatological incipit 'on that day' (*bayyôm hahû*'). Most of these would be more at home in a commentary on the book than as part of the text."

2. Manuscript Evidence for Revised Literary Editions

The preceding section described, briefly and impressionistically, the method by which the books of Scripture were composed. It is hypothetical, since no manuscript evidence survives to verify or disprove it. It is based on the literary-critical findings by myriads of scholars over the past centuries. But the discovery of the biblical scrolls from Qumran and other sites provided manuscript evidence from the late third century B.C.E. onward, documenting that same phenomenon, which continued throughout the Hellenistic and early Roman periods, including the time of the origins of rabbinic Judaism and Christianity.

Before the discovery of the Scrolls, the SP, the LXX, and Josephus demonstrated that there were variant, or revised, literary editions of certain books of Scripture in the late Second Temple period, though scholars did not see clearly the implications of this phenomenon. Now there is additional evidence for a number of variant, revised literary editions of the biblical books documented in the manuscripts found at Qumran. In certain cases the manuscript evidence from Qumran directly confirms the variant editions already discernible from the SP, the LXX, and Josephus.

Four different levels of development can be observed when comparing the Scrolls, the MT, the SP, and the LXX: (1) fuller orthography, or alternate spelling practices; (2) individual textual variants, such as errors, clarifications, or synonyms; (3) isolated insertions of commentary, supplements, or interpretation; and (4) large-scale revised literary editions. These four levels are distinct from one another, each operating independently. In order adequately to describe and differentiate the textual or literary activities of those producing such changes, at least four different terms will be required.

2.1. Genesis

It will prove instructive to explore examples of major, intentional work observable in the manuscript evidence. Though the main witnesses to Genesis display basically the same text throughout most of the book, the MT, the SP, and the LXX do present one interesting example of divergence. The chronologies in Gen 5 and 11 tabulating the ages of the prediluvian and postdiluvian ancestors display great variation between the three sources. In the SP version of Gen 5:3–32, Jared, Methuselah, and Lamech are still living when the flood begins. In the LXX version Methuselah is still living fourteen years beyond the start of the flood, when supposedly no humans remained except Noah and those with him in the ark (Gen 7:23–24). Moreover, the reports in Gen 11:10–32 indicate that many of the postdiluvian ancestors are still alive during Abraham's lifetime, while some even live past his death. The problem resulted from the joining of two sources with distinct chronologies: the Priestly genealogical schema and the traditional primeval narrative.

Ronald Hendel, following Ralph Klein's analysis,[8] concludes that the variant chronologies of the MT, SP, and LXX "are the result of conscious and systematic revisions of Genesis 5 and 11, motivated by problems implicit in the ages of the individuals at death.... Most remarkably, these problems were solved independently in the textual traditions ancestral to" the MT, SP, and LXX.[9] That is, three different individuals examining early copies of Genesis noticed the chronological inconsistencies, and each intentionally revised the text to resolve the problem, but with different numbers. The current MT, SP, and LXX were each copied from a different one of the three revised chronologies.

What term accurately fits the work of the three individual revisers? Since it is minor, isolated activity, "author" or "historiographer" is too elevated, nor does "editor" fit. "Attentive scribe" or simply "reviser" may come closest.

2.2. Exodus

Exodus offers a great deal of evidence for repeated growth in the text with up to five successive variant editions. First, there is one account of building the tabernacle in Exod 35–39 in the LXX, and a quite different, fuller and reordered account in the MT. The more persuasive explanation is that the LXX preserves an older account which has been revised in the MT tradition to agree more closely with the instructions given in Exod 25–31.[10] In either case, someone intentionally reworked five chapters to produce a

---

8. Ralph W. Klein, "Archaic Chronologies and the Textual History of the Old Testament," *HTR* 67 (1974): 255–63.

9. Ronald S. Hendel, *The Text of Genesis 1–11: Textual Studies and Critical Edition* (New York: Oxford University Press, 1998), 61.

10. See Anneli Aejmelaeus, "Septuagintal Translation Techniques—A Solution to the Problem of the Tabernacle Account," in *On the Trail of Septuagint Translators: Collected Essays* (ed. A. Aejmelaeus; Kampen: Kok Pharos, 1993), 116–30. For

revised edition of that account. Again, "author" is too elevated; "reviser" or "editor" may fit best.

A third edition of Exodus was discovered at Qumran. 4QpaleoExod[m] is clearly a biblical manuscript, though it differs from the MT in its spelling practices, displays a large number and a wide variety of textual variants and, though basically agreeing with the MT and LXX, frequently includes verses and even whole paragraphs that are not in the MT or LXX. Those large expansions are also found in the SP, though the single theological difference of Mount Gerizim as the site of the central Yahwistic shrine is not present in the scroll. The scroll thus exhibits a third edition of Exodus, intentionally, repeatedly supplementing the older narrative with two types of addition. There are frequent word-for-word insertions of pertinent parallel details from Deuteronomy into the Exodus narrative, as well as insertions that explicitly report that Moses and Aaron actually fulfilled God's commands, where the MT implicitly presumes the fulfillment. The person responsible for the new form of the text could be termed a "supplementer" or even an "editor," insofar as a modern publisher would list the work as a "new and expanded edition."

When viewed from a literary perspective, the differences between 4QpaleoExod[m] and the SP Exodus are minor: SP includes one long addition to the Ten Commandments after Exod 20:17 and the repeated formula that God "has chosen" Mount Gerizim as Israel's central shrine, in contrast to the Judean formula that God "will choose" Jerusalem. Literarily that would simply be a single expansion and a minor variant formula. Theologically, of course, it is a major and divisive challenge, sufficiently large that only one of the two versions would be acceptable to any particular individual or community. Thus a claim could be made that the SP forms a fourth edition of the book of Exodus. How might one describe this theological reviser?

A fifth edition of Exodus also surfaced at Qumran, which was published as a nonbiblical work under the title of 4QReworked Pentateuch. Already in 1993 I suggested that it should be considered a variant form of the Pentateuch, and increasingly this view is being accepted.[11] The editors of 4QRP describe the differences from the MT of Exodus thus:

---

the opposite view, see David W. Gooding, *The Account of the Tabernacle* (Cambridge: Cambridge University Press, 1959).

11. Eugene Ulrich, "The Bible in the Making: The Scriptures at Qumran," in *The Community of the Renewed Covenant: The Notre Dame Symposium on the Dead Sea*

The text presented here probably contained the complete Pentateuch, reworked by the author of 4QRP.... This composition contained a running text of the Pentateuch interspersed with exegetical additions and omissions. The greater part of the preserved fragments follows the biblical text closely, but many small ... elements are added, while other elements are omitted, or, in other cases, their sequence altered.[12]

If the form of "the Pentateuch" and "the biblical text" must necessarily be the Masoretic form or the MT/LXX/SP form, then 4QRP would not be classified as "biblical." But the evidence offered by the scriptural scrolls from Qumran as well as the SP and the LXX demonstrates that additions, omissions, and changed sequences are *characteristic* of the biblical text in this compositional period; they are not features that would disqualify a text from scriptural status. The work should now be labeled 4QPent instead.

The person responsible for the changed form of 4QPent would be at least a "supplementer": for example, after Gen 30:36 the scroll includes a report, absent from the MT and LXX, of what the messenger of God said to Jacob in a dream, the details of which are drawn from Gen 31:10–13.[13] Another copy has a large insertion concerning the wood offering and the festival of the new oil.[14] Thus we have documented five major stages, or

---

Scrolls (ed. E. Ulrich and J. C. VanderKam; Notre Dame, Ind.: University of Notre Dame Press, 1994), 77–93, esp. 92 n. 51 [repr., Ulrich, *Scrolls and the Origins*, 32]. See also Michael Segal, "4QReworked Pentateuch or 4QPentateuch?" in *The Dead Sea Scrolls: Fifty Years after Their Discovery* (ed. L. H. Schiffman, E. Tov, and J. C. VanderKam, with G. Marquis; Jerusalem: Israel Exploration Society/The Shrine of the Book, Israel Museum, 2000), 391–99; and Emanuel Tov now agrees that 4QRP is "to be reclassified as a biblical text, '4QPentateuch,'" and needs "to be studied as Hebrew Scripture." I thank Professor Tov for an advance copy of his article, "The Many Forms of Scripture: Reflections in Light of the LXX and 4QReworked Pentateuch," in *From Qumran to Aleppo: A Discussion with Emanuel Tov about the Textual History of Jewish Scriptures in Honor of His 65th Birthday* (ed. A. Lange, M. Weigold, and J. Zsengellér; Göttingen: Vandenhoeck & Ruprecht, 2009), 11–28.

12. Emanuel Tov and Sidnie White, "364–367. 4QReworked Pentateuch[b–e]," in *Qumran Cave 4.VIII: Parabiblical Texts, Part 1* (ed. H. Attridge et al., in consultation with J. C. VanderKam; DJD 13; Oxford: Clarendon, 1994), 187–351, esp. 187, 191.

13. 4QRP[b] (4Q364) frg. 4 b–e II, 21–26. Note the parallel phenomenon of dream repetition in all texts at Gen 31:24 + 31:29, and 41:1–7 + 41:17–24.

14. 4QRP[c] (4Q365 frg. 23, 5–11). Note that, though the wood offering does not appear in the traditional Pentateuch, Nehemiah in a passage about "obligations" already mentions the wood offering "as it is written in the Torah" (Neh 10:35 [34]; see also 13:31).

successive "new and expanded editions," of the developing text of Exodus, exhibiting different types of intentional literary work. Van Seters is correct that all five types would probably be attributed to "editors" by modern scholars, but adequate differentiation of roles does present a lexicographic challenge.

2.3. NUMBERS

Scholars were slow to accept the unforeseen new evidence for Exodus. But then a scroll from the book of Numbers (4QNum[b]) displayed a pattern identical to that seen in 4QpaleoExod[m], a pattern of recurrent expansions in general agreement with the SP, but lacking the specifically Samaritan theological claims. That meant that two of the books of the Torah were circulating in Jewish circles in two different, well defined forms, one based on the other but intentionally expanded. It also meant that generally the SP should rise in value as faithfully transmitting one of the forms of the common Jewish biblical text as it circulated in the first century B.C.E.

2.4. JOSHUA

4QJosh[a] presents an order of important events that differs from the MT and the LXX order. The scroll contains the earlier, uncomplicated order, whereas the MT has rearranged the order due to sectarian claims. In Deut 27:1–3 the command is given to build an altar and inscribe the law on it "on the day you cross over the Jordan." Accordingly, 4QJosh[a] places the building of the altar and accompanying Torah reading right after the crossing of the Jordan and entrance into the promised land (Josh 4), followed by the circumcision (Josh 5) and the beginning of the conquest (Josh 6). Weighty confirmation of the 4QJosh[a] order is supplied by the first-century Jewish historian Josephus (*Ant.* 5.20; cf. 5.45–57), who also places events in this order. Then, at Deut 27:4, in what looks like an addition, the SP and the Old Latin (OL)[15] insert "Mount Gerizim" into the text. At a third stage, the MT tradition reacted by replacing "Mount Gerizim" with the

---

15. It is impossible that the reading in the second century C.E. OL was translated directly from the text of the long-ostracized Samaritans. It was certainly accurately translated from an already augmented OG text, which means that the reading—though certainly northern—was earlier than the Samaritan split and not confined to the Samaritan sect.

enigmatic "Mount Ebal." As a consequence, the scene of the building of the altar and the reading of the Torah is moved to the end of chapter 8 in the MT and placed after 9:2 in the LXX.[16] The textual form of 4QJosh[a] appears to be simply the work of the original Dtr historiographer. The two-word insertion at Deut 27:4 in the SP, the OL, and the MT would be the work of theologically motivated scribes. But the major rearrangement of moving the building of the altar and the Torah reading from chapter 4 to the end of chapter 8 should be attributed to serious editorial activity.

2.5. JUDGES 6:7–10 INSERTED INTO MT

4QJudg[a] provides a marvelously clear example of a short original text into which the MT has inserted a theological passage featuring a prophet. Julio Trebolle published this oldest preserved manuscript of the book of Judges.[17] It dates from ca. 50–25 B.C.E. and survives in only a single fragment of 7.6 x 4.8 cm, but it offers an important piece of evidence. It contains text from Judg 6: verses 2–6 followed directly by verses 11–13. Verses 7–10 are not present. Trebolle notes that since the time of Wellhausen verses 7–10 have been "generally recognized by modern critics as a literary insertion" and that they are now seen as "a piece of late Dtr. redaction." On the basis of the 4QJudg[a] evidence he correctly concludes that "4QJudg[a] can confidently be seen as an earlier literary form of the book than our traditional texts."[18] The scroll apparently narrated the story of the Midianite oppression and the call of Gideon to deliver the Israelites. Whereas the early form of the story describes Gideon challenging "the angel of the Lord," the secondary text as preserved in the MT inserts this stereotypical passage which in fact contrasts with Gideon's challenge:

> When the Israelites cried out to the LORD on account of the Midianites, the LORD sent a prophet to the Israelites; and he said to them, "Thus says the LORD, the God of Israel: I led you up from Egypt, and brought you

---

16. This rearrangement in the MT and LXX creates the problematic situation that Joshua marches twenty miles north, builds the altar, and immediately returns south, leaving the altar abandoned and exposed in enemy Canaanite territory.

17. Julio Trebolle Barrera, "4QJudg[a]," in DJD 14:161–64; and idem, "Textual Variants in 4QJudg[a] and the Textual and Editorial History of the Book of Judges," *RevQ* 14/2 (1989): 229–45.

18. Trebolle, "4QJudg[a]," 162.

forth from the house of slavery.... But you have not given heed to my voice."[19]

2.6. JEREMIAH

A manuscript from Cave 4 at Qumran, 4QJer[b], has provided clinching proof for the reliability of the LXX, just as 4QpaleoExod[m] and 4QNum[b] validated the SP. It is well known that the Greek translation of Jeremiah is significantly shorter (about 16 percent shorter) than the form of the text in the MT, and that it presents a different order of the book. Its text had therefore been suspect. 4QJer[b], however, exhibits a starkly different Hebrew text form that proves to be the type of source text that the Greek has faithfully translated. Again, this vindicated the Septuagint as a faithful translation—it was simply not a translation of the Masoretic form but of an alternate ancient Hebrew form of the book. It represented an earlier edition of the book and showed the MT to be a secondary, expanded version that had developed beyond the earlier edition.[20]

2.7. EZEKIEL

Not quite as dramatic as the LXX of Jeremiah, but still instructive, is the Greek of Ezekiel, especially as seen in chapters 36–40. A second- or third-century papyrus, 967, shows the order of those chapters as 36, 38, 39, 37, 40, with the last section of chapter 36 absent. Johan Lust has studied the exegetical significance of this and persuasively argues that papyrus 967 accurately represents the original Greek translation which, like the Greek of Jeremiah, had been faithfully copied from a variant Hebrew tradition. A later Hebrew "editor" moved chapter 37 into its present position and added the last section of chapter 36 as an eschatological introduction to chapter 37.

---

19. The biblical translations in this essay are mainly from the NRSV with some adaptations.

20. Note that the relative status of the editions is here reversed: the MT was the earlier edition compared with 4QpaleoExod[m], 4QNum[b], and the SP, but is the later, secondary edition compared with 4QJer[b] and the LXX.

2.8. The Nature of the MT

Before the discovery of the Scrolls, scholars viewed the MT, the LXX, and the SP as three main text-types. For most books of the Bible, the basic text of the LXX was simply compared to the MT as a specimen held up for judgment against the presumed "correct" MT. Now, however, we can focus more clearly and render more exact appraisals. Scholars now realize that the MT is not "the original text" or the *Urtext* of the Hebrew Bible and, in fact, that it is not "a text" at all. It is a varied collection of texts—a different type of text for each of the books—each being simply a copy of one of the editions of that book which was circulating in late Second Temple Jewish circles. The MT is not "the original text"; it is rather the *only* collection of texts in the *original language* that was preserved (outside Samaritan circles) since the second century C.E. Moreover, the MT, the LXX, and the SP are not "three main text-types" but merely manuscript exemplars, each copied more or less accurately from one or other of the available editions of each book. Thus the Masoretic Texts must be judged on a par with and according to the same criteria by which the LXX, the SP, the Scrolls, the versions, and all other texts are judged, word by word. Perhaps it can be asked quite starkly: If we are comfortable with the conclusion that the original Greek translation is no longer available and attainable except through a critically established text, why do we hesitate to accept that the original Hebrew is no longer available except through a critically established text? Thus we should attempt to produce a critically established text of the Hebrew Bible, and so we turn to the present-day efforts to produce editions of the Hebrew Bible.

2.9. From Scrolls to Codex: Bible and Canon

This discussion has involved "texts" through most of the period described above, since the individual books developed separately and were copied on separate scrolls. Eventually the collection of texts coalesced into a single text. Books considered to have divine authority formed a special group distinct from other works. The group of five books seen as the revelation to Moses became "the Book of Moses" or "the Law of Moses"; it together with the group of prophetic books became "the Law and the Prophets," viewed as a special collection of authoritative Scripture in the late Second Temple period. Though that core of the collected writings was well established, books of the Writings, or Poetic and Wisdom books, were still finding their place in the first century C.E. Though the contents of the canon, or official collection, differed for each of the different communities, the process and general timeline were very similar in the several communities. By approximately the third century, the codex gradually supplanted the scroll as the preferred form, and the texts that had enjoyed only a mental unity were now transformed into a physical unity, a single text: the Tanak or the Old Testament.

3. CURRENT EDITIONS OF THE HEBREW BIBLE

There are English translations of the Jewish, Protestant, and Catholic forms of the Bible, for example, the New Jewish Publication Society Translation (based on the MT), the Protestant New Revised Standard Version (based mainly on the MT but using the LXX, Versions, and the Scrolls), and the Catholic New American Bible (based on "the Original Languages with Critical Use of All the Ancient Sources"). These Bibles each display a single clear text. The many forms of complexity, however, that lie behind those texts is betrayed by the fact there are five different critical editions of the Hebrew Bible currently in preparation: *The Hebrew University Bible* (ed. Moshe H. Goshen-Gottstein et al.); *Biblia Hebraica quinta editione* (ed. Adrian Schenker et al.); *The Oxford Hebrew Bible* (ed. Ronald Hendel et al.); *The Qumran Bible* (ed. Eugene Ulrich); and *Biblia Qumranica* (ed. Armin Lange et al.). They each offer a different form of the text based on varying perspectives and principles.

3.1. *THE HEBREW UNIVERSITY BIBLE*

The Hebrew University Bible is a huge undertaking, with each book meriting its own volume. To date only three volumes (Isaiah, Jeremiah, and Ezekiel) have been published. It is a diplomatic edition, in that it reproduces as its text at the top of each page a single manuscript: Codex Aleppo (dated to ca. 925). Beneath the text are five separate apparatuses. The first contains the variant readings from the ancient Greek, Aramaic, Syriac, and Latin versions. The second contains witnesses in the Hebrew language: the Dead Sea Scrolls and rabbinic literature; the third, variant readings from medieval Masoretic manuscripts; and the fourth, differences in orthography, vowels, and accents in the Masoretic manuscripts. Whereas those four apparatuses aim at objective presentation of the textual data, the fifth apparatus contains the editorial judgments that the editors consider appropriate to interject for the reader's consideration.

3.2. *Biblia Hebraica quinta editione*

The *Biblia Hebraica quinta editione* is an update of the current *Biblia Hebraica Stuttgartensia*, the generally best single-volume hand edition of the Hebrew Bible used by most academics today. It, too, is a diplomatic edition, which reproduces not the text of Codex Aleppo but of Codex Leningradensis (dated to ca. 1009). This updated edition should have all the best features of *BHS* and will include, for the first time, comprehensive witness in its critical apparatus of the readings from the biblical Dead Sea Scrolls, as well as editorial judgments assessing how the different variant readings arose.

3.3. *The Oxford Hebrew Bible*

The *OHB* will elevate Hebrew Bible studies to a new level, thanks to the Scrolls. (In their contributions to this volume, Eibert Tigchelaar and Sarianna Metso address this edition more fully.) Although virtually every other textual enterprise, including closely related fields studying the classics, the Septuagint, and the New Testament, operates with a critically established text, the Hebrew Bible has been limited to a diplomatic edition. That is, the text of a single manuscript (the Aleppo Codex or the Leningrad Codex containing the Masoretic Text) is printed, with an apparatus of variant readings from other preserved sources. But no single manuscript is without errors, and in a large collection such as the Bible, numerous errors are printed in the main edition. This was necessary because only one close family of Hebrew texts (the Masoretic Text) had been preserved since antiquity. Since both the SP and the LXX were discredited by most, there was a dearth of texts for comparison.

But this "default" situation of a diplomatic text for the Hebrew Bible can now be remedied. The biblical scrolls have revalidated the Samaritan text and the Greek text as reliable witnesses, and have provided over two hundred Hebrew and Greek manuscripts older by a millennium than our previously available MT manuscripts. Thus there is now a wide enough spectrum of texts to make a critically established text possible, desirable, and necessary.

3.4. *The Qumran Bible*

The Qumran Bible will present in a single volume the text of whatever portions of the traditional Hebrew Bible survived from the eleven caves at Qumran. Based on the format of *BHS*, it will present for each passage the text as witnessed by the most distinctive Qumran scroll preserved. An apparatus will list any Hebrew variants from other scrolls or from the MT or SP, and many of the more important Greek variants. It will be a one-volume hand edition, parallel to Rahlfs's single-volume *Septuaginta*.[21]

3.5. *Biblia Qumranica*

Biblia Qumranica also presents the textual data of the biblical scrolls, but in a larger context. Separate volumes are devoted to individual books or groups of books. Each volume presents in multiple columns in a two-page format the MT in the right column, the LXX in the left column, and the Scrolls in the columns between them. A separate column is devoted to each manuscript. If only one scroll is extant for the passages on that pair of pages, only one column is presented between the MT and the LXX. But at times there are four or five scrolls extant, and each is presented in its own column synoptically. To date only the Minor Prophets volume has appeared.

Each of these editions attempts a presentation of the text in light of different perspectives and principles. Perhaps from this pluriformity will emerge a sharper single focus on the text.

---

21. See provisionally Eugene Ulrich, *The Biblical Qumran Scrolls: Transcriptions and Textual Variants* (VTSup 134; Leiden: Brill, 2010).

Editing the Hebrew Bible:
An Overview of Some Problems

Eibert Tigchelaar

At present, three major projects, all aiming at major critical editions of the Hebrew Bible, are in progress.[1] The Hebrew University Bible Project (HUBP) was established in 1956 to undertake a comprehensive survey of the history of the textual development of the Hebrew Bible and to produce a major critical edition.[2] Three volumes of the *Hebrew University Bible* (*HUB*) have been published, and work on the fourth volume is in progress.[3] The Editorial Committee of the *Biblia Hebraica Quinta* (*BHQ*) was installed in 1990, but this project was heir to both the *Biblia Hebraica Stuttgartensia* (which had been completed in 1967), and the Hebrew Old

---

1. For more extensive overviews of both critical and noncritical editions of the Hebrew Bible, see Moshe H. Goshen-Gottstein, "Editions of the Hebrew Bible—Past and Future," in *"Sha'arei Talmon": Studies in the Bible, Qumran, and the Ancient Near East Presented to Shemaryahu Talmon* (ed. M. Fishbane and E. Tov, with the assistance of W. W. Fields; Winona Lake, Ind.: Eisenbrauns, 1992), 221–42; Emanuel Tov, "Hebrew Scripture Editions: Philosophy and Praxis," in *From 4QMMT to Resurrection–Mélanges qumraniens en hommage à Émile Puech* (ed. F. García Martínez et al.; STDJ 61; Leiden: Brill, 2006): 281–312; revised version in Emanuel Tov, *Hebrew Bible, Greek Bible, and Qumran—Collected Essays* (TSAJ 121; Tübingen: Mohr Siebeck, 2008), 247–70.

2. See the self-presentation of the HUBP archived at http://web.archive.org/web/20070107190040/http://jewish.huji.ac.il/research/Bible_Project.html.

3. Moshe H. Goshen-Gottstein, *The Hebrew University Bible, The Book of Isaiah* (Jerusalem: Magnes, 1995); Chaim Rabin, Shemaryahu Talmon, and Emanuel Tov, *The Hebrew University Bible, The Book of Jeremiah* (Jerusalem: Magnes, 1997); Moshe H. Goshen-Gottstein and Shemaryahu Talmon, *The Hebrew University Bible, The Book of Ezekiel* (Jerusalem: Magnes, 2004). It has been announced that by 2010, the HUBP will complete and publish the first volume (Hosea-Jonah) of a two-volume Twelve Prophets edition, under the edition of Michael Segal and Shlomo Naeh, and in 2014 the second volume.

Testament Text Project of the United Bible Societies which was consti-
tuted in 1969. Five fascicles of the *BHQ* have now been published.[4] In
2008 a third project, the *Oxford Hebrew Bible* (*OHB*), was officially presented.[5] Only samples have been published, both in print and on the
web.[6] All three projects have their own philosophy and take different
practical decisions, and these have been put forward and discussed in
many different publications.[7] The aim of the present overview is modest.
First I will briefly describe issues of the text of the Hebrew Bible and the
contribution of the Dead Sea Scrolls. I will then discuss two important
issues arising from the present projects. Finally, I will think beyond the
existing projects.

---

4. *Biblia Hebraica Quinta 18. General Introduction and Megilloth* (gen. ed. A.
Schenker; Stuttgart: Deutsche Bibelgesellschaft, 2004); David Marcus, *Biblia Hebraica
Quinta 20. Ezra and Nehemiah* (Stuttgart: Deutsche Bibelgesellschaft, 2006); Carmel
McCarthy, *Biblia Hebraica Quinta 5. Deuteronomy* (Stuttgart: Deutsche Bibelgesell-
schaft, 2007); Jan de Waard, *Biblia Hebraica Quinta 17. Proverbs* (Stuttgart: Deutsche
Bibelgesellschaft, 2007); Anthony Gelston, *Biblia Hebraica Quinta 13. The Twelve
Prophets* (Stuttgart: Deutsche Bibelgesellschaft, 2011).

5. Ronald Hendel, "The Oxford Hebrew Bible: Prologue to a New Critical Edition," *VT* 58 (2008): 324–51.

6. Sidnie White Crawford, Jan Joosten, and Eugene Ulrich, "Sample Editions of
the Oxford Hebrew Bible: Deuteronomy 32:1–9. 1 Kings 11:1–8, and Jeremiah 27:1–
10 (34 G)," *VT* 58 (2008): 352–66. For other samples (1 Sam 17:11, 32–37), see Ronald
Hendel, "Plural Texts and Literary Criticism: For Instance, 1 Sam 17," *Textus* 23 (2007):
97–114, as well as samples to be found on the website of the project: ohb.berkeley.edu/
samples.htm. On this same website one can find *The Oxford Hebrew Bible: Guide for
Editors* (rev. November 2008), which solves some problems of the sample editions and
introduces some improvements vis-à-vis the samples.

7. Here only a few, but important, examples are mentioned: Adrian Schenker,
"Eine Neuausgabe der Biblia Hebraica," *ZAH* 9 (1996): 58–61; James A. Sanders, "*The
Hebrew University Bible* and *Biblia Hebraica Quinta*," *JBL* 118 (1999): 518–26; Richard
D. Weis, "*Biblica Hebraica Quinta* and the Making of Critical Editions of the Hebrew
Bible," *TC: A Journal of Biblical Textual Criticism* 7 (2002) [http://purl.org/TC]; Tov,
"Hebrew Scripture Editions: Philosophy and Praxis"; Hendel, "Oxford Hebrew Bible";
H. G. M. Williamson, "Do We Need A New Bible? Reflections on the Proposed Oxford
Hebrew Bible," *Bib* 90 (2009): 153–75.

1. The Text of the Hebrew Bible
and the Impact of the Dead Sea Scrolls[8]

Up to the present day, all printed editions, both critical and noncritical, of the Hebrew Bible have been based on medieval Masoretic manuscripts, either eclectically, as the so-called first and second Rabbinic Bible, or following one specific manuscript such as the Codex Leningradensis (Firkovitch B 19 A) from 1009, or the tenth-century Aleppo Codex.[9] Of the present three major critical projects, the *HUB* uses as its basic text the Aleppo Codex, wherever it is preserved, and reconstructs the text where passages of the Aleppo Codex are not available.[10] The *Biblia Hebraica* series has, from its third edition on, used the Codex Leningradensis as its base text.[11] The *OHB* likewise takes as its so-called copy-text the same Codex Leningradensis.[12] The choice for medieval manuscripts was necessary because, before the discovery of the Dead Sea Scrolls, these were the oldest available Hebrew witnesses of the Hebrew Bible. Moreover, the Aleppo Codex and Leningrad Codex were seen as the most precise existing manuscripts of the Hebrew Bible.[13] The discovery of the Dead Sea Scrolls has changed

---

8. There are multiple discussions of the text of the Hebrew Bible, in manuscripts and editions. See for many of those aspects: Emanuel Tov, *Textual Criticism of the Hebrew Bible* (2nd rev. ed.; Minneapolis: Fortress, 2001); abbreviated forthwith as *TCHB*. For another succinct overview, see Arie van der Kooij, "The Textual Criticism of the Hebrew Bible Before and After the Qumran Discoveries," in *The Bible as Book: the Hebrew Bible and the Judaean Desert Discoveries* (ed. E. D. Herbert and E. Tov; London: British Library, 2002), 167–77. The following overview only aims at highlighting some aspects.

9. For a brief overview, see for example Goshen-Gottstein, "Editions of the Hebrew Bible."

10. The first examples of this reconstruction, based on the method of reconstruction of Menachem Cohen (Bar-Ilan) and refined at the HUBP, will appear in the next volume on the Twelve Prophets.

11. Thus the so-called *BHK*, that is the third edition of the *Biblia Hebraica*, edited by Rudolf Kittel and Paul Kahle (1929–1937); the *BHS* (*Biblia Hebraica Stuttgartensia*), edited by Kurt Elliger and Wilhelm Rudolph (1967–1977); and now the *BHQ*.

12. For a discussion of the use of the concept of copy-text by the *OHB*, see below.

13. Throughout his career, Goshen-Gottstein has criticized the Codex Leningradensis as an inferior codex in comparison to the Aleppo Codex (see, e.g., "Editions of the Hebrew Bible," 232. On this issue, see the *Biblia Hebraica Quinta 18*, xx, which characterizes the Leningradenis as an "excellent manuscript," but "not as carefully prepared as" the Aleppo Codex.

little in this respect: on the whole the biblical scrolls are too fragmentary to replace the medieval manuscripts of the Hebrew Bible as base texts.[14] Also, the text of the scrolls from Qumran and other locations in the Judean Desert only consists of the consonantal Hebrew text and some paragraphing, whereas the Textus Receptus of the medieval manuscripts contains, in addition, a full vocalization and accentuation system and the various Masoretic apparatuses. This raises the philosophical question about the different levels of the text of the Hebrew Bible and the practical issue of how critical editions deal with those different layers in the text. In the major critical editions we see three different approaches. The *HUB* pays full attention to matters of orthography, vowels, and accents in the medieval manuscripts, records such variants in a select group of ancient witnesses (Apparatus 4), and presents the Masorah of the Aleppo Codex. The *BHQ* presents the Masorah of the Codex Leningradensis diplomatically and gives notes on the Masorah in the commentary section. It does not record variants with regard to orthography, vowels, or accentuation in the Masoretic manuscripts. The *OHB* samples adopt the paragraphing, spelling, vowels, and accents of the Leningrad Codex as "accidentals" of the copy-text. Also, it regards the so-called Masoretic *ketiv-qere* readings as textual variants. In the case of the *OHB*, which aspires to reconstruct the archetype, or "earliest inferable textual state,"[15] the adoption of vowels and accents from a manuscript representing the latest textual state may seem practical, but inconsistent to some.[16]

Before the discovery of the first Dead Sea Scrolls in 1947, the medieval manuscripts were our oldest witnesses of the Hebrew text of the Hebrew

---

14. I am using here the term "Hebrew Bible" to refer to the cohesive entity of all the books that were collected in the large medieval codices such as the Aleppo and Leningrad Codices, later printed in the Rabbinic Bibles, and now in our Hebrew Bible editions. I also use the term to refer to the abstract entity of the texts of those books as transmitted since the Hellenistic period. The corpus of the Dead Sea Scrolls did not contain such comprehensive collections, but only scrolls with usually one book which was later included in the Hebrew Bible. For practical reasons, we call such scrolls that contain the text of books of the later Hebrew Bible "biblical scrolls," without claiming that at that time there already was a canonical or comprehensive concept of "Bible," or that those who copied those books made a clear distinction between biblical and nonbiblical scrolls or texts.

15. Hendel, "Oxford Hebrew Bible," 329–30.

16. See, for example, the critical discussion by Williamson, "Do We Need a New Bible?" 164–67.

Bible. It has become a common place to state that the Dead Sea Scrolls revolutionized our understanding of the text and transmission of the Hebrew Bible—but how have they affected the critical editions of the Hebrew Bible? Immediately after the publication of the Qumran Cave 1 Isaiah Scroll and the Habakkuk Commentary in 1950,[17] the "seventh edition"[18] of the *Biblia Hebraica* was extended by the addition of the variant readings for Isaiah and Habakkuk, in a separate apparatus below the already-existing apparatuses. The *BHS* did collate readings from the Dead Sea Scrolls in the apparatus, but many of the Cave 4 texts were not yet known to the *BHS* editors or were published too late to be included. Therefore, most references are to already published materials from the other caves.[19] It is only in the three present critical editions that the discoveries of the scrolls can be fully incorporated. The *HUB*, which aims at near-completeness, presents all variants between the biblical scrolls from the Judean Desert and the Aleppo Codex, "including erasures, corrections, and even evident scribal errors," and in the edition of Ezekiel it also includes quotations from the book of Ezekiel in nonbiblical compositions.[20] However, in accord with the philosophy of the *HUB*, it does not evaluate the evidence. The *BHQ* is selective, and generally presents only those variants that are both text-critically significant and potentially significant for translation or exegesis. Unlike the *HUB*, it does evaluate readings, and it sometimes expresses a preference for a variant reading. In the fascicle on Deuteronomy the latter happens about sixty times.[21] There are only a few cases where a preferred

---

17. Millar Burrows, with John C. Trever and William H. Brownlee, eds., *The Dead Sea Scrolls of St. Mark's Monastery Volume 1: The Isaiah Manuscript and the Habakkuk Commentary* (New Haven, Conn.: American Schools of Oriental Research, 1950).

18. This was actually a corrected and expanded reprint of the third edition, the *BHK*. New reprints or impressions after the third edition of 1937 were numbered as successive editions (thus the 4th and 5th ed. in 1949; the 6th in 1950; the 7th and 8th in 1951; the 9th in 1954, etc., up to the 16th in 1973). Later the *BHS* was seen as the fourth, and the *BHQ* as the fifth edition of the *BH* series.

19. A strange case is Hans Bardtke, *Biblia Hebraica Stuttgartensia 11 Liber Psalmorum* (Stuttgart: Württembergische Bibelanstalt, 1969), who gives the variants found in the first few columns of 11Q5, but not those found in cols. 5 to the end.

20. Goshen-Gottstein and Talmon, *The Book of Ezekiel*, xxviii. On the accuracy of the apparatus with respect to the Judean Desert materials, see my review in *JSJ* 36 (2005): 351–52.

21. I went through the entire apparatus searching for "|| pref" and found fifty-

variant reading is mentioned with reference to the Dead Sea Scrolls,[22] and only those in Deut 32 and 33 are of real interest.[23] The direct influence of readings from the Dead Sea Scrolls on the *OHB* cannot yet be established. The famous and much discussed case of Deut 32:8 turns up in the *OHB* sample of Deut 32:1–9, where Sidnie White Crawford emends בְּנֵי אל. In the sample on Gen 1:1–13, readings supported by both a Qumran scroll and the Septuagint are twice preferred over Masoretic readings.[24]

In view of the large number of fragmentary Qumran Deuteronomy manuscripts, this small number of preferred variant readings in the *BHQ* supported by the scrolls may seem surprising. One can observe also that none of the preferred variant readings in Deuteronomy is exclusively based on the scrolls, but always on evidence of the scrolls supported by other witnesses, usually the Septuagint, but also the Samaritan Pentateuch. This, in fact, characterizes the importance of the Dead Sea Scrolls for our understanding of the text of the Hebrew Bible. First, in spite of numerous small variants, the scrolls confirm the overall reliability of the transmission of the Hebrew Bible. Many manuscripts have a text that corresponds largely with the consonantal framework of the Masoretic Text. Second, there are biblical Dead Sea Scrolls that share individual readings, as well as typical features, with the Septuagint or the Samaritan Pentateuch against

---

eight cases, including twelve in Deut 22 where the editor "prefers" the M[qere] reading נַעֲרָה above the *ketiv* נַעַר. However, I still may have overlooked a few.

22. Deut 5:10 מִצְוֹתַי M[qere] Smr 4QDeut[n] G V S T; 22:15 הַנַּעֲרָה M[qere] Smr 4QDeut[f]; הַנַּעֲרָה M[qere] Smr 11QT[a]; 22:24 הַנַּעֲרָה M[qere] Smr 11QT[a]; 22:26 וְלַנַּעֲרָה M[qere] Smr 11QT[a]; 22:27 הַנַּעֲרָה M[qere] Smr 11QT[a]; 22:28 נַעֲרָה M[qere] Smr 11QT[a]; 22:29 הַנַּעֲרָה M[qere] Smr 11QT[a]; 24:14 שָׂכָר 1QDeut[b] G V S; 32:8 בְּנֵי אֱלֹהִים 4QDeut[j] G; 32:15 יֹאכַל יַעֲקֹב וַיִּשְׂבַּע יְשֻׁרוּן (correct וַיִּשְׂבַּע to יִשְׂבַּע; EJCT) Smr (4QPhyl[n]) (G); 32:43 שָׁמַיִם 4QDeut[q] G; עִמּוֹ 4QDeut[q] G; *foll* וְהִשְׁתַּחֲווּ לוֹ כָּל־אֱלֹהִים 4QDeut[q] (G); בָּנָיו 4QDeut[q] G; עַמּוֹ 4QDeut[q] G; לְצָרָיו וְלִמְשַׂנְאָיו יְשַׁלֵּם 4QDeut[q] G; אַדְמַת עַמּוֹ Smr 4QDeut[q] G; 33:8 הָבוּ 4QDeut[q] G; 33:8 לְלֵוִי תֻּמֶּיךָ (correct תֻּמֶּיךָ to תֻּמֶּיךָ; EJCT) 4QDeut[h] 4QTest (G).

23. The variants in Deut 32 and 33 were already included in the apparatus of the *BHS*, since the fragments had been published preliminarily by Patrick Skehan, "A Fragment of the 'Song of Moses' (Deut. 32) from Qumran," *BASOR* 136 (1954): 12–15; see also idem, "The Qumran Manuscripts and Textual Criticism," in *Volume de congrès, Strasbourg 1956* (VTSup 4; Leiden: Brill, 1957), 148–60.

24. White Crawford et al., "Sample Editions," 354 (text) and 358 (apparatus): "32:8 אל 4QDt[j] (אלוהים) G (θεοῦ)] ישראל M Sp (theol)." For another conjecture (בְּנֵי שֹׁר־אֵל), see Jan Joosten, "A Note on the Text of Deuteronomy xxxii 8," *VT* 57 (2007): 548–55. On Gen 1:1–13 see Ronald Hendel, "The Oxford Hebrew Bible: Sample of Genesis 1:1–13," accessed from ohb.berkeley.edu/samples.htm.

the Masoretic Text. The scrolls thus confirm what a minority of scholars had argued all along, namely that many readings and characteristics in the Septuagint and Samaritan Pentateuch were not idiosyncrasies introduced into the text by the Greek translator or the Samaritan community, but features going back to Hebrew Bible texts from Judea. Third, both the textual differences between the scrolls and the textual variety within one and the same scroll illustrate a phase in the transmission of biblical texts in which there was neither one fixed text, nor a clear distinction between different text-types.[25] Fourth, a small group of Qumran biblical manuscripts reflect not only textual variants but also literary editions of texts of the Hebrew Bible that are different from that transmitted in the Masoretic Text. Such "variant literary editions" of books or parts of books from the Hebrew Bible were already known from the Septuagint, but were often seen as a phenomenon related to translation. The Qumran scrolls now provide manuscript evidence of multiple variant literary versions in Hebrew, including one—in 4QJer[b]—corresponding to the Greek version of Jeremiah, coexisting in the same corpus.[26] Because of these variant literary

---

25. Emanuel Tov, for example in his "The Biblical Texts from the Judaean Desert—an Overview and Analysis of the Published Texts," in *The Bible as Book: the Hebrew Bible and the Judaean Desert Discoveries*, 139–66, esp. 152–57, classifies the biblical texts from Qumran on the basis of their degree of closeness to the Masoretic Text, the Septuagint, or the Samaritan Pentateuch. This results, according to this principle, in four categories: (1) Proto-Masoretic (or Proto-Rabbinic) Texts; (2) Pre-Samaritan (or: Harmonistic) Texts; (3) Texts Close to the Presumed Hebrew Source of LXX; and (4) Non-Aligned Texts, many of which are written according to Tov's "Qumran Scribal Practice." Note that many texts do not align exclusively with either the Masoretic Text, Septuagint, or Samaritan Pentateuch but often have, with respect to textual variants, a mixed character. For recent overviews on textual criticism of the Pentateuch and Tov's classification, see Armin Lange, *Handbuch der Textfunde vom Toten Meer: Band 1. Die Handschriften biblischer Bücher von Qumran und den anderen Fundorten* (Tübingen: Mohr Siebeck, 2009), 143–51; Hans Debel, "Greek 'Variant Literary Editions' to the Hebrew Bible?" *JSJ* 41 (2010): 161–90, esp. 163–71.

26. The terminology "double/variant/multiple literary editions" with respect to texts from the Hebrew Bible, seems to have been introduced by Eugene Ulrich, initially in "Double Literary Editions of Biblical Narratives and Reflections on Determining the Form to be Translated," in *Perspectives on the Hebrew Bible: Essays in Honor of Walter J. Harrelson* (ed. J. L. Crenshaw; Macon, Ga.: Mercer University Press, 1988), 101–16; repr. in *The Dead Sea Scrolls and the Origins of the Bible* (Grand Rapids, Mich.: Eerdmans, 1999), 34–50; see also idem, "Pluriformity in the Biblical Text, Text Groups, and Questions of Canon," in *The Madrid Qumran Congress: Proceedings of*

forms of texts, it has become clear that textual criticism, literary criticism, and redaction criticism are all relevant for determining the development of the Hebrew text.[27]

In short, the prime importance of the Dead Sea Scrolls is not found in individual textual variants, which may or may not reflect a more original state of the text. Instead, the contribution of the scrolls is more comprehensive. They testify that already in the Second Temple period there were manuscripts with texts virtually identical to the consonantal framework of the Masoretic Text. But they also shed a light on the pluriformity of the biblical text in the late Second Temple period (ca. 200 B.C.E. to 100 C.E.), and underscore the importance of the Septuagint and Samaritan Pentateuch as witnesses to forms of the text of the Hebrew Bible in this period.

2. Some Issues Arising from the Present Projects

2.1. Variant (Literary) Editions and Archetypes

The concept of variant literary editions is based on the phenomenon of a literary unit being attested in two or more parallel forms in our textual witnesses. Three classic examples from the Hebrew Bible are: (1) the book of Jeremiah, having a shorter form in the Septuagint than in the Masoretic Text, and a different arrangement of the sections in these two main textual witnesses; (2) the story of David and Goliath in 1 Sam 17–18 in the Old Greek and the Masoretic Text; (3) Daniel 4–6 in the Old Greek and Maso-

---

the International Congress on the Dead Sea Scrolls, Madrid 18–21 March 1991 (ed. J. C. Trebolle Barrera and L. Vegas Montaner; STDJ 11; Leiden: Brill, 1992), 23–41, esp. 32–37; repr. in The Dead Sea Scrolls and the Origins of the Bible, 79–98; idem, "Multiple Literary Editions: Reflections Toward a Theory of the History of the Biblical Text," in Current Research and Technological Developments on the Dead Sea Scrolls: Conference on the Texts from the Judean Desert, Jerusalem, 30 April 1995 (ed. D. W. Parry and S. D. Ricks; STDJ 20; Leiden: Brill, 1994), 78–105; repr. in The Dead Sea Scrolls and the Origins of the Bible, 99–120. See further the other literature cited in Hendel, "Oxford Hebrew Bible," 326 n. 4.

27. Note that here, as so often, the changes in insight and approach should be related only to a limited extent to the new material evidence. Equally important are general tendencies in scholarship. Note, for example, how Jerome J. McGann (A Critique of Modern Textual Criticism [Chicago: University of Chicago Press, 1983]) emphasizes the relationships between textual and literary criticism (see also the preface in the 1992 edition).

retic Text.[28] In all three cases the multiple textual differences and partial rearrangements cannot be explained as resulting from a series of unrelated intentional or accidental textual variants. Rather, the differences follow a consistent pattern of intentional modifications.[29]

Here, as with textual variants, one can ask how two variant literary editions are related: which is the primary, and which the secondary edition, or are both independent secondary editions of a now lost older form? Such variant literary editions pose problems for a critical edition of the Hebrew Bible. Literary analysis suggests that in some cases the Greek translation reflects a Hebrew text that preceded the Masoretic Text, and that in other cases the Greek represents the secondary version. In the case of Dan 4–6, all transmitted versions seem to be secondary. Reflecting on the question as to which form of the biblical text one should translate, Ulrich argues that one can, for practical or confessional reasons, systematically choose the only text that has been transmitted and preserved in full in Hebrew (Aramaic), the Masoretic Text. However, if one prefers to base one's choice on arguments of priority or of latest careful edition, then one should choose for the Old Greek version in one case, and for the Masoretic in the next, even with regard to different literary units in one and the same book.[30]

The *HUB* and *BHQ* present the text of the Aleppo Codex and Leningrad Codex respectively, and in their apparatuses only refer to individual textual variants, not to variant literary editions.[31] The *OHB* announces that

---

28. See, for example, Ulrich, "Double Literary Editions," with brief discussions and relevant bibliography; and Tov, *TCHB*, 313–50, esp. 319–27 (Jeremiah), 334–36 (1 Sam 16–18). Both also include other examples. The phenomenon of multiple editions is amply attested in other literatures. See, for example, Luigi Giuliani, Herman Brinkman, Geert Lernout, and Marita Mathijsen, eds., *Texts in Multiple Versions: Histories of Editions* (Amsterdam: Rodopi, 2006) = *Variants. The Journal of the European Society for Textual Scholarship* 5 (2006), with articles dealing with both ancient and modern examples.

29. For a more sophisticated discussion, see especially the work of Peter L. Shillingsburg, as, for example, "Text as Matter, Concept, and Action," *Studies in Bibliography* 44 (1991): 31–82. It should be noted that the term "edition," as in "variant editions," is rather typical of biblical scholarship, whereas literary critics would use the term "version."

30. For example, with regard to the David and Goliath (1 Sam 17–18) and Hannah (1 Sam 1–2) stories in 1 Samuel.

31. Goshen-Gottstein and Talmon, *The Book of Ezekiel*, xxii n. 43 "The question

when there are "multiple editions" (as found in the Masoretic Text, the Septuagint, or the Samaritan Pentateuch) it "aims to produce critical texts of each ancient edition, which will be presented in parallel columns," and that "in cases where one edition is not the textual ancestor of the other(s), a common ancestor to the extant editions will be reconstructed, to the extent possible."[32] Two of the three samples in the sample article, namely 1 Kgs 11:1–8 and Jer 27:1–10 (34 G), indeed present two editions in parallel columns. The *OHB* suggests that in 1 Kings the Masoretic Text is the textual ancestor of the Greek, and in Jeremiah it is the other way round.[33] In these samples, the editions in the parallel columns are of the reconstructed archetypes[34] of the Proto-Masoretic Text and of the Old Greek. In practice, the reconstruction of one archetype can influence the reconstruction of the other, because of the presumed relationship between the two.[35]

This is an interesting endeavor, and such a parallel presentation of archetypes will certainly facilitate the comparison of the witnesses. Of course, the short introduction and the samples do not yet answer all questions. For one, it is not clear to what extent Hendel's "multiple editions" or "plural texts" correspond to Ulrich's concept of "variant/multiple literary editions," or to one or more of Tov's examples of different kinds of literary differences between versions, or even within a version.[36] Whereas, for example, Ulrich emphasizes editorial intentionality and consistency as those elements that characterize a variant literary edition (as distinct

---

of the importance of 967 as a witness to the Old Greek and its possible reflection of a variant Hebrew tradition cannot be treated here." The general introduction in *Biblia Hebraica Quinta 18*, xvii states: "Readings that are judged to derive from another literary tradition for a book will be characterized as 'lit.'"

32. Hendel, "Oxford Hebrew Bible," 326.

33. White Crawford et al., "Sample Editions," 357–66. See also the sample on the *OHB* website of 2 Kgs 1:1–6, edited by Andrés Piquer Otero.

34. On "archetype," see Hendel, "Oxford Hebrew Bible," 329, where he describes it as the "earliest inferable textual state," and passim. See also further below, in section 3.1.

35. For example, the Masoretic Text of 1 Kgs 11:1–8 is thought to be derived from the primary edition (Edition A), and the Greek from the secondary one (Edition B). But the *OHB* text of Edition A lacks in 11:7 the words בהר אשר על פני ירושלם, on the supposition they were added in the transmission of this text after the translation by the Greek.

36. Hendel, "Oxford Hebrew Bible," 326 n. 4, refers to the work of Tov, Ulrich, and others when he introduces "multiple editions," but does not commit himself to any particular view.

from either unintentional variants, or unrelated intentional variants), those criteria are not clear with respect to 1 Kgs 11, and the *OHB* concept of "multiple editions" may be broader than Ulrich's "variant literary edition."[37] Hendel does not explain what exactly constitutes "plural texts" and "multiple editions," and when and why the *OHB* will present distinct texts in parallel columns. This lack of clarity also makes it uncertain how the *OHB* is going to distinguish between the original characteristics of variant editions—which should be attributed to an editor or author who consciously and consistently reworked a literary unit—and (subsequent) textual changes in the course of that edition's transmission[38]—or, for that matter, whether the *OHB* thinks it useful to distinguish between these at all.

The concept of multiple editions should be related to models of the genesis and development of texts. In the present discussion, two sets of alternatives are being discussed. The first is whether textual growth should be conceptualized as proceeding through a limited number of authorized substantial editions or, alternatively, as resulting from a continuous process of revision and expansion.[39] The second is whether the creation of books took place in a linear fashion, or whether one can also have "parallel versions of the same biblical book."[40] I am not sure that we need to choose absolutely between the alternatives. Van der Toorn's proposal for the reconstructed successive editions of Deuteronomy might hold true for the period up to the Persian period,[41] but clearly not for the successive edi-

---

37. The editor, Jan Joosten, comments (about the problems in 1 Kgs 11:1) "Edition A is a mess, edition B an unsuccessful attempt to clean it up," which hardly suggests intentionality and coherency on the part of the editor of edition B, but at best the attempt to make sense of a problematic text. Joosten's comment is also problematic, because it suggests that edition B knew edition A as it is presented in the archetype.

38. A problem addressed by Tov, *TCHB*, 350.

39. Karel van der Toorn, *Scribal Culture and the Making of the Hebrew Bible* (Cambridge, Mass.: Harvard University Press, 2007), 143–72, esp. 144–45.

40. See, for example, Emanuel Tov, "Some Thoughts about the Diffusion of Biblical Manuscripts in Antiquity," in *The Dead Sea Scrolls: Transmission of Traditions and Production of Texts* (ed. S. Metso, H. Najman, and E. Schuller; Leiden: Brill, 2010), 151–72.

41. Van der Toorn (*Scribal Culture*, 143–72) argues for a single master copy of the *Urdeuteronomium*, and of the successive literary editions. Since large scale scribal interventions cannot be carried out on a master copy written neatly on a papyrus scroll (van der Toorn does not consider the possibility of leather scrolls, but that is

tions of Jeremiah or Ezekiel as reflected in the Masoretic and Greek texts. The single master copy period clearly had ended by the time a copy of the Torah could be sent to Egypt in the early Hellenistic age. Van der Toorn's argument against a continuous process of expansion and revision might again hold true for the period of Deuteronomy's editing, but the scrolls from Qumran, in particular those that are called "reworked" and "harmonizing," do testify to such a continuous process. The discussion about linear and parallel literary editions is more problematic, since the word "parallel" is not always used in the same sense, even by the same author, and because the evidence for true parallel editions, as opposed to linear ones, is ambiguous.[42]

The brief comments about multiple versions in the prologue to the *OHB* and in the few available samples do not answer the principal question one should ask, and which Ulrich already posed with respect to the issue of translations.[43] If the *OHB* seeks to construct an archetype ("the earliest inferable textual state") with regard to the text, why does it not seek to reconstruct an earliest inferable literary edition? Here it seems that the *OHB* chooses for a compromise between two different objectives. It wants

---

immaterial to his argument), new editions would only have been produced every forty years or so, when the existing master copy had deteriorated after heavy use and was in need of replacement. The overall reconstruction is attractive, but the details of this hypothesis are either entirely conjectural or not spelled out. For example, the period of forty years or so between the editions is based on historical-literary analysis, not on any evidence pertaining to the life span of papyrus. The one and only copy of the second to fourth editions of Deuteronomy would have been preserved in Babylonia, where they apparently suffered from heavy use by scribal exiles.

42. See, for example, Emanuel Tov, "The Nature of the Large-Scale Differences between the LXX and MT S T V, Compared with Similar Evidence in Other Sources," in *The Earliest Text of the Hebrew Bible. The Relationship between the Masoretic Text and the Hebrew Base of the Septuaginta Reconsidered* (ed. A. Schenker; SCS 52; Atlanta, Ga.: Scholars Press, 2003), 121–44; rev. version in *Hebrew Bible, Greek Bible, and Qumran—Collected Essays* (TSAJ 121; Tübingen: Mohr Siebeck, 2008), 155–70. In the revised version (158) he states, "In the Song of Hannah, three parallel editions in MT, LXX, and 4QSam[a] display distinct theological tendencies," and later (167 and n. 58), argues that "the existence of pristine parallel editions ... cannot be supported by the preserved evidence ... most cases of [early] different literary editions ... reflect development in a linear way, one edition having been developed from an earlier one," and that cases that suggest otherwise show "that scholars are often unable to decide which text developed from another one."

43. See above.

to reconstruct the earliest inferable literary form (either Edition A or a reconstructed common ancestor of multiple editions), as well as to restore and present the (textual archetypes of the) major ancient editions. From a practical point of view, this is perhaps the better part of wisdom, but the *OHB* offers no theoretical foundation for this choice.

2.2. The Use of Copy-Text

In a section of the prologue to the *OHB*, Hendel introduces Walter Greg's concept of "copy-text" as a "theoretically cogent response" to the problem of orthography, vocalization, and accents of a critical text.[44] In a very influential essay,[45] Greg theorized on the use of "copy-text" as that text—generally the earliest printed edition—that should govern in the matter of "accidentals," such as "spelling, punctuation, word-division, and the like, affecting mainly its formal presentation,"[46] whereas "the choice between substantive readings belongs to the general theory of textual criticism and lies altogether beyond the narrow principle of the copy-text."[47] The theory is concerned specifically with sixteenth- and seventeenth-century English printed literature, and stems from the insight that the so-called accidentals (spelling, punctuation, etc.) in an early edition are most likely to have departed least from the author's manuscript, whereas in cases of variations with regard to substantive readings, other editions may, and often do, have the better reading. Greg briefly refers to the basic difference in this respect between the editing of classical texts and that of English texts: since editors of classical texts follow the practice of normalizing the spelling, "the function of an editor is limited to choosing between those manuscript readings that offer significant variants."[48] In contrast, editions of English texts aim to present the author's individual peculiarities, even with regard to "accidentals." Greg emphasized the need to accept the accidentals of a

---

44. Hendel, "Oxford Hebrew Bible," 343–46, here 343.

45. Walter W. Greg, "The Rationale of Copy-Text," *Studies in Bibliography* 3 (1950–51): 19–36; the entire *Studies in Bibliography* can be accessed and searched online through http://etext.virginia.edu/bsuva/sb/; repr. in *Sir Walter Wilson Greg: A Collection of His Writings* (ed. J. Rosenblum; The Great Bibliographers Series 11; Lanham, Md.; Scarecrow, 1998), 213–28 (pagination from both).

46. Ibid., 21/215. Note that, according to Greg, some types of words tend to fall in between the categories of "substantive readings" and "accidentals."

47. Ibid., 26/219.

48. Ibid., 20/214.

copy-text, because he did not consider it possible to evaluate the authority of accidentals.[49] In further theoretical and methodological extensions on the concept of copy-text, G. Thomas Tanselle reformulated and broadened the concept: "the idea of copy-text as presumptive authority, which one accepts (for both accidentals and substantives) whenever there is no other basis for choosing among the variants," as a "concept of copy-text relevant for materials of any period."[50]

Hendel mainly refers to Greg's original concept of "copy-text," especially with respect to the distinction between substantives and accidentals, as the solution to the problem of vocalization and accentuation. Hendel thus appropriates Greg's terminology, but uses it in a way entirely alien to Greg's original theory, and even at odds with Tanselle's broader application of the concept to classical, biblical, and medieval textual criticism. What then are the tensions?

First, the so-called Greg-Bowers-Tanselle theory of copy-text is ultimately concerned with the reconstruction of a text, including the accidentals, according to its author's practice or intentions, and Greg's choice of a particular copy-text is largely based on the assumption that with respect to accidentals it stands closest to the author. Tanselle extensively discusses the issue of spelling and other accidentals in ancient literature,[51] and concludes:

> Indeed, one must ask whether for a work of any period there is ever a justification, from a scholarly point of view, of any aim regarding accidentals other than the reconstruction of the author's own practice; however imperfectly that aim may be realized in many instances, it is the only aim consistent with the view that accidentals are integral to a text and that modernization therefore has no place in scholarly editing.[52]

---

49. See, for example, G. Thomas Tanselle, "Editing without a Copy-Text," *Studies in Bibliography* 47 (1994): 1–22.

50. G. Thomas Tanselle, "Classical, Biblical, and Medieval Textual Criticism and Modern Editing," *Studies in Bibliography* 36 (1983): 21–68; repr. in *Textual Criticism and Scholarly Editing* (Charlottesville: University Press of Virginia, 1990), 274–321; quotes from 64–65 and 317–18.

51. He does this in discourse with Martin L. West's *Textual Criticism and Editorial Technique Applicable to Greek and Latin Texts* (Stuttgart: Teubner, 1973).

52. Tanselle, "Classical, Biblical, and Medieval Textual Criticism," 43/296.

Of course, the concept of an author, and of authorial intention and practice, is not directly applicable to most texts of the Hebrew Bible, which are seen as the product of multiple expansions, rewritings, rearrangements, and so on, by the hands of editors and scribes, sometimes over a period of many centuries. Nonetheless, the view remains that accidentals are integral to a text, and that if one constructs an archetype with respect to substantive readings, one should do the same with respect to accidentals—according to the theory of copy-text. The proponents of this theory would never have condoned a critical edition with ancient substantive readings and medieval accidentals. In short, even though Hendel claims he is applying the concept of copy-text, his practice is at odds with the concept of copy-text.

Second, Greg meant the distinction between "substantive readings" and "accidentals" to be practical, not philosophical. Although he admits that spelling and punctuation can in principle alter the meaning of a text, in practice they mainly affect its formal presentation. Here we need not discuss theoretically the legitimacy of the distinction between "substantive readings" and "accidentals," but rather the question of the extent to which the Masoretic vocalization and accentuation signs can be seen as "accidentals" in the sense suggested by Greg and adopted by Hendel. In the passage quoted by Hendel, Greg differentiates "substantive readings" and "accidentals" by referring to scribal behavior. In general scribes reproduce substantive readings, but "as regards accidentals they will normally follow their own habits or inclination, though they may, for various reasons and to varying degrees, be influenced by their copy." However, the Masoretic vocalization is not a matter of form or presentation that sometimes also affects meaning, nor is it a matter in which scribes follow their own habits and inclinations. On the contrary, in the Masoretic manuscripts the vocalization has been implemented as an integral part of the substantive reading of the text, intended to convey a precise meaning, reflecting ancient exegetical traditions or the views of the Masoretes themselves, and it is clear that scribes reproduced these elements as cautiously as the consonantal framework.[53] Likewise, one of the functions of the accentuation is to express the syntactical relationships between words. It is therefore exegetical; it indicates meaning.[54] Here we have to remind ourselves that

---

53. See discussion and examples in Tov, *TCHB*, 39–49, esp. 39–43.
54. For discussion and examples, see ibid., 67–71.

Greg did not intend to provide a theoretical framework.[55] He was primarily interested in the editions of English Renaissance literature, and the distinction was a practical one for the period with which he was working. It does seem clear, though, that regardless of how one wants to describe the Masoretic vocalization and accentuation signs, they certainly are not accidentals in the way Greg meant, and Greg's rationale of copy-text can therefore not validate the *OHB*'s procedure of reproducing the orthography, vocalization, and accents of the Leningrad Codex.[56]

Third, in the samples that have been made available, the use of the Leningrad Codex as a copy-text that governs in the matter of "accidentals" (as Hendel sees them) demonstrates occasional departures and inconsistencies. These indicate some problems with this procedure. (Note, however, that the present "Guide for Editors," published after the samples, solves some of the inconsistencies.) In the case of those accidentals that were already used in antiquity, the *OHB* samples prefer the ancient evidence above those of the copy-text, whereas it uncritically reproduces the typically Masoretic "accidentals." A few examples will illustrate the problems.

(1) Hendel declares paragraphing to be one of the accidental matters, for which the *OHB* will use the Leningradensis in its accidentals.[57] A first exception occurs immediately in the first sample, where Sidnie White Crawford presents Deut 32:1–9 laid out stichometrically, because "the most ancient manuscript evidence for this passage, 4QDeut^c and 4QDeut^q, indicates that by the second century B.C.E. the Song of Moses, of which these verses are a part, was arranged on the scroll stichometrically."[58] Here the layout of the proclaimed copy-text, the Leningrad Codex, which does not take into account the meaning or poetic structure, is not followed, but rather the stichometry of two old Hebrew manuscripts from Qumran.[59] This certainly occurs for good reasons: virtually all our manuscripts,

---

55. Of the three, Walter W. Greg, Fredson Bowers, and Thomas Tanselle, it was the latter who was most interested in the broader application of the theory.

56. In short, Hendel's claim that "we can make a legitimate distinction between substantives and accidentals in the textual history of the Hebrew Bible" ("Oxford Hebrew Bible," 344) does not hold true for the Masoretic vocalization and accentuation.

57. Ibid., 344–45.

58. White Crawford et al., "Sample Editions," 354.

59. For a description of the colometry of Deut 32 in ancient Hebrew manuscripts, see Paul Sanders, *The Provenance of Deuteronomy 32* (OtSt 37; Leiden: Brill, 1996), 102–11. For a description and graphic presentation of the different types of

ancient and medieval, except the copy-text, present the text stichometrically. However, this goes against the assigned importance of the copy-text,
which would usually govern such issues. A minor point is that in the oldest
manuscripts Deut 32 is written in different stichographic systems.

(2) In Deut 32:5a שִׁחֵת לוֹ לֹא בָּנָיו מוּמָם, White Crawford emends
the singular שִׁחֵת of MT into a plural שחתו and omits מוּמָם altogether,
offering a long discussion of the text and its emendation. The emended
text therefore runs: שחתו לו לא בניו, "His not-children acted corruptly
towards him." However, the emended text in the sample has reproduced
for the nonemended words the vocalization and accentuation of the copy-
text, resulting in the unintelligible שׁחתו לוֹ לֹא בָּנָיו,[60] with under לֹא the
disjunctive accent *ṭifḥā*, whereas the emendation, if one used the system
of accentuation at all, demands a conjunctive accent, most probably the
munāḥ (this would also entail the use of a different accent, probably
ṭifḥā, with the preceding לוֹ). A similar problem pertains to the *dāgeš* and
the conjunctive *munāḥ* in בָּנָיו which, in the emended text should read,
according to the Masoretic system, בָנָיו. In other words, if the Masoretes
would have read the text שחתו לו לא בניו and understood it as "His not-
children acted corruptly toward him," then most likely they would have
vocalized and accented the text as follows: שִׁחֲתוּ לוֹ לֹא־בָנָיו. The Masoretic
accentuation has been reproduced here without attention to its Masoretic
function or meaning.[61]

(3) In Deut 32:6 the editor changes the letter spacing in הֲ־לַיהֹוָה and
emends to הליהוה. She removes all Masoretic signs and comments that
she has selected the letter spacing that represents ancient practice.[62] It
seems at first sight that we have here another case of preferring accidentals of ancient texts above those of the copy-text, illustrating exactly why

---

stichometry of Deut 32 in Qumran manuscripts, see Emanuel Tov, *Scribal Practices
and Approaches Reflected in the Texts Found in the Judean Desert* (STDJ 54; Leiden:
Brill, 2004), 171.

60. The present "Guide for Editors" has somewhat changed the manner of presentation of the critical text, which (if I understand it correctly) would now be presented
as follows: שִׁחֲתוּ לוֹ לֹא בָּנָיו.

61. This is not the only example of this practice in the samples. See, for example,
the *tvir* in Edition B of 1 Kgs 11:(1) נָכְרִיּוֹת. Also in the "Guide for Editors," 4, we still
find examples of Masoretic signs that because of changes in the text do not function
as intended any longer.

62. White Crawford et al., "Sample Editions," 357.

Greg chose copy-texts that were close to the author, generally the earliest.[63] However, the issue is more complex. First, the spacing in the word in the copy-text is exceptional, and the normal Masoretic practice accords with the ancient practice, namely of joining the interrogative particle ה without space to the next word. The editor's change, with reference to ancient practice, is actually a case of normalization, and it is not clear to what extent the *OHB* will also normalize other cases, according to either the specific practice of the copy-text, the more general Masoretic practice, or ancient scribal practice. Second, the large variety of variants in the Masoretic manuscripts representing this word (or combination of words)[64] underlines its exceptionality. Since this verse has not been preserved in earlier Hebrew manuscripts, we have no way of determining how ancient manuscripts wrote the text in this specific case. This example therefore opens up several text-critical options: (1) adopting the reading of a copy-text with respect to accidentals; (2) adopting the attested reading of extant ancient manuscripts; (3) applying ancient scribal practices with respect to some or all accidentals; or (4) normalizing peculiar forms.

(4) The sample edition of 1 Kgs 11:1–8 raises new kinds of issues. The edition presents two archetypes, Edition A (≈ M) and Edition B (≈ G). The latter edition presents the Hebrew archetype of the Greek, and has been vocalized and accentuated with the Masoretic signs of the copy-text whenever the reconstructed clauses correspond to the Masoretic Text. In the sample, it has no Masoretic signs when the retroverted or reconstructed word does not appear in that form in the corresponding Masoretic Text. But the more recent "Guide for Editors" prescribes a new approach. For example,

---

63. Hendel, "Oxford Hebrew Bible," 343, is formally correct, but nonetheless misleading, when he states that Greg "recommends that the textual critic select a good manuscript (not necessarily the earliest) as a copy-text." Within the context of editing English Renaissance literature, Greg would never have chosen such a late manuscript. In this respect, Tanselle's thinking about copy-text (see below) is more relevant.

64. With regard to spacing, we find the following options: ה־ליהוה (Leningradensis), ה ליהוה (with a small space; Aleppo Codex and the Damascus Pentateuch), הל יהוה and הליהוה (see the critical apparatus to *BK2*). In addition, many manuscripts, as well as the Second Rabbinic Bible and those editions dependent on it, have a large *he*, and the vocalization varies between הֲ־לְיהֹוָה (Leningradensis), הֲ לַיהוָה (Aleppo Codex) or הַ לְיהֹוָה (Second Rabbinic Bible).

Edition A (≈ M) 1 Kgs 11:8	Edition B (≈ G)

וְכֵן עָשָׂה לְכָל־נָשָׁיו הַנָּכְרִיֹּות   וְכֵן עָשָׂה לְכָל־נָשָׁיו הַנָּכְרִיֹּות מקטר

מַקְטִירֹות וּמְזַבְּחֹות לֵאלֹהֵיהֶן: ומזבח לֵאלֹהֵיהֶן (Sample)

וְכֵן עָשָׂה לְכָל־נָשָׁיו הַנָּכְרִיֹּותˈוּמִזַבֵּחַ

מְקַטֵּרˈלֵאלֹהֵיהֶן:‏[65] (Guide for Editors)

The system used in the sample of not vocalizing or accentuating words that did not appear in that form created a problem in verse 1 below (I here reproduce only the first four words):

Edition A (≈ M) 1 Kgs 11:1	Edition B (≈ G)

וְהַמֶּלֶךְ שְׁלֹמֹה אָהַב נָשִׁים   וְהַמֶּלֶךְ שְׁלֹמֹה אֹהֵב נָשִׁים (Sample)

נָשִׁיםˈאֹהֵבˈוְהַמֶּלֶךְˈשְׁלֹמֹה (Guide for Editors)

The Greek translation καὶ ὁ βασιλεὺς Σαλωμων ἦν φιλογύναιος suggests that the translator interpreted אהב as a participle, which with Masoretic vowel signs would have been אֹהֵב, and probably not as a perfect, as in the Masoretic אָהַב. Of course, the texts of the two archetypes would have had the same unvocalized form אהב, which only in the later traditions was interpreted differently. This example shows again that the Masoretic vowels are not so-called "accidentals," but express interpretations of the texts and convey meaning, but also that these accidentals do not belong to the level of the archetype.[66] The solution of the "Guide for Editors" is more consistent than that of the sample, but still shows the problem of including an anachronistic system and later exegesis in the archetype.

---

65. Or, instead of מְקַטֵּר, construct the form מַקְטִיר.

66. Every scholar will realize that the archetype of the text was simply והמלך שלמה אהב נשים, but the *OHB* presentation might suggest that the variant interpretations of אהב as perfect or participle took place on the level of the editions, which can only be substantiated on the basis of the grammar of the different clauses of 1 Kgs 11:1–2, not on the attested forms in MT and LXX.

It is clear that the *OHB* system of editing is still in development, and that other practical improvements may be expected. Nonetheless, one must conclude that its only available discussion on editing lacks theoretical reflection on the application of the concept of "copy-text" to Hebrew Bible editing, in particular with respect to the distinction between substantive readings and accidentals in Hebrew Bible manuscripts. One must also observe that the concept of "copy-text" as proposed by Greg, and as articulated in Hendel's prologue, is applied inconsistently. In practice, the approach to "copy-text" comes closer to Tanselle's later (but not his latest) theorizings, in which he describes "copy-text" as "the presumptive authority, which one accepts (*for both accidentals and substantives*) whenever there is no other basis for choosing among the variants."[67] Unfortunately, the brief discussion of the concept of "copy-text," and the uncritical acceptance of the idea of accidentals, followed by the statement that the Leningrad Codex would be the most reasonable choice of "copy-text," has precluded any discussion about which layers of the Leningrad Codex should be included in a critical text.

3. Thinking beyond the Projects

3.1. The Editions and Their Texts

Behind every edition lies a concept of the text. Whereas in general textual scholarship there has been a great deal of theorizing about concepts such as "text," "work," and "version,"[68] it is not always clear which theoretical

---

67. Tanselle, "Classical, Biblical, and Medieval Textual Criticism and Modern Editing," 64–65/317–18 (emphasis added). But one should follow Tanselle's development in thinking about copy-text. In "Editing without a Copy-Text," *Studies in Bibliography* 47 (1994): 1–22, Tanselle proposes to "move beyond this often useful but nevertheless inherently restrictive concept" (2), and argues for the process "of building up a new text rather than making changes to an old one" (19).

68. See, for example, Francisco Rico, "Scholarly Editions and Real Readers," *Variants* 5 (2006): 1–13, here 8: "what is a text, and where is the text? Is it only one, or rather each and every one of its specific, physical manifestations, each of them unavoidably different, because they are inextricably linked to a production and custom context, to a time, a place and a set of "bibliographical codes"? Is it an abstraction out of all these specific manifestations? Or the succession of all of them, considered simultaneously? Is it a material object, or an immaterial entity? Does it reside in the author's mind, in a set of graphic signs, in the reader's perception?"

concepts govern the Hebrew Bible editions. For the *HUB* the text of the Hebrew Bible is found in all the different witnesses included in the apparatus, which together reflect the transmission history of the biblical text. The *HUB* does not evaluate the evidence given in the apparatuses. However, the physical presentation of the material, with a near-diplomatic edition of the Aleppo Codex as the base text, and the organization of the apparatus as notes to this base text, does in fact place one form of the text at the center of its organization. Some evaluation of the evidence has taken place before the editing.

The *BHQ* employs a near-diplomatic edition of the Leningrad Codex as its base text, to which it adds "a critical apparatus offering the evidence of the text's transmission in relation to the point of reference provided by the base text,"[69] but—unlike the *HUB*—includes proposals for readings to be preferred above those of the base text. By declaring the base text as point of reference for the apparatus, it chooses, in the case of the existence of other literary traditions, for the tradition that has led to the Masoretic Text. The *BHQ*'s preferred readings do not seek to present a form of the text at one specific earlier stage, but rather to present individual corrections of the base text that are preferably based on older readings.[70] Essentially, the *BHQ* thus presents a slightly emended Masoretic Text.

The *OHB* presents one or more reconstructed texts or archetypes, as attempts to represent the "best set of readings," that is, "the earliest or more original readings."[71] The view that the "earliest or more original" readings are the best stems from the understanding of archetype as the form "which explains or makes transparent the introduction of error or change."[72] For the same reason, Hendel speaks about "restoring the text … towards its archetype(s)."[73] Since the archetype only pertains to the textual state, multiple archetypes are presented whenever

---

69. *Biblia Hebraica Quinta 18*, viii.

70. Weis, "*Biblia Hebraica Quinta* and the Making of Critical Editions," 5 states that the *BHQ* editors "aim to reconstruct the earliest *available* form of the text, whether that can be said to be the original form of the text or not," but *Biblia Hebraica Quinta 18*, ix, is critical of attempts of such reconstructions.

71. Hendel, "Oxford Hebrew Bible," 331.

72. Ibid., and n. 21 quoting Frank Moore Cross, and substituting "change" for Cross's "corruption."

73. Ibid., n. 19. Note that here, and ibid., 330, where he mentions "an archetypal reading not extant in the textual evidence," he extends the traditional meaning of "archetype" from the text reconstituted by *recensio* (of the latest common ancestor of

there are multiple literary editions. Essentially, the *OHB* therefore aims at an approximation of the text(s) of biblical books as they existed in the Second Temple Period.[74]

All three projects clearly reject the editorial scholarship of the first part of the twentieth century—still represented in some editions of the *BHS*—where some editors aimed to reconstruct an original (authorial) text in the apparatus, partly on text-critical grounds, but mainly through the literary methods of their time.[75] But the *BHQ* and the *OHB* share with the *BHS* the focus on one specific form of the text, or one particular stage in its existence: with the exception of some emendations, the *BHQ* focuses on its more or less final form as the stage reached after its transmission; the *OHB* focuses on its form before the errors and changes of its transmission.

Here it is helpful to return to the Dead Sea Scrolls, which include—in Homeric terms—many "wild texts"[76] with respect to eccentric variants, but also various forms of rewriting and reworking of the texts we now refer to as biblical.[77] The latter clearly testify to the biblical texts' existence as social products composed by communal authors which, after their origin, develop over time. Although from the perspectives of *BHQ* and *OHB* those texts would probably be—apart from possible textual variants—peripheral, from a viewpoint of the work as a process these are of equal impor-

---

all surviving manuscripts, whose individual variant readings are compared) to include also *emendatio*.

74. As a result, the relation between text and apparatus is different from that in the *HUB* or *BHQ*.

75. The *BHS* is very heterogeneous in this respect. At the one end of the extreme is the edition of Samuel by Piet A. H. de Boer, who only lists variants, in the *HUB* fashion, without any expression for preferred readings, and at the other end, for example, Karl Elliger on the Twelve Prophets, whose apparatus reflects his literary analysis of layers, and who reconstructs the original form of the text, according to his *Das Buch der zwölf Kleinen Propheten 2: Die Propheten Nahum, Habakuk, Zephanja, Haggai, Sacharja, Maleachi* (ATD 25; Göttingen: Vandenhoeck & Ruprecht, 1949; 6th ed., 1967).

76. See Martin L. West, "The Textual Criticism and Editing of Homer," in *Editing Texts = Texte edieren* (ed. G. W. Most; Aporemata 2; Göttingen: Vandenhoeck & Ruprecht, 1998), 94–110. On p. 102 he compares the relationship between the Qumran fragments and the Masoretic Text to that between the papyrus fragments and the medieval Homeric tradition.

77. See, for example, a group of manuscripts that originally were described by their editor, Emanuel Tov, as "Reworked Pentateuch" manuscripts and classified as nonbiblical, whereas later Tov changed his opinion and views them as biblical ones.

tance for the development of the text. One of the aims of modern editions is therefore not to print the best text, or to restore the earliest one, but to present the variety and complexity of the text as it has been transmitted.

3.2. FUTURE EDITIONS OF THE HEBREW BIBLE: FROM TEXTS TO HYPERTEXT

At this stage, with three major projects running simultaneously, and most competent scholars[78] being involved in one of the projects, it makes little sense to propose even more editions. The following are therefore general remarks, not a program.

In the case of editions of the Hebrew Bible, the aim is not to present for the first time the text of the Hebrew Bible to a lay or scholarly audience, but rather to present either a specific form or version of the text or, in the case of critical editions, to present a commentary to the user. The present three major editions have clearly differing philosophies and practices and therefore different audiences. The *HUB* is a diplomatic edition of books of the Aleppo Codex and at the same time, in its apparatus, a depository of evidence intended for specialists, with only very limited discussion. The *BHQ* and *OHB* are aimed at both specialists and nonspecialists and contain not only apparatus but also extensive commentary. It is to be expected that nonspecialists such as students and biblical scholars with little text-critical training will mainly consult the *BHQ*. Unfortunately, the system of presentation of the *BHQ* may easily authorize the widely held view that ultimately, with few exceptions, the Masoretic codices contain the best form of the Hebrew Bible.[79] One would wish for theological students and other nonspecialists an edition that, like the *OHB*, visually indicates that the Masoretic Text is one of many texts of the Hebrew Bible.

One such edition could be a multicolumn one, such as Tov suggests as a means to "educate the users toward an egalitarian approach to the textual

---

78. But see the comments by West, *Textual Criticism and Editorial Technique*, 62, on the qualifications required!

79. Williamson ("Do We Need a New Bible?" 161) believes that only "the most extreme orthodox Jews" believe "that the masoretic tradition must always be superior." However, the practice that in exegesis the Masoretic Text must be followed, unless grammatically impossible and with regard to content meaningless (quote from guidelines for exegesis used in a Faculty of Theology), is not exactly uncommon among continental Protestant theologians and biblical scholars.

witnesses."[80] According to Tov, "such an edition would present MT, LXX, the SP, and some Qumran texts, on an *equal* basis in parallel columns.... This equality is needed for literary analysis and exegesis, and less so for textual specialists."[81] The *OHB* sample system of presenting variant editions (archetypes) in parallel columns is one way to alert the nonspecialist reader to the existence and equality of variant editions. The *Biblia Qumranica* series also records the biblical texts from the Judean Desert in parallel columns (together with MT and LXX) and utilizes a special system of markings to help the reader find correspondences and differences. Of course, users of Bible software such as Accordance or Bibleworks can to some extent emulate a multicolumn edition on their screens.

In a sense, the *OHB* as a whole is a helpful visualization of text-critical conclusions described in the commentary in connection with a special understanding of the history of development of the Hebrew Bible. One may agree with Williamson's critical appraisal that we do not really need such a visualization, and that scholarship would be served best by a "full and sober textual commentary."[82] It seems that the *OHB* fits first of all in a series of publications that aim to visualize in print the conclusions of specialist biblical scholarship to those who read Biblical Hebrew. In more general terms, and with an eye to future text-critical work and editions, one should raise the question of how to deal with the relationship between text, apparatus, and commentary. The examples of *BHK*, *BHS*, *BHQ*, and *HUB* show that within years of publication, new fragments in Hebrew or Greek turned up which one would have liked to have included in the apparatus, and which would have had an impact on the commentary. In the case of the *OHB* the emergence of new material may influence not only the apparatus but also its reconstruction of the archetype. In addition, not only new evidence but new theories or insights will arise, which scholars will want to translate into different approaches, commentaries, conclusions, and editions. In my opinion, not all this metatextual scholarship ought to be transposed into full-blown new critical editions.

Instead, the study of the text of the Hebrew Bible will profit much more from the creation, sooner or later, of hypertextual archives and databases which will ultimately allow one to generate virtual electronic editions. With the Hebrew Bible, this will probably be indefinitely more com-

---

80. Tov, "Hebrew Scripture Editions," 309–11, here 309.
81. Ibid., 310.
82. Williamson, "Do We Need a New Bible?" 170, 174–75, here 175.

plex than with *Don Quixote*,[83] and even a few years ago this would have been technologically problematic. As a hypertextual archive and database, it would include the text of actual manuscripts, codices, editions, and critical editions, as well as images of each of those, but also that of text-critical commentaries. Not being restricted by space constraints, it would include the entire transmission of the Hebrew Bible in its different forms and languages, from its first attestations up to the most recent editions that are generated. In addition, a dynamic hypertextual system would provide tools to perform tasks automatically such as, for example, collating and indexing textual variants.[84] Such a hypertext, as a much fuller, stronger, and flexible system that allows analysis of multiple texts, will eventually generate a new generation of critical editions.

---

83. See the Electronic Variorum Edition of Don Quixote (EVE-DQ), of the Cervantes Project (http://cervantes.tamu.edu).

84. See the EVE-DQ, which is composed of databases, various modules including a multi-variant editor, as well as data entity management system. See for a description of the EVE-DQ, as well as the changes it has brought about in editing: Eduardo Urbina, Richard Furuta, Carlos Monroy, Neal Audenauert, Jie Deng, and Erika Pasquel, "The *Electronic Variorum Edition of 'Don Quixote'* at the Cervantes Project," in *Framing the Quixote, 1605-2005* (ed. A. F. Sherman Jr.; Provo: Brigham Young University, 2007), 205–19. This article, and all other articles relating to the Cervantes Project, are accessible through the Cervantes website (http://cervantes.tamu.edu/V2/CPI/variorum/publ.htm).

Evidence from the Qumran Scrolls for the Scribal Transmission of Leviticus[*]

Sarianna Metso

Compared to the sparse witnesses to Leviticus among the medieval codices, the Dead Sea Scrolls provide us with a wealth of material.[1] Fourteen Hebrew manuscripts of Leviticus were found in the Judean caves; of these fourteen, twelve were found at Qumran and two at Masada. Four are written in the Paleo-Hebrew script. In addition, two Greek manuscripts, called Septuagint Leviticus[a] and Septuagint Leviticus[b], and one manuscript of an Aramaic targum of Leviticus were found, for a total of seventeen manuscripts of the book. Compared to many other biblical books, the text of Leviticus survived well; of the twenty-seven chapters of Leviticus, only chapter 12 is not represented among the scrolls. The dates of the Leviticus manuscripts range from the middle of the third century B.C.E. to the middle of the first century C.E. Thus the manuscripts of Leviticus found at Qumran and Masada are over a thousand years older than the Hebrew manuscripts available prior to the discovery of the Dead Sea Scrolls.[2]

In what follows I will examine a few examples of cases to show (1) how the Dead Sea Scrolls manuscripts enhance our knowledge of the early text of Leviticus and provide readings superior to the Masoretic Text; (2) how, in the course of its textual development, the book of Leviticus gradually evolved from priestly ritual directives into a book of Scripture; (3) how

---

[*] This essay is a revised form of an article published in *Houses Full of All Good Things: Essays in Memory of Professor Timo Veijola* (ed. J. Pakkala and M. Nissinen; Helsinki: Finnish Exegetical Society; Göttingen: Vandenhoeck & Ruprecht, 2008), 507–19.

1. See appendix 1.

2. Fragments of two additional manuscripts, Schøyen MS 4611 and Nahal Arugot MS, were found and await official publication.

the Dead Sea Scrolls manuscripts of Leviticus show that the Old Greek text was faithfully translated from an ancient Hebrew text that was simply different from the traditional Masoretic Text; and (4) how the text of Leviticus was used in the Jewish literature of the Second Temple period.[3]

1. The Hebrew Text of Leviticus

The uniqueness of the Dead Sea Scrolls is that they open a window onto the time period during which the text of the Hebrew Bible was still in the process of dynamic development. The manuscripts copied during this first period display variation at the level of individual textual variants, but also at the level of intentionally different editions.[4] In regard to the books of the Torah, the books of Exodus and Numbers also appear in pluriform state; both of them display two or more literary editions. The situation in the case of Leviticus is not quite as dramatic, but the manuscripts found at Qumran still shed significant new light on the textual history of Leviticus. These manuscripts provide numerous individual variants. However, at the level of textual editions, evidently Leviticus had basically achieved a uniform state by the second half of the Second Temple period. This is a conclusion already reached by many scholars before me: Kenneth Mathews, Eugene

---

3. This essay presents a preview of a project that aims at preparing a critical edition of the book of Leviticus for the *Oxford Hebrew Bible*. In this project, critical editions will be published for all the books of the Hebrew Bible, taking into account for the first time the full Hebrew manuscript evidence from the Dead Sea Scrolls. Unlike earlier, "diplomatic" editions of the Hebrew Bible, in which a single manuscript is selected as the base text against which textual variants in other manuscripts are mirrored, this "critical" edition will present a text that is a compilation of the best readings from all the manuscripts available, whether from the Dead Sea Scrolls or from other important ancient textual witnesses. Each edition will be accompanied by a text-critical commentary. My work in this project is still in progress, but this essay provides my initial reflections on some of the issues central to the edition of Leviticus.

4. This distinction between individual textual variants and intentional literary editions follows the widely accepted system of classification developed by Eugene Ulrich. See his "Multiple Literary Editions: Reflections toward a Theory of the History of the Biblical Text," in *Current Research and Technological Developments on the Dead Sea Scrolls: Conference on the Texts from the Judean Desert, Jerusalem, 30 April 1995* (ed. D. W. Parry and S. D. Ricks; STDJ 20; Leiden: Brill, 1996), 78–105; repr. in Eugene Ulrich, *The Dead Sea Scrolls and the Origins of the Bible* (Studies in the Dead Sea Scrolls and Related Literature; Grand Rapids: Eerdmans; Leiden: Brill, 1999), 99–120.

Ulrich, Emanuel Tov, and Esther Eshel, to name a few.[5] It is plausible that the Jerusalem priesthood had carefully guarded the transmission of the text of Leviticus. Evidently, their rationale was *not* careful preservation of a "standard text" of the *scriptural* book—otherwise, why were Exodus and Numbers allowed textual development?—but preservation of instructions for *standard praxis* for the sacred rituals and orthodox priestly traditions to be practiced in the temple and beyond.[6] I will return to this point later.

The following are a few examples of cases where the Qumran manuscripts have arguably preserved a more original text than the Masoretic manuscripts.

(1) 1:17   היא 4QLev[b]] היא אשה MT SP; ἐστιν θυσία LXX

(2) 17:4   (ואל פתח אהל מועד לא הביאו) [לעש]ות אתו עלה או
שלמים ליהוה לרצונכם ל]ריח ניחח וישחטהו בחוץ ואל
פתא אהל מו[עד לא יביאנו SP 4QLev[d]

ὥστε ποιῆσαι αὐτὸ εἰς ὁλοκαύτωμα ἢ σωτήριον κυρίῳ δεκτὸν
εἰς ὀσμὴν εὐωδίας καὶ ὃς ἂν σφάζῃ ἔξω καὶ ἐπὶ τὴν θύραν τῆς
σκηνῆς τοῦ μαρτυρίου μὴ ἐνέγκῃ αὐτό OG] > 11QpaleoLev
MT (for יביאנו in 4QLev[d] see v. 9 MT)

(3) 22:31   אתם 4QLev[b] SP OG] + אני יהוה MT LXXmss

In the first case, 4QLev[b] gives a shorter text for the priestly regulations regarding the burnt offering of birds in Lev 1:17: "[And the priest shall burn it on the altar, on the wo]od that is on [the fir]e; it is a *burnt offering*, of pleasing odor to the Lord." For the latter part of the verse,

---

5. Kenneth A. Mathews, "The Leviticus Scrolls (11QpaleoLev) and the Text of the Hebrew Bible," *CBQ* 48 (1986): 171–207; Eugene Ulrich, "4QLev-Num[a]" and "4QLev[b]," in *Qumran Cave 4.VII: Genesis to Numbers* (ed. E. Ulrich and F. M. Cross; DJD 12; Oxford: Clarendon, 1994), 153–87; Emanuel Tov, "4QLev[c]," "4QLev[d]," "4QLev[e]," and "4QLev[g]," in Ulrich and Cross, *Qumran Cave 4.VII*, 189–204; Esther Eshel, "Book of Leviticus," in *Encyclopedia of the Dead Sea Scrolls* (ed. L. H. Schiffman and J. C. VanderKam; 2 vols.; Oxford: Oxford University Press, 2000), 1:488–93.

6. See Sarianna Metso and Eugene Ulrich, "The Old Greek Translation of Leviticus," in *The Book of Leviticus: Composition and Reception* (ed. R. Rendtdorff and R. Kugler; The Formation and Interpretation of Old Testament Literature; VTSup 93; Leiden: Brill, 2003), 247–68, esp. 267.

the Masoretic Text, Samaritan Pentateuch, and the Septuagint provide a slightly longer text, adding the term אשה, "an offering by fire," a synonym for the term עלה, "burnt offering," that is already in the text. Adding explanations by way of synonymous words is typical scribal activity; thus the longer version is likely to be secondary. The Masoretic Text reads at the end of the verse: "... *a burnt offering, it is an offering by fire* of pleasing odor to the Lord."

In the second case, a manuscript of Leviticus from Cave 4 (4QLev^d), like the Samaritan Pentateuch and the Septuagint, includes a lengthy reading with sacrificial aspects that is not found in the Masoretic Text, nor in the paleo-Hebrew Leviticus manuscript from Cave 11 (11QpaleoLev^a). The situation could be judged either way: that the Masoretic Text has lost the reading through parablepsis due to homoioteleuton (הביאו—יביאו) or, that an early widespread Hebrew tradition had added extra material. If it is a case of parablepsis, it is a perfect example of the scrolls providing a superior text for the priestly sacrificial system in Israel. If 11QpaleoLev and MT are in fact the sound original text, and 4QLev^d exhibits a secondary addition, then at least we have an interesting example of the dynamic growth of the biblical text as laws were still being expanded in the light of current practice.

In the third case, 4QLev^b, the Samaritan Pentateuch and the Greek version have simply: "Therefore shall you keep my commandments and do them." The Masoretic Text, however, adds the formulaic "I am the Lord" at the end of the verse. By the normal principles of textual criticism, the Masoretic Text is to be judged a secondary expansion: the frequent formula could have been added, mirroring its occurrence at the end of the previous verse.

Although definitive conclusions regarding the textual witnesses of Leviticus may be premature, it appears that there was only one principal edition of Leviticus in circulation, with numerous manuscripts each displaying a modest number of predictable variants within that single edition. Many of the readings newly offered by Qumran agree with those long since attested in the Septuagint and the Samaritan Pentateuch. But remarkably, they also offer a significant number of independent readings that were unknown to us from other textual witnesses. 11QpaleoLev^a, in particular, is of special importance in this respect.[7] Thus in the preserved

7. For the edition of 11Qpaleo-Lev^a, see David N. Freedman and Kenneth A. Mathews, *The Paleo-Hebrew Leviticus Scroll (11QpaleoLev)* (Winona Lake, Ind.: ASOR/Eisenbrauns, 1985).

manuscripts there are many variants, but they are mostly minor and betray no clear patterns in the affiliations between the textual traditions. The single main edition is in contrast to many other books of the Hebrew Bible, for which there were two or more intentionally developed editions in circulation. The single edition is understandable, insofar as there may well have been a single priestly tradition preserved and guarded by the temple priesthood in charge of administering the sacrificial rituals.

2. FROM RITUAL DIRECTIVES TO SCRIPTURE

Normal textual criticism combined with source and redaction criticism provides a major breakthrough for understanding the process of composition of the biblical book and the process by which it became a book of Scripture. Viewed from the perspective of source and redaction criticism, it appears that an earlier form of traditions about how to perform the priestly rituals was a "source" for proper practices, which became transformed into a "scriptural" text by a redactor who joined this source material with other divinely ordered legal materials. As Ulrich has noted, the introductory and concluding sentences in chapters 1, 4, 7, and 27 appear to be a redactor's transformation of a text that had functioned simply as the priests' ritual directives. The source at 7:37 may well have read: "This is the ritual of the burnt offering, the grain offering, the sin offering, the guilt offering, the offering of ordination, and the sacrifice of well-being...." The redactor's conclusion in 7:38 incorporates that source into the framework of God's revelation on Sinai: "which the Lord commanded Moses on Mount Sinai, when he commanded the people of Israel to bring their offerings to the Lord, in the wilderness of Sinai" (7:38). Current temple ritual practice is retrojected back to the time of Moses and the revelation at Sinai. What had been the priests' ritual directives now became the Word of God.[8]

---

8. Eugene Ulrich, "From Literature to Scripture: Reflections on the Growth of a Text's Authoritativeness," *DSD* 10 (2003): 3–25, esp. 9. Similar processes of authorization of legal materials can be seen, e.g., in the books of Deuteronomy and Ezra, see Hindy Najman, *Seconding Sinai: The Development of Mosaic Discourse in Second Temple Judaism* (JSJSup 77; Leiden: Brill: 2003), 20–40; and idem "Torah of Moses: Pseudonymous Attribution in Second Temple Writings," in *The Interpretation of Scripture in Early Judaism and Christianity: Studies in Language and Tradition* (ed. C. A. Evans; JSPSup 33; SSEJC 7; Sheffield: Sheffield Academic Press, 2000), 202–16. For further discussion on the issues of scriptural authority, see Lee Martin McDonald and James A. Sanders, eds., *The Canon Debate* (Peabody, Mass.: Hendrickson, 2002).

Thus the book of Leviticus contains diverse materials originating from different time periods that were produced by editors and scribes with different agendas. The classic Documentary Hypothesis saw the Priestly edition of the Pentateuch as a composition of the postexilic period, but increasingly the existence of such a composition of priestly traditions has been questioned, and it is claimed that "P" should rather be seen as simply one late editorial layer in a long process of redactional overworking of this material. Recently, however, some scholars have argued that Leviticus was produced during the early monarchical period and reflects the rituals of the First Temple, rather than the Second.[9]

There is merit in each of these theories. That is, it is possible to identify in the book certain textual entities that with all likelihood enjoyed independent existence before being incorporated into the larger collection of materials. The sacrificial regulations in Lev 1–7 and the Holiness Code in Lev 17–26 provide the most obvious examples, but the overall book can be viewed as a compilation of previously existing legal collections, some of which may go as far back as Israelite sanctuaries of the monarchic period. The rituals of the Second Temple undoubtedly reflected in some measure those of the First Temple: cultic regulations and practices tend to remain the same from age to age.

As the later redactors worked through a theological lens to conjure up an ideal pattern of worship and society, which they ascribed to Moses, they did so both in order to legitimize the current practice and to shape community identity. As such, their purpose was to express a religious and social philosophy. Not only do we have materials that reflect the real practice of various periods, but we also have late materials that present themselves as ancient. All of this suggests that we should appreciate the ancient background of some parts of Leviticus while still viewing the final form of the book as having originated in the Second Temple period.

---

9. For differing opinions regarding the dating of different layers of material in Leviticus, compare Jacob Milgrom, *Leviticus 1–16: A New Translation with Introduction and Commentary* (AB 3; New York: Doubleday, 1991), 13–35; Erhard Gerstenberger, *Leviticus: A Commentary* (OTL; Louisville: Westminster John Knox, 1996), 6–10; Israel Knohl, *The Sanctuary of Silence: The Priestly Torah and the Holiness School* (Minneapolis: Fortress, 1995), 199–224; Frank Crüsemann, *The Torah: Theology and History of Old Testament Law* (Edinburgh: T&T Clark, 1996), 282–90.

3. The Old Greek Text of Leviticus[10]

The Hebrew manuscripts also teach us a great deal about the Old Greek translation. The question guiding this part of my article concerns the character of the original Greek as a translation of an ancient Hebrew text. The textual evidence demonstrates that the Masoretic Text was *not* the *Vorlage* of the Old Greek, but that nonetheless the Old Greek *is* a reliable witness to the ancient Hebrew text. Let us explore these questions.

A number of the variants show that the Old Greek was based on ancient Hebrew readings that differ from the Masoretic Text.[11] Some readings demonstrate that when Old Greek differs from the Masoretic Text, it is often supported both by a Jewish manuscript from Qumran and by the Samaritan version.

(1) 3:1   ליהוה 4QLev[b] OG La[100] (*deo*)] > MT SP LXX[mss]

(2) 15:3   [טמא הוא] בו כל ימי ז[ב בשרו או החתים בשרו מזובו]
             11QpaleoLev[a] SP(> בו) OG] > MT (מזובו 1 ˚⌢2˚)[11]

(3) 17:3   לא בישרֹאֵ֯ל [והגר ה]גֵ֯ר 4QLev[d] (cf. 𝕲[ABFM] ἢ τῶν προσηλύτων
             τῶν προσκειμένων ἐν ὑμῖν; and cf 16:29; 17:8, 10, 13)] >
             11QpaleoLev MT SP LXX[ed]

---

10. This part of the essay draws from my earlier co-authored article listed in n. 5, "The Old Greek Translation of Leviticus," esp. 258–61.

11. Of course, the OG also shows much agreement with the MT. That fact, however, does not detract from the present argument, but rather bolsters it, showing that the OG reflects an ancient Hebrew text that was partly in agreement with the MT but also partly in disagreement from it.

12. Kenneth Mathews correctly notes that the SP, though in the main agreeing with 11QpaleoLev[a] and OG, nonetheless varies from them in lacking בו; see David Noel Freedman and Kenneth A. Mathews, *The Paleo-Hebrew Leviticus Scroll (11Qpa-leoLev)* (Winona Lake, Ind.: ASOR/Eisenbrauns, 1985), 32; and Kenneth A. Mathews, "The Leviticus Scroll (11QpaleoLev) and the Text of the Hebrew Bible," *CBQ* 48 (1986): 171–207, esp. 198. For the purposes of this limited study, however, focus will be kept on the main lines of affiliation, ignoring minor variants (such as לוא יביאנו 4QLev[d] versus לא הביאו SP in the next reading at 17:4) within readings that do demonstrate major affiliation.

(4) 17:4 [לעשות אתו עלה [אֹו שלמים ליהוה לצֹונֹכֹם לֹ]ריח ניחח
4QLev^d SP וישחטהו בחוץ ואל פתח אוהל מועד לוא יביאנו
OG] > 11QpaleoLev MT

(5) 22:5 טמא 4QLev^e SP OG] > 1QpaleoLev (vid) MT

(6) 22:31 אתם 4QLev^b SP OG] + אני יהוה MT LXX^mss

These examples[13] display variants for which one or more Hebrew manuscripts attest the type of *Vorlage* used by the Old Greek rather than the
Masoretic Text. The double witness from Qumran and from the Samaritan
Pentateuch in examples 2, 4, 5, and 6 confirms the validity of other examples in which the Old Greek agrees with a single extant Qumran manuscript against the Masoretic Text, irrespective of the Samaritan Pentateuch.
From these readings it should be clear that, though there is a large degree
of agreement among all witnesses to Leviticus, the Old Greek frequently
shows faithful dependence upon an ancient Hebrew text which was simply
at variance with the form of the text transmitted as the Masoretic Textus
Receptus.[14] Some of the simple, commonplace variants may have arisen
separately and coincidentally, but for the most part it can be argued for
Leviticus, as it has also been demonstrated for many other books, that generally the Old Greek is a faithful translation of its ancient Hebrew parent

---

13. Two of these examples are the same as before, but the point in this section is
different: the focus here is on the Greek text that is identical with some Hebrew text,
not necessarily on superior readings as in the previous section.

14. Thus the evidence available in the Scrolls has methodological implications
for the work of a textual critic, supportive of the principle that when the LXX reading
is at variance with the MT, the first consideration should be whether it is likely that
the LXX is faithfully rendering an alternate Hebrew reading; see Anneli Aejmelaeus,
"What Can We Know about the Hebrew *Vorlage* of the Septuagint," in *On the Trail
of Septuagint Translators*, 77–115, esp. 92–93 (*ZAW* 99 [1987]: 58–89, esp. 71). This
contrasts with the approach suggested, e.g., by John William Wevers (*Notes on the
Greek Text of Leviticus* [Atlanta: Scholars Press, 1997], xxxii): "One should not automatically presuppose a different parent text when differences between the Greek and
the Hebrew obtain; rather one should first seek for and pursue other explanations. It is
only through such details that a picture of the attitudes, the theological prejudices, as
well as of the cultural environment of these Jewish translators can emerge."

text, and that this parent text was similar but not identical to the one that eventually became the Masoretic Text.

The Old Greek translator of Leviticus was faithfully attempting to translate the contents of a certain ancient Hebrew scroll into a Greek form that had strong and primary fidelity to the details of the original rituals while still attempting to make sense to the Hellenistic Jewish community. Scholars agree that the Old Greek of Leviticus is the most literal of the pentateuchal translations.[15] To the extent that it is compared to its proper Hebrew *Vorlage* rather than to the MT, the fidelity and literalness of the translation can now be appreciated even more. The Old Greek is best represented by codices Vaticanus and Alexandrinus and Minuscule 121 throughout the book,[16] but the fragmentary Greek manuscripts from Qumran, where they are extant, provide some readings closer to the Old Greek translation than Vaticanus, Alexandrinus, and 121, which are at least four centuries later.

When attempting to judge variants in the Septuagint, one should consider the various phases that result in the text one now reads. Those phases include (1) the Hebrew source text which lay before the OG translator; (2) the rendering of the Hebrew text into the Greek language by the translator with his specific techniques; (3) the changes that undoubtedly entered the Greek text tradition during the long period of its transmission; and (4) the work of Aquila, Symmachus, and Theodotion as they revised the various Greek versions during the second and third centuries.

For the first phase, the Hebrew text which the Old Greek translator inherited already included layers of editorial and scribal activity. The particular scroll of Leviticus that the translator inherited, however, was close to but not identical with the Masoretic Text, and should not be judged by comparison with the Masoretic Text. For the second phase, the translator primarily performed a single operation: he attempted, as best he could, to translate the particular Hebrew scroll he had into the Greek language. For the third phase of transmission, indeterminable amounts of unintentional changes, such as errors and losses, as well as intentional changes, such as clarifications and exegetical insertions, undoubtedly occurred. These, however, now stand alongside original readings as part of "the LXX." The

---

15. See Paul Harlé et Didier Pralon, *La Bible d'Alexandrie: Le Lévitique* (Paris: Cerf, 1988), 49.

16. John William Wevers, *Text History of the Greek Leviticus* (MSU 19; Göttingen: Vandenhoeck & Ruprecht, 1986), 59–71, esp. 71.

fourth phase involved intentional but mostly mechanical revision with little attempt at exegetical activity. All four phases must be considered when evaluating Greek variants. But the Old Greek translation, and the Qumran Greek manuscripts in particular, should be viewed as important witnesses to the ancient Hebrew text.

4. Use of Leviticus in Ancient Jewish Literature

In the first three parts of this essay, I have dealt with the development of the scriptural text of Leviticus. In the concluding part, I would like to consider briefly its influence on other ancient Jewish literature and the importance of Leviticus for the life of the Jewish communities in the Second Temple period. Again, the evidence from Qumran proves to be of high importance. Surveying the nonbiblical manuscripts found at Qumran, we learn that nonbiblical works with quotes from Leviticus total over twenty, and of the twenty-seven chapters of Leviticus, twenty-two are quoted somewhere in the nonbiblical scrolls.[17] The book of Leviticus clearly was instrumental in shaping the life and self-understanding of the priestly community at Qumran and in creating a unique culture of elitist ritual purity with clearly defined boundaries toward the outside world.[18]

---

17. Martin Abegg also calls attention to the high level of influence the book of Leviticus exercised in the Essene community, providing helpful examples. Subsequently in a private communication he indicated that he had slightly revised his data: "Astonishingly, every chapter of the book of Leviticus is referenced somewhere in the nonbiblical scrolls. Because only the book of Deuteronomy approaches this preeminence, it appears safe to conclude that Leviticus was the heart and soul of the priestly community at Qumran. The Temple Scroll by itself quotes or paraphrases portions of twenty-three chapters. Of the two dozen rulings of 4QMMT, more than half are discussions based on legal issues concerning ritual purity from the text of Leviticus. The laws of the Damascus Document are also to a great extent rehearsals of various Levitical commands. The assorted collection of legal discussions recorded in A Commentary to the Law of Moses (4Q251) is also largely levitical in origin" (Martin Abegg, Jr., Peter Flint, and Eugene Ulrich, *The Dead Sea Scrolls Bible* [San Francisco: HarperSanFrancisco, 2002], 78).

18. In addition to halakhic expositions, Leviticus played a significant role in shaping and establishing community discipline and cohesion. Quotes from the book of Leviticus were used as explicit or implicit prooftexts in discussions of, e.g., (1) separation from the outsiders (CD 6:14–21 [Lev 10:10]; 1QS 5:14–15 [Lev 22:16]); (2) rebuke of transgressors (4QRebukes Reported by the Overseer; CD 9:2–4 [Lev 19:17]; 1QS 5:24–6:1 [Lev 19:17]; 4QBerakhot 4Q286–4Q290) [Lev 19:17–18]); (3) destiny of a

It is also interesting to observe that Leviticus continued to exert significant influence on Jewish writers of the first century. Philo makes frequent
references to the text of Leviticus, especially in his *De specialibus legibus*. [19]
In fact, Philo's writings contain parallels from every chapter of Leviticus.
Similarly, Josephus in his *Antiquities* uses parallels from twenty out of the
twenty-seven chapters of Leviticus;[20] Josephus's biblical sources, of course,
originated before the destruction of the Temple and should be considered
Second Temple witnesses.[21] Thus, the book of Leviticus was foundational
in shaping Jewish life both in Palestine and the Diaspora, and the direct
or indirect references to Leviticus in nonbiblical writings of the Second
Temple period shed further light on its textual traditions.

---

traitor (CD 9:1 [Lev 27:29]); (4) painting of apostates as those ruled by the spirits of
Belial (CD 12:1b–2a/4QD^f 5 I 18–19 [Lev 20:27]); (5) picturing insiders as those to
be saved by Melchizedek (11QMelch (11Q13) [Lev 25:13; 25:9]); and (6) banning of
disabled from the community (1QSa 1:5–9 [Lev 21:17–21; 22:21–23]).

19. Interesting cases of Philo's exegesis of Leviticus are, e.g., (1) widowed, child-
less daughter of a priest returning to live in her father's house (*Spec.* 1.129–130 [Lev
22:13]); (2) laws regarding menstruation and intercourse (*Spec.* 3.32–33 [Lev 18:19]);
and (3) prohibition of adultery (*Spec.* 4.203 [Lev 19:19]). These cases have been discussed by Adele Reinhartz, "Philo's *Exposition of the Law* and Social History: Methodological Considerations," in *SBL Annual Meeting 1993 Seminar Papers* (ed. E. H.
Lowering Jr.; Atlanta: Scholars Press, 1993), 6–21, esp. 14 and 17. For further literature, see, e.g., David T. Runia, *Exegesis and Philosophy: Studies on Philo of Alexandria*
(Hampshire, U.K.: Variorum, 1990), 185–98; Burton L. Mack, "Exegetical Traditions
of Alexandrian Judaism: A Program for Analysis of the Philonic Corpus," *SPhilo* 3
(1974–1975): 71–112; Yehoshua Amir, "Philo and the Bible," *SPhilo* 2 (1973): 1–8;
Richard D. Hecht, "Preliminary Issues in the Analysis of Philo's *De Specialibus Legibus*," *SPhilo* 5 (1978): 1–56.

20. Louis H. Feldman, *Josephus's Interpretation of the Bible* (Berkeley: University
of California Press, 1998); idem, "Josephus's Biblical Paraphrase as a Commentary
on Contemporary Issues," in *Interpretation of Scripture in Early Judaism and Christianity* (ed. C. A. Evans; Sheffield: Sheffield Academic Press, 2000), 124–201; Étienne
Nodet, "Josephus and the Pentateuch," *JSJ* 28 (1997): 154–94; Steve Mason, "Josephus
on Canon and Scriptures," in *Hebrew Bible /Old Testament: The History of Its Interpretation*, vol. 1, part 1 (Göttingen: Vandenhoeck & Ruprecht, 1996), 217–35.

21. In *Vita* 416–418 Josephus states that Titus allowed him to take some sacred
scrolls from Jerusalem to Rome.

5. Conclusion

The publication of the Dead Sea Scrolls—now complete—gives us an opportunity to take a fresh look at the textual traditions and historical development behind Leviticus and the other biblical books. To sum up the main points of this essay: (1) The Dead Sea Scrolls manuscripts of Leviticus show a textual diversity larger than was previously known. (2) Textual criticism provides a necessary step for establishing a solid foundation for source- and redaction-critical analysis. Such analysis shows that, in the course of its textual development, the book of Leviticus gradually evolved from cultic directives into a book of Scripture. (3) The Dead Sea Scrolls manuscripts are roughly contemporary with the Old Greek translation and provide a window onto the nature of the Hebrew text from which the Septuagint was translated. It confirms that the Old Greek was a faithful translation of a Hebrew text in circulation at that time. (4) The nonbiblical Dead Sea Scrolls, combined with the contemporary evidence from Philo and Josephus, attest to the high importance that Leviticus continued to have in the life of ancient Jewish communities.

Appendix 1
Manuscripts of Leviticus from Qumran and Masada

Text Number	Publication	Name	Manuscript Date
		Hebrew	
1Q3, frgs. 1–7, 22–24	DJD I	1QpaleoLev	
2Q5	DJD III	2QpaleoLev	100–1 B.C.E.
4Q17	DJD XII	4QExod-Lev^f	ca. 250 B.C.E.
4Q23	DJD XII	4QLev-Num^a	150–100 B.C.E.
4Q24	DJD XII	4QLev^b	ca. 50 B.C.E.
4Q25	DJD XII	4QLev^c	30–1 B.C.E. (?)

4Q26	DJD XII	4QLev[d]	
4Q26a	DJD XII	4QLev[e]	100–30 B.C.E. (?)
4Q26b	DJD XII	4QLev[g]	
6Q2	DJD III	6QpaleoLev	250–150 B.C.E.
11Q1	Freedman-Mat-thews	11QpaleoLev[a]	ca. 100 B.C.E.
11Q2	DJD XXIII	11QLev[b]	ca. 50 C.E.

Greek

4Q119	DJD IX	4QLXXLev[a]	125–1 B.C.E.
4Q120	DJD IX	4QpapLXXLev[b]	100–1 B.C.E.

Aramaic

4Q156	DJDVI	4QtgLev	

Masada

Mas 1a	Masada VI	MasLev[a]	50–1 B.C.E.
Mas 1b	Masada VI	MasLev[b]	ca. 50 C.E.

GREEK PAPYRI AND THE TEXTS OF THE HEBREW BIBLE

Kristin De Troyer

1. INTRODUCTION

In this contribution I would like to comment on a couple of readings from the Joshua and Leviticus Schøyen papyri (resp. MS 2648 and MS 2649)[1] in order to demonstrate that there are two tendencies visible in these Old Greek papyri. On the one hand they preserve some readings that witness to a pre-Masoretic Text of the Hebrew Bible, and on the other hand they clearly contain pre-Hexaplaric corrections toward the MT. A Greek reading that witnesses to a pre-MT reading is a Greek reading that hearkens back to a Hebrew text which came before the Masoretic Text (or proto-Masoretic Text).[2] In other words, it witnesses to a stage prior to the one in the MT. A pre-Hexaplaric correction is a correction of the Old Greek text toward the MT attested in the period and literary texts before Origen's

---

1. Kristin De Troyer, "Leviticus" in *Papyri Graecae Schøyen II* (ed. D. Minutoli and R. Pintaudi; Papyrologica Florentina 40/Manuscripts in the Schøyen Collection, Greek Papyri 5.3; Firenze: Gonnelli: 2010), 1–68 + plates I–XVI; idem, "Joshua" in *Papyri Graecae Schøyen I* (ed. R. Pintaudi; Papyrologica Florentina 35/Manuscripts in the Schøyen Collection, Greek Papyri 5; Firenze: Gonnelli, 2005), 79–145 + plates XVI–XXVII. These papyri come from the Oxyrhynchus area in Egypt and were dated by Guglielmo Cavallo to the end of the second or beginning of the third century C.E. (see De Troyer, "Joshua," 92). They are rather similar to the Chester Beatty Papyri, esp. VI, IX–X. The Joshua papyrus is the oldest witness of the Old Greek text; for Leviticus, there are two older witnesses (4QLXXLev[a] [= Ra 801; second–first century B.C.E.] and 4QpapLXXLev[b] [= Ra 802; first century B.C.E.]), but the Schøyen papyrus is the largest witness. See www.schoyencollection.com.

2. As the proto-MT differs from the MT only in reading vowels, accents, and marginal notes and as there are no differences in the consonantal text, the proto-MT and the MT are treated in the same way in this essay. See Emanuel Tov, *Textual Criticism of the Hebrew Bible* (2nd ed.; Minneapolis: Fortress, 2001), 23.

Hexapla.[3] Both these readings can help define the place of the manuscripts under consideration in the textual history of the biblical text.

The two sorts of readings reflect two tendencies in the history of the biblical text and play a role in the larger current debate about the plurality of texts on the one hand and the uniformity, or at least dominance of the MT, on the other. The choices one makes in the debate about plurality or uniformity of the text have an impact on the question of which text to use in biblical studies. The second section of my contribution will be devoted to that issue.

This essay follows up on conclusions that I wrote after comparing the two Greek Schøyen manuscripts and outlining their contribution to the study of the Hebrew Bible at large.[4] With regard to Joshua, I noticed some variants that "pointed to the existence of a Hebrew text that was different from the Masoretic Text.... In the text of the papyrus, there were in my opinion clear examples which indicate that the Old Greek was translated from a pre-Masoretic Text."[5] But I also noted that "the papyrus ... contains variants that point toward pre-Hexaplaric corrections toward the MT."[6] Similarly for the Greek Leviticus text as attested in the papyrus, I noted pre-Hexaplaric corrections toward the MT[7] as well as some, albeit smaller, variants that witness to a pre-Masoretic text.[8] In other words, on the one hand, pluriformity of text is still visible in the Leviticus and Joshua Greek texts, witnessing to the presence of Hebrew texts that were (slightly) different from the Masoretic Text, and on the other hand, the clear trend is to conform to the texts of the Masoretic Text. A closer look at some examples will demonstrate these two opposing tendencies.

---

3. See Natalio Fernández Marcos, *The Septuagint in Context: Introduction to the Greek Versions of the Bible* (trans. W. G. E. Watson; Leiden: Brill, 2000), 247–52.

4. Kristin De Troyer, "From Leviticus to Joshua: The Old Greek Text in Light of Two LXX Manuscripts from the Schøyen Collection," *Journal for Ancient Judaism* 2 (2011): 29–78.

5. Ibid., 76–77.

6. Ibid., 77.

7. Ibid., 49–51.

8. Ibid., 55–57.

2. Corrections in the Old Greek Texts

2.1. Pre-MT and Pre-Hexaplaric Corrections in Joshua

2.1.1. Example of Attestation to a Pre-MT Different from the MT: Josh10:11b

In Josh 10:11b the MT reads אבנים גדלות מן־השמים: God is throwing "big stones from heaven" on the enemies. These big stones are often translated in English as hailstones. Origen's text[9] reflects the Hebrew: λίθους μεγάλους χαλάζης. That should come as no surprise, since Origen revised the Old Greek toward the MT. Codex Vaticanus reads λίθους χαλάζης. I refer here to the text of Codex Vaticanus, since there is not yet a volume in the Göttingen major edition of the Old Testament in Greek,[10] and since the text of Codex Vaticanus is often taken as the best witness to the Old Greek text.[11]

The text of καιγέ reads the same: λίθους χαλάζης.[12] The latter text is known to correct toward the Hebrew text. In this case it is clear that it does not revise toward the Hebrew text attested in the MT.

The text of MS 2648 offers a small variant: λίθοις χαλάζης. It too seems to lack the additional word μεγάλους, found in Origen and MT. Thus neither kaige/Theodotion nor 2648 have μεγάλους, which is a translation of גדלות. Since there is no clear indication of dependence of MS 2648 on kaige/Theodotion, and since the Old Greek as attested in Codex Vaticanus also lacks the additional adjective, I believe that the pre-MT and the

---

9. See Ilmari Soisalon-Soininen, *Der Charakter der asterisierten Zusätze in der Septuaginta* (Suomalaisen Tiedeakatemian Toimituksia/Annales Academiae Scientiarum Fennicae, Series B; vol. 114; Helsinki: Suomalainen Tiedeakatemia, 1959), 172 and note 7 ad v. 11.

10. The Cambridge edition has the same reading as Codex Vaticanus. See Alan England Brooke, Norman McLean, and Henry St. John Thackeray, eds., *The Old Testament in Greek according to the Text of Codex Vaticanus, Supplemented from Other Uncial Manuscripts, with a Critical Apparatus Containing the Variants of the Chief Ancient Authorities for the Text of the Septuagint* (3 vols. in 9; Cambridge: Cambridge University Press, 1917), 1.4:711.

11. I acknowledge that there are already some pre-Hexaplaric corrections in the text of Codex Vaticanus, but not in this case. See De Troyer, *Joshua*, 142. Also, idem, "From Leviticus to Joshua," 73–74.

12. For the kaige readings, see Leonard J. Greenspoon, *Textual Studies in the Book of Joshua* (HSM 28; Chico, Calif.: Scholars Press, 1983), case number 70.

Vorlage of the Old Greek only read אבנים. This is confirmed by 4QJosh[a], which reads אבנים מן השמים.[13]

2.1.2. Example of a Pre-Hexaplaric Correction toward MT: Josh 10:23

There are many examples in the Greek Joshua papyrus witnessing to a text that is different from the Old Greek text as given by Codex Vaticanus, but at the same time similar to the MT. In 10:23, for instance, the text of the Schøyen papyrus reads βασιλεῖς τούτους, whereas Codex Vaticanus only reads βασιλεῖς.[14] Tov suggested that the word "these" is a small elucidation of "(the) five kings."[15] The OG does not have the element "these." Moreover, Soisalon-Soininen states that the addition of τούτους is "kein origenischer Zusatz," in other words, the addition does not stem from the hand of Origen.[16] And as this addition is already visible in the older Greek Joshua Schøyen papyrus, it surely must stem from pre-Hexaplaric times. Thus the Greek Joshua Schøyen papyrus surely shows examples of pre-Hexaplaric corrections of its text toward the MT.

2.2. Pre-MT and Pre-Hexaplaric Corrections in Leviticus

2.2.1. Example of Attestation to a Pre-MT That Is Different from the MT: Lev 11:28

There are not that many clear examples of readings in the Greek Leviticus Schøyen papyrus. Although I argued elsewhere that the clearest example

---

13. The text of 4QJosh[a] does not have the word גדלות. Cf. Ulrich, "4QJosh[a]," 151–52. Cf. also Greenspoon, *Textual Studies*, 69–70; idem, "The Qumran Fragments of Joshua: Which Puzzle Are They Part of and Where Do They Fit?" in *Septuagint, Scrolls and Cognate Writings: Papers Presented to the International Symposium on the Septuagint and Its Relation to the Dead Sea Scrolls and Other Writings* (ed. G. J. Brooke and B. Lindars; SBLSCS 33; Atlanta: Scholars Press, 1992), 159–94, esp. 174.

14. Again, the Cambridge edition follows the text of Codex Vaticanus in this reading; see Brooke, McLean, and Thackeray, *Old Testament in Greek*, 1.4:713.

15. See Emanuel Tov, *The Greek and Hebrew Bible: Collected Essays on the Septuagint* (VTSup 72; Leiden: Brill, 1999), 391, repr. from "The Growth of the Book of Joshua in the Light of the Evidence of the LXX Translation," *Scripta Hierosolymitana* 31 (1986): 321–39, esp. 332.

16. Soisalon-Soininen, *Der Charakter*, 174.

was 11:28,[17] I now think 25:31 is a better example of a reading that harks back to a pre-MT that is (slightly) different from the MT. In 25:31, the text of the papyrus reads: λογι]σθησονται. The reading in the reconstructed critical edition of Leviticus,[18] with its main witnesses being Codex Vaticanus and Alexandrinus, is λογισθήτωσαν. I noted that 11Q1 reads with the reconstructed *Vorlagen* of the Greek Leviticus Schøyen papyrus and Symmachus, and also with the text of the Samaritan Pentateuch, a plural (יחשבו), against the singular of the MT (although with a plural subject) and with an indicative against the imperative of the OG, against the indicative of the MT. The reading of the papyrus is thus attested in the Old Greek as edited by Wevers, but also in 11Q1, the Samaritan Pentateuch, and Symmachus. Surely this must indicate that the text in front of the Old Greek translator of the book of Leviticus was slightly different from the MT.

2.2.2. Example of a Pre-Hexaplaric Correction of the Old Greek Text toward MT: Lev 11:28

Whereas there were not many examples of readings that buttress a pre-MT different from the MT in the Old Greek of Leviticus, there are plenty of examples of pre-Hexaplaric corrections. The best example in my opinion is again in Lev 11:28.[19] In 11:28 the papyrus offers the following reading: ιματια αυτου; the Old Greek text, however, according to Wevers, only read: ἱμάτια. The longer reading appears in witnesses that are normally Hexaplaric, in other words, it is clearly attested in manuscripts that belong to a tradition that revises the text in a Hexaplaric way toward the MT.[20] The main codices have the shorter text. Wevers thus correctly opted for the shorter text as representing the Old Greek.[21] As the correction toward the

---

17. See Kristin De Troyer, "The Hebrew Text behind the Greek Text of the Pentateuch," in *Proceedings from the IOSCS Meeting in Helsinki 2010* (ed. M. Peters; SCS; Atlanta: Society of Biblical Literature, forthcoming).

18. John William Wevers, *Leviticus* (Septuaginta Vetus Testamentum Graecum, Auctoritate Academiae Scientiarum Gottingensis editum 2.2; adiuvante Udo Quast; Göttingen: Vandenhoeck & Ruprecht, 1986), 274.

19. De Troyer, *Leviticus*, 61–62. See also, idem, "From Leviticus to Joshua," 50.

20. John William Wevers, *Text History of the Greek Leviticus* (MSU 19; Göttingen: Vandenhoeck & Ruprecht, 1986), 14.

21. Wevers, *Leviticus*, 274.

Hebrew text already appears in the Greek Leviticus Schøyen papyrus, it most likely is a pre-Hexaplaric correction toward the MT.

2.3 The Two Tendencies in the Greek Schøyen Papyri

Two conclusions can be drawn from the above examples. First, the examples of pre-Hexaplaric corrections in both the Leviticus text and the Joshua text demonstrate that there was in these codices a tendency to correct the Old Greek text toward the MT, most likely attesting to its growing importance and dominance. Second, there are readings in both papyri that attest to a Hebrew text that is slightly different from the MT. In other words, there is textual plurality, albeit in small details, in both the Leviticus and the Joshua codices. That there is still textual plurality in Joshua in the period in which the Old Greek was produced seems already to have been accepted in scholarship. Emanuel Tov, for instance, has argued for the existence of two parallel editions of Joshua.[22] That there is also textual plurality in Leviticus may come as a surprise, since it is part of the Torah/Pentateuch. My examples, however, support the conclusions of Armin Lange, who claims that with regard to Leviticus the Dead Sea Scrolls display textual fluidity and plurality.[23]

Now, what impact do these conclusions have on our investigations into the text of the Hebrew Bible?

3. Which Text Do We Use When Doing Biblical Scholarship?[24]

3.1. Goals of Textual Criticism

In his recent book *A Student's Guide to Textual Criticism*, Paul D. Wegner lists six goals of what he calls Old Testament Textual Criticism, each time appending the name of a scholar or project famous for that goal.[25] The

---

22. See Tov, *Greek and Hebrew Bible*, 385–96.

23. See Armin Lange, *Die Handschriften biblischer Bücher von Qumran und den anderen Fundorten* (vol.1 of *Handbuch der Textfunde vom Toten Meer*; Tübingen: Mohr Siebeck, 2009), 69–75.

24. See also Kristin De Troyer, "Which Text Are We Using for Our Studies of Dtr?" in *Proceedings of the IOSOT Meeting in Helsinki 2010* (ed. M. Nissinen, forthcoming).

25. Paul D. Wegner, *A Student's Guide to Textual Criticism: Its History, Methods*

goals are: (1) restore the original composition (Roland K. Harrison); (2) restore the final form of the text (Ellis R. Brotzman, Ferdinand E. Deist, Ernst Würthwein); (3) restore the earliest attested form (Hebrew University Bible Project, United Bible Society Hebrew Old Testament Text Project); (4) restore accepted texts (James A. Sanders, Brevard Childs); (5) restore final texts (Emanuel Tov, Bruce K. Waltke); and (6) restore all various "literary editions" of the Old Testament (Eugene Ulrich). Whereas I can understand the attempt to restore the earliest attested form of the biblical text or to restore accepted texts, for me as a text critic the most compelling goals are the ones formulated by Tov and Ulrich, restoring final texts or literary editions.

3.2. Evaluating the Approaches of Ulrich and Tov

According to Ulrich a multiple literary edition is:

> A literary unit—a story, pericope, narrative, poem, book, etc.—appearing in two or more parallel forms (whether by chance extant or no longer extant in the textual witnesses), which one author, major redactor, or major editor completed and which a subsequent redactor or editor intentionally changed to a sufficient extent that the resultant form should be called a revised edition of that text.[26]

Ulrich distinguishes this sort of creative scribal activity from, for instance, the activity that resulted in "individual variant readings," that is, variant words or phrases in the MT.[27] The model that Ulrich has in mind for all forms of editorial activities is the scribe: "Indeed, the scribes of scriptural manuscripts often intended simply to produce a new copy of an older *Vorlage*, and from time to time they made mistakes."[28] Ulrich does not focus on their "smaller errors and corruptions" and on the smaller variants, however, but on their larger editorial and creative changes.[29] He has pointed to

---

and Results (Downers Grove, Ill.: InterVarsity Press, 2006), 31. Wegner summarizes the work of Bruce K. Waltke in this section of his book.

26. Eugene Ulrich, *The Dead Sea Scrolls and the Origins of the Bible* (Studies in the Dead Sea Scrolls and Related Literature; Grand Rapids: Eerdmans, 1999), 63. See also his essay in this volume, "The Evolutionary Composition of the Hebrew Bible."

27. Ulrich, *Dead Sea Scrolls*, 62.

28. Ibid., 61.

29. Ibid.

many examples of revised editions of biblical texts, especially those found in the history of the books of Exodus, Samuel, Jeremiah and Daniel. For all of these books, Ulrich distinguishes between an earlier version (MT and LXX Exodus; MT 1–2 Sam[30]; LXX Jeremiah; no longer existing Old Hebrew Daniel) and a later version (4QpaleoExod[m] and SamEx; LXX 1–2Sam[31]; MT Jeremiah; MT and LXX Dan 1–4).[32] It is also important to note that according to Ulrich all the editing and reworking happened at the Hebrew level and thus cannot be ascribed to the Old Greek.[33] He notes:

> The parallel editions were current, available forms of the sacred text in the original language, and apparently up to the end of the first century of the common era they were seen as having equally valid claims to being "the biblical text."[34]

In his discussion of the book of Jeremiah, Tov states that it is "unlikely that the translator would have abridged his Hebrew *Vorlage*." Thus "the brevity of the LXX reflects a short Hebrew text."[35] In other words, Tov acknowledges two Hebrew texts of Jeremiah. Similarly, but to a lesser extent, there are "two different redactional stages" in the book of Ezekiel. Again, the "additional layer of the MT added exegetical remarks and harmonizing details, explained contextual difficulties, and in one instance changed the sequence of the text."[36]

Ulrich and Tov have very similar views. Both point to more than one Hebrew text existing for some of the biblical books. Both emphasize that these texts were indeed Hebrew texts and that the process of editing happened at the Hebrew stage.[37] They might differ, however, when it comes to labeling the person doing this sort of editorial work. When describing the nature of the work done by the editor of Jeremiah II, Tov remarks: "The anonymous editor II was not a scribe, but he produced one of the stages of the literary work now called MT." He further elaborates: "He had access

---

30. Except for 1 Sam 17–18, where LXX has the earlier form and MT has the secondary form.

31. See n. 30.

32. See Ulrich, *Dead Sea Scrolls*, 72.

33. Ibid., 72.

34. Ibid., 73.

35. Tov, *Greek and Hebrew Bible*, 363.

36. Ibid., 410.

37. Ulrich, *Dead Sea Scrolls*, 42–44.

to genuine Jeremianic material not included in Edition I, he rearranged sections, and he also added new material."[38] Tov connects scribal activities with scribal practices, and thus thinks in categories of writing materials, technical aspects of writing, writing practices, layout of poetical units, scribal marks, correction procedures, scripts, special scribal characteristics of certain types of text, and scribal traditions.[39] Thus whereas Ulrich defines the editor as a scribe, Tov does not see her or him as a scribe. Yet how these editors do their work seems almost the same.

What Ulrich stresses is that all the different texts of a given biblical book seem to be related to each other in a sequential way and that each edition further elaborates an earlier one. For instance, in his table showing "grouping of manuscripts according to editions," he organizes the witnesses in the following categories: n+1, n+2, n+3, n+4.[40] For Exodus, the grid looks like this:[41]

n+1	G-Exod
n+2	MT-Exod
n+3	4QpaleoExod^m
n+4	SP-Exod

Ulrich writes:

> the OG has one edition of [Exod] 35–40 which the MT superseded; the entire book as in the MT was expanded systematically by one or more Jewish scribes into a form very close to the SP; and the Samaritans used the latter as their base text into which they inserted their two minor specific confessional changes.[42]

---

38. Tov, *Greek and Hebrew Bible*, 365.

39. Emanuel Tov, "Scribal Practices Reflected in the Texts from the Judaean Desert," in *The Dead Sea Scrolls after Fifty Years: A Comprehensive Assessment* (ed. P. W. Flint and J. C. VanderKam; 2 vols.; Leiden: Brill, 1998), 1:403–29, esp. 403. See also his book: *Scribal Practices and Approaches Reflected in the Texts Found in the Judean Desert* (STD 54; Leiden: Brill, 2004).

40. With regard to the "n+1" form, Ulrich writes: "The 'n+1' type of designation for successive editions of a text assumes that there has been a series of editions during the composition of the text which constitutes its growth leading up to the first extant witness to a given book." See Ulrich, "The Scrolls and the Biblical Text," in *Dead Sea Scrolls After Fifty Years*, 1:79–100, esp. 85 n. 21.

41. See Ulrich, "Scrolls and the Biblical Text," 79–100, esp. 85.

42. Ibid., 79–100, esp. 87.

Given the rather linear and sequential way in which the different editions come to be, Ulrich opts to restore all various editions of the text.

In his research on the texts of Jeremiah, Tov also recognizes a sequential and linear development. He writes of "the premise that the Hebrew *Vorlage* of the LXX and 4QJer[b,d] represent an early edition of Jeremiah which was expanded by the editor of MT into Edition II."[43] He presumes similarly for the texts of Joshua: "The working hypothesis suggested here is that a short text like the LXX was expanded to a long text like MT."[44] And concerning Ezekiel: "In most instances the short text of the LXX reflects a more original text … and the long text of MT a secondary one."[45] But Tov leaves space for developments that fall outside the linear sequential model: "It is suggested that several sequence differences between the MT and LXX relate to late additions of sections whose position was not yet fixed when the archetypes of these texts were composed."[46]

The latter remark by Tov should reinforce the importance of restoring all literary editions of a given biblical book. Next, the restoration of all literary units ought to result in the study of the different literary editions of any given biblical book. Given the multiplicity of texts already at hand and those that are now being produced, which text should one use when doing biblical studies? It is one thing to have a text-critical goal in mind, and another to actually choose a text to work on.[47] The production of the different literary editions of biblical books should lead to the use of all literary editions in biblical scholarship. We can no longer choose to work only with MT Joshua or MT Leviticus, but need to integrate the other versions, whether or not they are sequentially linked to each other. The study of the Greek papyri therefore leads us back to the study of *texts* of the Hebrew Bible, and not only to its *text*.

---

43. Tov, *Greek and Hebrew Bible*, 364.

44. Ibid., 389.

45. Ibid., 400.

46. Ibid., 411 (with regard to Numbers, Joshua, 1 Samuel, 1 Kings, and Jeremiah, for which examples are further elaborated on 411–19).

47. My thanks to Allen Jones for making this distinction.

What Text Is Being Edited?
The Editing of the New Testament

Michael W. Holmes

1. Introduction

The text of the New Testament, extant today in more than 5,300 manuscripts, is better attested than any other text from the ancient world.[1] Yet approximately 85 percent of those manuscripts were copied in the eleventh century C.E. or later; very few of the 15 percent or so that were written during the first millennium of the text's existence can be dated any earlier than the beginning of the third century; and the entire group comprises a premier example of a cross-pollinated (or "contaminated") textual tradition, rendering traditional Lachmannian genealogical analysis impossible.[2] In these circumstances, nearly all editors and textual critics have

---

1. For an illuminating analysis (both quantitative and qualitative) of the number and extent of manuscripts of the New Testament during the first millennium of its existence, see Eldon Jay Epp, "Are Early New Testament Manuscripts Truly Abundant?" in *Israel's God and Rebecca's Children: Christology and Community in Early Judaism and Christianity* (ed. D. B. Capes et al.; Waco, Tex.: Baylor University Press, 2007), 77–117, 395–99. Epp lists only three or four second-century manuscripts: P52, P90, P104, and perhaps P98 (pp. 83, 98). A slightly more generous estimate of the number of second-century texts is offered by J. Keith Elliott, "The Nature of the Evidence Available for Reconstructing the Text of the New Testament in the Second Century," in *The New Testament Text in Early Christianity/Le text du Nouveau Testament au début du christianisme* (ed. C. -B. Amphoux and J. K. Elliott; Lausanne: Éditions du Zèbre, 2003), 10–11.

2. For a brief analysis of the impact of "contamination" on a textual tradition, see Michael W. Holmes, "Working with an Open Textual Tradition: Challenges in Theory and Practice," in *The Textual History of the Greek New Testament: Changing Views in*

adopted an approach known most widely as reasoned eclecticism.[3] In contrast to a Lachmannian approach, which seeks to identify the manuscript or archetype from which all other extant manuscripts descend, reasoned eclecticism seeks to identify, on a variant by variant basis, the reading from which all other readings at that point of variation originate. A Lachmannian stemmatic approach implies a specific goal (the recovery of the archetype), whereas with a reasoned eclectic approach, any of a number of goals are possible. Therefore the question "what text is being edited?" is a substantive matter in the context of contemporary New Testament textual criticism. In pursuing this question, we will find that (1) a surprising range of answers have been given to that question in recent decades; (2) the ways editors have characterized the same printed text has shifted over time; and (3) that shift is reflective of a significant development within the discipline itself. A survey of some recent critical editions will provide an appropriate *point de départ*.

2. A Survey of Selected Critical Editions

The Greek New Testament: so reads the title of the first book I purchased when I commenced graduate studies.[4] The second edition of the text published by the United Bible Societies, it was printed in a beautiful eye-pleasing Greek font, had a useful dictionary in the back, and was encased in what proved to be a wretched maroon plastic cover.

Eventually I acquired another Greek Testament, this one entitled *Novum Testamentum Graece ... editione vicesima sexta*—the twenty-sixth edition of the famous Nestle-Aland text.[5] Smaller in format (just 11.5 x 16.2 x 2.6 cm, versus 13.5 x 19.2 x 3.2 cm for the UBS text), this edition

---

Contemporary Research (ed. K. Wachtel and M. W. Holmes; Atlanta: Society of Biblical Literature, 2011), 65–78.

3. See further on this topic Michael W. Holmes, "The Case for Reasoned Eclecticism," in *Rethinking New Testament Textual Criticism* (ed. D. A. Black; Grand Rapids: Baker Academic, 2002), 77–100; idem, "Reasoned Eclecticism," in *The Text of the New Testament in Contemporary Research: Essays on the* Status Quaestionis (ed. B. D. Ehrman and M. W. Holmes; SD 46; Grand Rapids: Eerdmans, 1995), 336–60.

4. Kurt Aland, Matthew Black, Carlo M. Martini, Bruce M. Metzger, and Allen Wikgren, eds., *The Greek New Testament* (2nd ed.; New York: United Bible Societies, 1968).

5. Kurt Aland et al., *Novum Testamentum Graece* (26th ed.; Stuttgart: Deutsche Bibelgesellschaft, 1979).

utilized a more ornate font, had a considerably more extensive critical apparatus at the foot of the page, and was bound in a sturdy blue pebble-grained cover.

A later acquisition was *The New Testament in the Original Greek according to the Byzantine/Majority Textform.*[6] Larger in size (16 x 23.5 x 3.7 cm), this critically edited edition of the Byzantine textform presents a distinctive appearance to the eye: according to its editors, "The basic format ... is designed to resemble an ancient Greek manuscript," combining "the best features of uncial and minuscule manuscript style."[7] It is printed entirely in lowercase font with no accentuation, no breathings, no punctuation, no diacritical marks, no paragraphing, and no critical apparatus; on the other hand, individual words are separated; *nomina sacra* are printed in full; there is no word division at the end of a line; and chapter and verse numbers are included.[8]

In recent years I have been accumulating the various fascicles of yet another critical edition, this one entitled *Novum Testamentum Graecum: Editio Critica Maior.*[9] Four installments covering the Catholic Epistles have appeared to date. It stands out from the others not only with respect to its large page size (21 x 29.7 cm) but also its layout: typically only one or two lines of text appear on each page, the rest being devoted to the apparatus (thus the 108 verses of James occupy 102 pages). Moreover, the edition prints a number under each word in every verse in the text (consecutive even numbers for the words, with the unprinted odd numbers applying by

---

6. Maurice A. Robinson and William G. Pierpont, *The New Testament in the Original Greek according to the Byzantine/Majority Textform* (Atlanta: Original Word Publishers, 1991).

7. Ibid., xliii.

8. In a subsequent publication by the same editors (*The New Testament in the Original Greek: Byzantine Textform, 2005*, compiled and arranged by Maurice A. Robinson and William G. Pierpont [Southborough, Mass.: Chilton, 2005]—apparently not a "second edition" of the 1991 work), the distinctive features of the 1991 edition (lowercase font with no accentuation, no breathings, no punctuation, no diacritical marks, no paragraphing, and no critical apparatus) have been abandoned.

9. Barbara Aland, Kurt Aland, Gerd Mink, Holger Strutwolf, and Klaus Wachtel, eds., *Catholic Letters* (vol. 4 of *Novum Testamentum Graecum: Editio Critica Maior*; 4 installments; The Institute for New Testament Textual Research; Stuttgart: Deutsche Bibelgesellschaft, 1997–2005): (1) *James* (1997; 2nd rev. impr., 1998); (2) *The Letters of Peter* (2000); (3) *The First Letter of John* (2003); (4) *The Second and Third Letter of John. The Letter of Jude* (2005).

implication to the spaces between them), thus facilitating a very precise specification of the location of every variant reading in the apparatus.

These four representations of the Greek New Testament—the two most widely used editions of the Greek New Testament today, a critical edition of an alternative form of the New Testament text, and the first part of a long-awaited major critical edition—are each very different in appearance, layout, and features. But what about the *texts* they convey? How do the editors of these editions characterize the text that they have edited? What, in other words, do they claim to be producing as a result of their editorial activities? What historical form or stage of the Greek New Testament do our modern editions reproduce? It turns out that in some cases these are not easy questions to answer, as a brief survey of the four editions will indicate.

3. A Comparison of Four Editions

3.1. *The New Testament in the Original Greek according to the Byzantine/Majority Textform*

This is the only edition to characterize its text in its title. In their introduction to the volume, editors Maurice Robinson and William Pierpont offer a double characterization of their text. First, they characterize their text as "the closest approximation yet produced to a true Byzantine-Text edition of the Greek New Testament"—a textform they define as the one that "represents the pattern of readings found in the Greek manuscripts predominating during the 1000-year Byzantine era."[10] Second, in their introduction they offer "evidence to support the hypothesis that the Byzantine Textform more closely represents the original autographs than any other texttype."[11] In contrast to their careful definition of the Byzantine textform, however, they do not indicate how they define the term "original autographs." To be fair, this is hardly a cause for surprise, for in 1991 the meaning of that term was still widely considered to be self-evident and unproblematic.

---

10. Robinson and Pierpont, *Byzantine/Majority Textform*, xiii, xvi.
11. Ibid., xiii.

3.2. THE GREEK NEW TESTAMENT

The second edition (1968) of the UBS *Greek New Testament* (= UBS²), the first edition of which was published in 1966, has subsequently appeared in the third (1975), third corrected (1983), and fourth revised (1993) editions. In none of these editions does either the preface or the introduction say anything about the character of the text presented by the editors. The preface to the first edition informs the reader about the purpose of the edition (to serve the needs of Bible translators). It mentions that Westcott and Hort's edition of the Greek New Testament served as the initial basis from which the UBS editors worked and that "the Committee carried out its work in four principal stages": (1) it determined "which of the variant readings warranted further study"; (2) it gathered "data on several thousand sets of variants"; (3) it selected and compared variations in punctuation"; and finally (4) "the Greek text was established."[12] It also informs the reader of "the intention of the Committee from time to time to revise its work in order to take into account new discoveries and fresh evidence."[13] It says nothing, however, about how the text was established, or about the character of the resulting text. Similarly the prefaces and introductions to the second, third, and fourth editions, while alerting users to textual changes of various sorts from the previous edition (or, in the fourth edition, the lack thereof), are completely silent with regard to the character of the text.[14]

Already in 1964, however, one of the UBS editors, Bruce Metzger, began to compile a *Textual Commentary* to accompany the UBS text.[15]

---

12. Kurt Aland, ed., *The Greek New Testament* (New York: United Bible Societies, 1966), v–vi.

13. Ibid., vii.

14. "This Second Edition of the Greek New Testament incorporates a number of typographical corrections, 45 changes in evaluation of the evidence (i.e., changes in the ratings of A, B, C, and D), 11 alterations involving brackets, and five modifications of text or punctuation" (UBS 2nd ed., viii); "As a result of the Committee's discussions, more than five hundred changes have been introduced into this Third Edition" (Kurt Aland et al., eds., *The Greek New Testament* [3rd ed.; London: United Bible Societies, 1975], viii); in the 4th edition the apparatus has been thoroughly revised, while the text is identical to that of the 3rd edition (Kurt Aland et al., eds., *The Greek New Testament* [4th ed.; Stuttgart: Deutsche Bibelgesellschaft and United Bible Societies, 1993], 1).

15. Bruce M. Metzger, *A Textual Commentary on the Greek New Testament* (London: United Bible Societies, 1971; corr. ed., 1975; 2nd ed., 1994).

When finally published in 1971, it was intended to accompany the third edition of the UBS text, which was not published until 1975. In it Metzger, working (to quote the title page) "on behalf of and in cooperation with the Editorial Committee," makes the following claim:

> During the twentieth century, with the discovery of several New Testament manuscripts much older than any that had hitherto been available, it has become possible to produce editions of the New Testament that approximate ever more closely to what is regarded as the wording of the original documents.[16]

Since over five hundred changes from the second edition were introduced into the third edition, it seems reasonable to infer that the editorial committee considered the third edition to "approximate ever more closely" what they "regarded as the wording of the original documents." Here we find both a characterization of the text and an apparent indication of the editors' goal (recovering "the wording of the original documents").

The text of the fourth revised edition (1993) is identical to that of the third. The Committee declares, however, that:

> This should not be misunderstood to mean that the editors now consider the text as established. Work on the text of the Holy Scriptures continues to be a task of concern for each of the editors who will offer the results of their research in future editions of the *Greek New Testament*. Yet the editors feel that at the present time this responsible research has not yet advanced sufficiently to authorize making specific changes in the text.[17]

To summarize: first, the editors say nothing in any of the editions about the character of the text produced or the goal of their work; nevertheless, one may infer from the accompanying textual commentary that their goal was to "approximate" as closely as possible "the wording of the original documents." Second, in the editors' opinion work on the text is not fin-

---

16. Metzger, *Textual Commentary* (1971), xxiii–xiv. Compare this formulation to that of B. F. Westcott and F. J. A. Hort: "Our own aim ... has been to obtain ... the closest possible approximation to the apostolic text itself" (Brooke Foss Westcott and Fenton John Anthony Hort, eds., *The New Testament in the Original Greek*, [2:] *Introduction* [and] *Appendix* [Cambridge: Macmillan, 1881; 2nd ed., London: Macmillan, 1896], 288).

17. UBS 4th ed., vi.

ished, but in the present state of knowledge, no further progress can be made. One still wonders, however, just how close to that goal the Committee thinks it has come. To infer a possible answer to that question, we must turn to another edition prepared under the supervision of the same editorial committee: the twenty-sixth edition of the Nestle-Aland text.

3.3. NESTLE-ALAND, *NOVUM TESTAMENTUM GRAECE*

While five editions (21st–25th) of what is now commonly referred to as the "Nestle-Aland" text appeared between 1952 and 1963, it was not until 1979 that the twenty-sixth edition appeared (= NA[26]). That long interval was the result of major changes to both text and apparatus undertaken for that edition. Two major changes had already become known in 1975 with the publication of the third UBS edition: the same Editorial Committee would be responsible for both the UBS and the Nestle-Aland texts, and the texts of the UBS[3] and the (at that time still forthcoming) NA[26] editions would be identical (though they would continue to differ in other respects, in accordance with their different purposes).

At first glance, the introduction to the NA[26] text says no more about the character of its text than does the introduction to the UBS text. In contrast to that text, however, it does include a brief description of how the editors established the text of NA[26]:

> After carefully establishing the variety of readings offered in a passage and the possibilities of their interpretation, it must always then be determined afresh on the basis of external and internal criteria which of these readings (and frequently they are quite numerous) is the original, from which the others may be regarded as derivative.[18]

On the basis of this short statement one could reasonably infer that the editors believed that they were, to some extent at least, establishing the "original" reading at each place of variation. But what does this "original" reading represent—an archetype from which the other readings are derived, the "original text," or something else? The reader receives no guidance in this regard. A few lines later, the text of this edition is described as "the Standard Text"—but no explanation or definition of this term is given.

---

18. NA[26], 43*.

Once again, however, a volume written by one of the editors of this text provides additional information. In the 1981 handbook co-authored by Kurt Aland and Barbara Aland (who joined the Editorial Committee in 1982) entitled *Der Text des Neuen Testaments*, the NA[26] text is discussed in some detail.[19] There we learn, for instance, that the frequently-used "Standard text" label[20]—a name that "did not come from the editors but from reviews of the new Nestle-Aland[26] in the popular press and in scholarly journals"—designates "the text officially published and distributed by the United Bible Societies and also officially by the Catholic church."[21] It is, in other words, an indication of this text's status rather than a description of its character.

With respect to that character, the Alands are quite clear: in their estimation, the text of NA[26] does not merely come "closer to the original text ['Urtext'] of the New Testament than did Tischendorf or Westcott and Hort." It "approximates the original form of the New Testament ['ursprünglichen Neuen Testaments'] as closely as possible, at least according to the five members of its editorial board."[22] To be sure, the editors of the "Standard text" certainly do not claim infallibility. They do, however, recognize that to the best of their knowledge and abilities, and with resources unmatched for any manual edition of the New Testament in modern times, they have edited a text that comes as close as possible to the original form ["ursprünglichen Fassungen"] of the New Testament writings.[23]

Here also, as in the case of Metzger earlier, we find both a characterization of the text and an apparent indication of the editors' goal. In contrast to Metzger, however, the Alands do give some indication of what they mean by "ursprünglich" in these and other phrases (such as "ursprüngli-

---

19. Kurt Aland and Barbara Aland, *Der Text des Neuen Testaments* (Stuttgart: Deutsche Bibelgesellschaft, 1981; 2nd ed., 1989); idem, *The Text of the New Testament* (trans. E. F. Rhodes; Grand Rapids: Eerdmans; Leiden: Brill, 1987; 2nd ed., 1989).

20. It occurs at least thirty times in the volume; see the index for details.

21. Aland and Aland, *The Text*[1], 30 (= *Der Text*[1], 41).

22. Aland and Aland, *The Text*[1], 24, 218 (= *Der Text*[1], 34, 227).

23. Aland and Aland, *The Text*[1], 306 (= *Der Text*[1], 313); see also Kurt Aland ("Der neue 'Standard-Text' in seinem Verhältnis zu den frühen Papyri und Majuskeln," in *New Testament Textual Criticism: Its Significance for Exegesis: Essays in Honour of Bruce M. Metzger* [ed. E. J. Epp and G. D. Fee; Oxford: Clarendon, 1981], 274): "A hundred years after Westcott-Hort, it seems that the goal of an edition of the NT 'in the original Greek' has been reached."

che Text").[24] In an important statement near the end of the book, they acknowledge that "the competence of New Testament textual criticism is restricted to the state of the New Testament text from the moment it began its literary history through transcription for distribution"[25]—that is, by "original text" they mean the text in the form in which it was first copied for circulation.

In addition to the observations just noted, there is an interesting mixture of assertion and tentativeness evident in the statements quoted above. This can be seen elsewhere in their handbook as well. For example, on the one hand, it is acknowledged that:

> Of course the new "Standard text" itself is not a static entity. The members of the editorial committee as well as all others responsible for the edition agree on the tentative nature of the publication. Every change in it is open to challenge—requiring only that arguments for proposed changes be convincing.[26]

On the other hand, this apparent openness to arguments for change is sharply curtailed just a few lines later, where the reader is warned that "Rash decisions should always be avoided. Many will undoubtedly feel strongly inclined to make improvements here and there in the 'Standard text.' This temptation should be resisted."[27]

So, even as the text of NA[26] is described as open to improvement and not static, the reader is informed that it "approximates the original form of the New Testament as closely as possible" and all "temptations" to make changes should be "resisted." With all due effort to balance the tension between these statements, it is difficult to avoid the conclusion that a very strong claim is made on behalf of NA[26] (it "comes as close as possible to the original form"), one that goes beyond anything claimed in regard to UBS[3]—which prints, of course, the identical text. In short, two of the text's editors (Metzger and Aland) give two rather different characterizations of the same text.

---

24. This last phrase ("ursprüngliche Text") is apparently their most widely used expression (see, e.g., *Der Text*[1], 303, 304, 308 (4x), 313 [= *The Text*[1], 296, 297, 301, 306]); for "Urtext," see also *Der Text*[1], 314 (= *The Text*[1], 307).

25. Aland and Aland, *The Text*[1], 292 (= *Der Text*[1], 298).

26. Aland and Aland, *The Text*[1], 35 (= *Der Text*[1], 45).

27. Ibid.

That same text is also printed in the twenty-seventh edition of the Nestle-Aland text published in 1993, where it receives yet a third characterization. In the introduction to this edition, the Editorial Committee (now composed of Barbara Aland, Kurt Aland, Johannes Karavidopoulos, Carlo Martini, and Bruce Metzger) informs readers "that this text is a *working text* ["Arbeitstext"] (in the sense of the century-long Nestle tradition): it is not to be considered as definitive, but as a stimulus to further efforts toward defining and verifying the text"; that is, "it intends to provide the user with a well-founded working text together with the means of verifying it or alternatively of correcting it."[28] This is a rather different sort of characterization, one that sidesteps the question of whether or to what extent the edited text approximates the "original text."

3.4. *Novum Testamentum Graecum: Editio Critica Maior*

A fourth characterization of what is virtually the same text may be found in the introduction to the *Editio Critica Maior* (= *ECM*). The production of a comprehensive critical edition has been a long-term goal of the Institut für Neutestamentliche Textforschung in Münster,[29] and decades of work by a multitude of co-workers at the Institute began to bear fruit in 1997 when the first installment, presenting the text and data for James, was published. This has been followed by three additional installments covering 1–2 Peter (2000), 1 John (2003), and 2–3 John and Jude (2005).[30] It is important to note the publication dates of the various installments, because these initial installments represent a work in progress, and the characterization of the edited text has shifted somewhat during the course of editorial work on the *ECM*.

In the introduction to the first installment (James) the text of the *ECM* is not characterized. The reader is, however, informed that "the text of the present edition has been established afresh ["neu konstituiert"], on the basis of all the evidence presented," that is, a presentation of "the full range

---

28. NA[27] introduction, 45*, 45*–46* (emphasis added). Despite this invitation to correct the text, the reader continues to be warned that "it is advisable, even imperative, to let the text of this edition remain unaltered" (49*).

29. Kurt Aland, "*Novi Testamenti graeci editio maior critica.* Der gegenwärtige Stand der Arbeit an einer neuen grossen kritischen Ausgabe des Neuen Testamentes," *NTS* 16 (1969–1970): 163–77.

30. Aland et al., *Catholic Letters.*

of resources necessary for scholarly research in establishing the text and reconstructing the history of the New Testament text during its first thousand years."[31]

In the preface to the second installment (1 and 2 Peter), "new methodological developments and their effects on the reconstruction of the text" are mentioned, and in the introduction (which builds upon the introduction to the first installment) two new concepts are briefly introduced and defined: "coherence" and "Ausgangstext" (or "initial text"). "Coherence within a group of witnesses means that the members of the group are connected by a direct genealogical relationship," while "the initial text is the form of a text that stands at the beginning of a textual tradition. The constructed text of an edition represents the hypothetical reconstruction of this initial text."[32] In comparing the introductions to the first two installments, one begins to realize that a new analytic tool, in development for a number of years, is now being employed as a means of better understanding the external criteria, in particular the relationships between the various Greek manuscript witnesses to the text of these letters.[33]

In the preface to the third installment (1 John), the new methodological development is given a name: the "Coherence-Based Genealogical Method," or CBGM.[34] In addition, the introduction provides a fuller description of how the text of the *ECM* is established, and what the "initial text" represents.

In order to gain "a first impression" of the available manuscript witnesses for 1 John, the text of UBS[4]/NA[27] was utilized as a collation base, since it is "a reconstruction which we believe to be the best hypothetical initial text that has been reached up to now without the knowledge of the extensive material being offered in the ECM."[35] So here we have a fourth

---

31. *ECM James*, 11*.

32. *ECM 1–2 Peter*, 23*.

33. It was also applied retroactively to the text of James, with the result that "earlier textual decisions were mainly confirmed, although sometimes weakened. Yet the new findings did not support a variant reading over the primary line except in one instance (2:4/2–4)" (*ECM 1–2 Peter*, 24* n. 4).

34. See Gerd Mink, "Problems of a Highly Contaminated Tradition, the New Testament: Stemmata of Variants as a Source of a Genealogy for Witnesses," in *Studies in Stemmatology II* (ed. P. van Reenen, A. den Hollander, and M. van Mulken; Amsterdam: Benjamins, 2004), 13–85.

35. *ECM 1 John*, 28*. This initial use of UBS[4]/NA[27] had already been hinted at in the introduction to the James installment: after specifying the two places where the

characterization of the UBS$^{3-4}$/NA$^{26-27}$ text, this time as "a hypothetical initial text."

This initial collation provides a starting point for the eventual application of the CBGM as a tool for assessing the external evidence for each instance of variation. This evidence, in conjunction with the results of an assessment of internal evidence by means of the customary criteria, provided a basis for making textual decisions on a passage-by-passage basis. The results of these decisions comprise the primary text line of the *ECM*— an even better representative of the initial text than UBS^4/NA^{27}, inasmuch as it was able to take into account the genealogical coherence of the witnesses in a way never before possible.

The initial text itself is defined as "the form of a text that stands at the beginning of a textual tradition."[36] If one defines an archetype as "the manuscript, whether lost or extant, from which the manuscript tradition is descended," then one may define the initial text as the reconstructed text that is imperfectly conveyed by the archetypal manuscript.[37] It is thus to be distinguished from an authorial text, with which it may or may not have a close relationship (that is a question to be investigated, rather than assumed), and also from the text as preserved in the archetypal manuscript(s), in that the initial text, reconstructed by means of the tools of textual criticism, is something more than the archetype.[38]

The text of the *ECM*, however, is not identical to that of the initial text, as the editors explain:

> The hypothetical initial text, an artificial witness referred to as *A* (Aus-gangstext), is not identical with the NA/GNT text or with the primary text line of the ECM. The text of *A* corresponds largely to the primary line, but not completely, because in any passage where the case for

---

text of *ECM* differs from that of NA^{27}/UBS^4, it informs the reader that "Apart from these there was no need to alter the text" (*ECM James*, 11*)—of what? Presumably that of UBS^4/NA^{27}.

36. *ECM 1–2 Peter*, 23* n. 4.

37. Klaus Wachtel and David C. Parker, "The Joint IGNTP/INTF Editio Critica Maior of the Gospel of John: Its Goals and Their Significance for New Testament Scholarship" (paper presented at the SNTS meeting, Halle, 15 August 2005). Online: http://epapers.bham.ac.uk/754/1/2005_SNTS_WachtelParker.pdf, p. 9.

38. Ibid., 10.

attributing a reading to *A* is too uncertain or cannot be made at all, the
decision is suspended and A is regarded as having a lacuna.[39]

In other words, "The constructed text of an edition represents the hypothetical reconstruction of this initial text."[40] This means that the initial text
is the *goal* toward which the editors strive, and the lead text of the *ECM* is
the *closest approximation* to it that can be achieved in the present circumstances and conditions. Here we have a clear characterization of the text
of the *ECM*.

How closely does the *ECM* approximate the hypothetical initial text?
In the 432 verses[41] that make up the Catholic Letters, there are some
eighty instances where the text of the *ECM* is bracketed by bold dots (as
at, e.g., Jas 1:20, •οὐκ ἐργάζεται•). In some of these instances the bold dots
mark places where in the editors' estimation the reading of the initial
text is undeterminable, and in others they mark places where agreement
between the *ECM* and initial text is probable but not certain.[42] This means
there are no more than eighty possible differences between the *ECM* and
the initial text (many of which involve word order variation, rather than
differences in wording[43]); the actual number is less, and in any case it is
not large.

4. Comparing Some Answers

It is now possible to begin to summarize (if only in a tentative way) and
compare some answers to the framing questions posed earlier: What are

---

39. *ECM 1 John*, 29*. Those places where the decision with respect to the reading
of the initial text is suspended are marked by bold dots (• … •) in the primary line, and
the bold dot signals the alternative reading in the apparatus.

40. *ECM 1–2 Peter*, 23* n. 4.

41. So Aland and Aland, *The Text*, 29.

42. A precise number is difficult to ascertain because sometimes the bold dots
signal "alternative readings which were considered of equal value," and sometimes
they mark instances where "the reasons for the reading in the primary line were
regarded as superior, but not sufficiently to rule out with complete confidence the
claims of the indicated alternative reading" (*ECM 1–2 Peter*, 24*, where, according to
p. 37* n. 2, "the significance of the bold dot is explained better than in the Introduction
11*" [James]; cf. also 30* [1 John].

43. Five of eleven instances in James.

the editors of these several editions aiming at, and what do they claim to be producing as a result of their editorial activities?

The editors of the Byzantine/Majority text offer an exemplary model in this regard, indicating clearly both the character of their text ("a true Byzantine-Text edition of the Greek New Testament"), their goal (the "original autographs"), and the relationship between the two. The critical edition of the Byzantine text of the Gospel of John offers another excellent example in this regard.[44]

The situation is rather different for the editions that stand in what may be termed the UBS/NA/*ECM* textual tradition. Here we find (when we find anything at all) an interesting range of responses. If we combine statements from the prefaces and introductions to these editions with other statements by some of the individual editors, as has been done above, the following set of answers emerges.

Regarding the goal of New Testament textual criticism:

Textual Commentary **(1971):** to approximate the wording of the original documents (with [on UBS[3] 1975] "original" left undefined)
Aland and Aland (1982): to recover the original (ursprünglich) text, that is, the text as it first circulated
NA[27] (1993): (not specified)
ECM **(1–2 Peter, 2000):** reconstruction of the *Ausgangstext* (initial text)

Regarding the characterization of the resultant text:

Textual Commentary **(1971):** the *GNT*[3] text approximates more closely than any previous edition the wording of the original documents (but there is no indication as to how close it may come to that goal)
Aland and Aland (1982): the NA[26] text comes as close to the original text as possible in the present circumstances
NA[27] (1993): NA[27] represents a well-founded working text, in the Nestle-Aland tradition

---

44. Roderic L. Mullen, Simon Crisp, and David C. Parker, *The Gospel according to John in the Byzantine Tradition* (United Bible Societies; Stuttgart: Deutsche Bibelgesellschaft, 2007).

ECM (1–2 Peter, 2000): the best representation to date of the *Ausgangstext*

What is of particular interest is the observation that over the course of about three decades it is evident that there have been multiple characterizations of what is essentially the same text (in the 432 verses of the Catholic letters, UBS$^{3–4}$/NA$^{26–27}$ differs from the *ECM* in only twenty-four instances[45]). Both the characterizations of the texts produced and the goals toward which editorial committees have worked have changed even as the resultant text has remained virtually identical.

In short, there has been a fundamental shift in how the editorial committees responsible for these editions understand their task or goal: whereas the editorial committee responsible for the NA^{26}/UBS^{3} text viewed their goal as recovering or approximating the wording of the original text, the two organizations currently at work on the *Editio Critica Maior*—the Institut für Neutestamentliche Textforschung (INTF) and the International Greek New Testament Project (IGNTP)[46]—have set as their goal the recovery of the Ausgangstext: the reconstructed form of text from which all surviving witnesses descend.

5. The Broader Context

This change in goal on the part of those editing the *ECM* exemplifies a growing realization within the discipline of the problematic nature of the concept of "original text" (or any similar formulation, such as "original," "autograph," or "original documents"). The term "original text," which frequently has been used in an undefined and/or unreflective manner, and whose definition is easily colored by Platonic, Idealistic, or Romantic preconceptions,[47] is an inherently ambiguous term. To what does it refer: the

---

45. Three in James, seven in 1 Peter, eight in 2 Peter, three in 1 John, none in 2–3 John, and three in Jude.

46. Regarding the current cooperative and collaborative working agreement between the two organizations, see Wachtel and Parker, "Joint IGNTP/INTF Editio Critica Maior," 1–2.

47. Lee Patterson, "The Logic of Textual Criticism and the Way of Genius," in *Textual Criticism and Literary Interpretation* (ed. J. J. McGann; Chicago: University of Chicago Press, 1985), 55–91; Jerome J. McGann, *A Critique of Modern Textual Criticism* (Chicago: University of Chicago Press, 1983).

text as it existed in the mind of its author,[48] or as it was written down by the author's amanuensis, or as it left the author's hand after correction, or some other form (perhaps the one in which it first circulated)?

In the early 1990s, William Petersen and I independently raised the question of the meaning of the term "original text" with regard to New Testament textual criticism, as did Emanuel Tov with regard to the Hebrew Bible.[49] This issue was then taken up most notably by Eldon Epp in a series of essays, in particular his now famous essay on "The Multivalence of the Term 'Original Text' in New Testament Textual Criticism,"[50] in which he clearly demonstrates the ambiguity of the term "original text" in both past and current usage.[51]

---

48. Note how Léon Vaganay, e.g., distinguishes between "text" and "autograph": "In restoring the text of any document the obstacles to be overcome are evident. If we possess the actual autograph … the thing is easy. It is just a matter of noting the evident faults due to the writer's inattention" (Léon Vaganay, *An Introduction to the Textual Criticism of the New Testament* [trans. B. V. Miller; St. Louis: Herder, 1937], 10).

49. William L. Petersen, "What Text Can New Testament Textual Criticism Ultimately Reach?" in *New Testament Textual Criticism, Exegesis, and Early Church History* (ed. B. Aland and J. Delobel; CBET 7; Kampen: Kok Pharos, 1994), 136–52; Holmes, "Reasoned Eclecticism," 353– 54; Emanuel Tov, *Textual Criticism of the Hebrew Bible* (Minneapolis: Fortress; Assen and Maastricht: Van Gorcum, 1992), 164–80, (2nd rev. ed., 2001).

50. Eldon Jay Epp, "Textual Criticism in the Exegesis of the New Testament, with an Excursus on Canon," in *Handbook to Exegesis of the New Testament* (ed. S. E. Porter; NTTS 25; Leiden: Brill, 1997), 45–97 (repr. in Epp, *Perspectives on New Testament Textual Criticism: Collected Essays, 1962–2004* [Leiden: Brill, 2005], 461–95); idem, "The Multivalence of the Term 'Original Text' in New Testament Textual Criticism," *HTR* 92 (1999): 245–81 (repr. in Epp, *Perspectives*, 551–93); idem, "It's All about Variants: A Variant-Conscious Approach to New Testament Textual Criticism," *HTR* 100 (2007): 275–308.

51. Indeed, Epp extends and applies the term "original" in so many different ways that the term becomes virtually meaningless. Moreover, even as these essays successfully problematize the term "original," they also sow conceptual confusion in some respects. In the "Multivalence" essay, for example, the description of the views of Dahl and Gamble regarding the textual history of Romans and Ephesians as "explorations of prior compositional levels" ("Multivalence," 267) is fundamentally misleading; Dahl and Gamble are dealing with *post*-compositional levels of editing and alteration (cf., e.g., Harry Y. Gamble, *Books and Readers in the Early Church: A History of Early Christian Texts* [New Haven: Yale University Press, 1995], 97–98). This is symptomatic of this essay's confusion of the differing roles of source, literary, and textual criticism (263) and of source, literary, traditions, and textual criticism (269). Furthermore, the

In these essays Epp discusses matters primarily in theoretical or conceptual terms. One may also approach the issue from a more pragmatic perspective. In the case of a Pauline letter, taking 1 Corinthians as an example, does the "earliest recoverable form of the text" represent: (1) the letter that Paul sent to Corinth; (2) the copy he almost certainly kept for his own archives[52] (which would be a close but not perfect copy of the sent letter); or (3) some later copy of either one that became part of a collected edition (*corpus Paulinum*) of the Pauline letters that some scholars (e.g., Günther Zuntz[53]) think is the source of all known copies? If the answer is the first option, then effectively the "earliest recoverable form" would be identical to the letter Paul sent, that is, the "autograph"; but if the answer is the third, then it is possible for there to be a gap of a generation or more between the "earliest recoverable form" of 1 Corinthians and the letter Paul sent.

Or consider as another example the Gospel of Luke (or Acts, for that matter): one may imagine Luke sending a carefully executed and personally corrected manuscript of his volume off to its dedicatee, Theophilus, and presumably Luke retained a similar manuscript for himself; was there also a third such manuscript that he "published," that is, made available for copying (which is what "publication" amounted to in those days[54])? Given the realities of the copying process, none of the three would be identical, and so a question arises: does our textual tradition descend from one or

---

essay's definition of a *"predecessor text-form"*—"a form of text … discoverable behind a New Testament writing that played a role in the composition of that writing," or the reference a few lines later to "an earlier stage in the composition of what became a New Testament book" ("Multivalence," 276; cf. also the reference to "preliterary" layers behind New Testament books [p. 258])—describes a form or stage of activity that by virtually any definition of the discipline (other than the new one proposed in the essay ["Multivalence," 268]) is not the province (and lies beyond the reach) of textual criticism. Alongside this conceptual confusion, it may be not insignificant to observe that once the essay turns to contemporary developments (255–81), there is virtually no mention of an author or of authorial activity (a surprising omission, given the topic).

52. E. Randolph Richards, *The Secretary in the Letters of Paul* (WUNT 42; Tübingen: Mohr Siebeck, 1991), 3–4; Gamble, *Books and Readers*, 100–101.

53. Günther Zuntz, *The Text of the Epistles: A Disquisition on the* Corpus Paulinum (London: Oxford University Press, 1963), 274–83.

54. Michael W. Holmes, "Codex Bezae as a Recension of the Gospels," in *Codex Bezae: Studies from the Lunel Colloquium, June 1994* (ed. D. C. Parker and C.-B. Amphoux; Leiden: Brill, 1996), 123–60, here 144; Gamble, *Books and Readers*, 93–147.

more than one of these hypothetical copies? And if more than one, does that mean we are dealing with multiple "originals"? Further, suppose Luke later revised his personal copy to some degree, and made the revised version—in effect, a second edition[55]—available for distribution? How might one define "original text" in these sorts of situations?

It was in the context of this continuing discussion about the meaning of the term "original text" that the concept of the *Ausgangstext* (or "earliest recoverable form" of the text) emerged as an alternative goal. In many respects this is a healthy development; in any case it certainly offers a more clearly defined description of both the goal of and the results achieved by the editors of our printed texts than do the titles typically given to them, such as "The New Testament in the Original Greek" or more simply "The" Greek New Testament. Rather than assuming, as has traditionally been done, that the recovered text is the original, this new goal carries with it an acknowledgement that the initial text may or may not be the original text (however one may define it). In other words, an ultimate goal has been replaced by a penultimate one.

From a methodological perspective, this is an important development. Recall that in theory the textual criticism of classical or biblical texts typically involves three (or sometimes four) stages: *recensio*, *selectio* (only if required by a split tradition), *examinatio*, and *divinatio* (i.e., emendation).[56] In a closed (or uncontaminated) tradition, such as one sometimes finds in the classics, *recensio* is used to determine an unequivocal *stemma codicum*; once the archetype (or archetypes) of the *stemma* has been determined, the rest of the witnesses may be eliminated from consideration. But in an open (or contaminated or cross-pollinated) tradition, of which the New Testament is the example *par excellence*, the construction of a *stemma* is impossible. In such cases, *recensio* involves not the elimination of witnesses but rather an assessment of all the available witnesses using the methodology and tools of a reasoned eclecticism.[57] The goal is to identify, variant by variant, the *reading(s)* closest to

55. Markus Mülke, *Der Autor und sein Text: Die Verfälschung des Originals im Urteil antiker Autoren* (Untersuchungen zur antiken Literatur und Geschichte 93; Berlin: de Gruyter, 2007), 11–94, 202–60; Hilarius Emonds, *Zweite Auflage im Altertum* (Leipzig: Harrassowitz, 1941).

56. See, e.g., Paul Maas, *Textual Criticism* (Oxford: Clarendon, 1958).

57. Zuntz, *Text of the Epistles*, 8–12; Holmes, "Working with an Open Textual Tradition," 70–75.

the archetype at any given point in the tradition.[58] That is, one seeks to identify, on a variant-by-variant basis, the reading (or occasionally readings) best explaining the origin of all the other readings, and thus is most likely to represent the archetypal text.

These readings are then subjected to *examinatio*, which seeks to assess "the quality of the most ancient reading or readings attained by *recensio*."[59] Those readings that prove satisfactory in terms of internal criteria are accepted as original,[60] but in those cases "where the tradition fails to yield such a reading, *emendatio* strives to recover, by means of conjecture, the original wording which failed to reach the archetype or archetypes of the extant evidence."[61]

Examinatio is a critical step, because while *recensio* can indicate the oldest surviving reading, it cannot tell us whether it is also the original reading.[62] This is where the further stage of *examinatio* (and, if necessary, *emendatio*) comes into play. Yet it is precisely this step that has often been neglected or ignored, because it is widely assumed that the original reading must have survived somewhere among the extant witnesses. Some affirm this as a matter of conviction;[63] others, who decline to consider even the possibility of the need for emendation of the New Testament, do so by

---

58. This is essentially the same methodology as the Alands' "local-genealogical" approach: "applying to each passage individually the approach used by classical philology for a whole tradition" (Aland and Aland, *The Text*[2], 34).

59. Zuntz, *Text of the Epistles*, 12.

60. As Hort observes regarding "the task of discriminating between existing various readings, one variant in each case being adopted and the rest discarded": "The utmost result that can be obtained under this condition is the discovery of what is relatively original: whether the readings thus relatively original were also the readings of the autograph is another question." Consequently, "any investigation of the ultimate integrity of the text is governed by no theoretical presumptions: its final conclusions must rest on the intrinsic verisimilitude or suspiciousness of the text itself" (Westcott and Hort, *Introduction*, 66–67).

61. Zuntz, *Text of the Epistles*, 12.

62. Westcott and Hort, *Introduction*, 66–69; Zuntz, *Text of the Epistles*, 282–83; Colwell, "Genealogical Method," 109–33 (reprinted in *Studies*, 63–83).

63. E.g., Aland and Aland, *The Text*[2], 291–96 (e.g., "any reading ever occurring in the New Testament textual tradition, from the original reading onward, has been preserved in the tradition and needs only to be identified" [296]); J. Keith Elliott, "Thoroughgoing Eclecticism in New Testament Textual Criticism," in *The Text of the New Testament in Contemporary Research: Essays on the Status Quaestionis* (ed. B. D. Ehrman and M. W. Holmes; SD 46; Grand Rapids: Eerdmans, 1995), 322.

default. In other words, the assumption that the original reading always has survived (especially when it is also assumed that there is a single point of origin for the text) has short-circuited the methodological process. On these assumptions, whatever is the outcome of *recensio* must be the "original text," and so the additional steps of *examinatio* and especially *divinatio* have been felt to be unnecessary.

Identifying the initial text as the goal of editorial activity, however, challenges both assumptions, in that it requires one to ask about, rather than to assume, the relationship between the initial text and the "source text" (i.e., the form of text in which an early Christian book first began to be copied and made available for circulation).[64] What traditionally has been assumed now becomes a substantive question; indeed, as David C. Parker observes, "The distance between the critical text [i.e., the initial text] and the beginning of the existence of this text is an important matter for consideration, providing often the biggest unsolved problems in New Testament textual criticism."[65]

Raising this question does not mean that the ideas of a single "source" text and of the survival of the original reading at every point of variation are necessarily wrong. It does mean, however, that those ideas ought to function as hypotheses to be tested against the evidence rather than as assumptions that shape or channel an analysis of the evidence. Furthermore, it cannot be assumed that the answer to this question will be the same across the New Testament corpus; it is a question which must be answered not merely for each sub-corpus within the New Testament, but in the case of the Gospels and Catholic letters, on a book-by-book basis.

---

64. I am using "source" text—defined for the purposes of this essay as "the form of text in which an early Christian book first began to be copied and made available for circulation" (whenever and in whatever form that was for a particular document) in lieu of more traditional phrases such as "original" text or even "authorial" text because of the inherent ambiguity of these terms. (Of course, in some quarters even the word "text" has become a problematic term; cf., e.g., Elizabeth A. Clark, *History, Theory, Text: Historians and the Linguistic Turn* [Cambridge: Harvard University Press, 2004], 130–55, or Joseph Grigely, "The Textual Event," in *Textual Editing and Criticism: An Introduction* [ed. E. Kelemen; New York: W. W. Norton, 2009], 194–225; he proposes "a model of a text that is as radically unstable as our interpretations for that text" [213]).

65. David C. Parker, *An Introduction to the New Testament Manuscripts and Their Texts* (Cambridge: Cambridge University Press, 2008), 180.

For some books, *examinatio* almost certainly suggests that the initial text is virtually identical to the source text. The introductions to each letter in the *ECM* of the Catholic Letters provide general descriptions of the detailed studies of the textual history of each letter, conducted with the assistance of the CBGM in preparation for the *ECM*. These descriptions (at least as I read them) indicate that in the case of 1–2–3 John, it is highly likely that the initial text (wherever it can be established) is virtually identical to the source texts of these letters.[66] For each of these books, it does appear that there was a single source text and that the original readings have survived in the extant witnesses.

The original reading, however, does not appear to have survived in the case of 1 Cor 6:5. Here the phrase "to judge between a brother"—the reading found in every known Greek manuscript—makes no more sense than it does to speak of "traveling between Toronto."[67] It appears that here we have a case of universal agreement in error—evidence that the earliest recoverable text is apparently not the same as the source text, and thus an example of the need for emendation to recover that source text. Such a conclusion will have major implications for both how one envisions the relationship between the initial text and an authorial text and how one reconstructs the history of the transmission of that text between those two stages or forms.

To return to the Catholic Letters, the same situation that is found in 1 Cor 6:5 is also the case in regard to 2 Peter in at least one instance. At 2 Pet 3:10, the *examinatio* stage—carried out with the assistance of the CBGM—revealed that none of the extant readings in the Greek witnesses satisfied the requirements of genealogical coherence.[68] A proposed conjectural emendation, however, does meet the required level of coherence. Therefore at this point the editors followed the logic of their method and printed the conjecture (οὐχ εὑρεθήσεται) as the reading of the initial text.

---

66. Cf. *ECM 1 John*, 29–30; *ECM 2–3 John, Jude*, 35–37.

67. See Jeffrey Kloha, "1 Corinthians 6:5: A Proposal," *NovT* 46 (2004): 132–42; cf. Zuntz, *Text of the Epistles*, 15.

68. In this instance the use of the CBGM offers a striking confirmation of the judgment of Westcott and Hort on this passage: "External evidence is here strongly favourable to εὑρεθήσεται. ... Internal evidence of transcription is absolutely certain on the same side, for εὑρεθήσεται fully accounts for all four other readings. ... Yet it is hardly less certain by intrinsic probability that εὑρεθήσεται cannot be right: in other words, it is the most original of recorded readings, the parent of the rest, and yet itself corrupt" (*Introduction*, 280).

By positioning the ideas that there is a single source text and that the original reading has survived somewhere in the tradition as hypotheses rather than as assumptions, the editors of the *ECM* are following in the methodological footsteps of predecessors such as Zuntz, Westcott, and Hort. For example, Zuntz's efforts to understand the complex mixture of both authentic and secondary readings in the earliest surviving major witness (P46), together with the implications of cases such as that of 1 Cor 6:5, led him to propose that all the surviving manuscript traditions of the Pauline letters descends from an early edition of the *Corpus* that had, in addition to the text, a large number of alternative readings in the margins.[69] As for Westcott and Hort, perhaps due to the influence of the title of their edition, it is often disregarded that in an easily overlooked section of their introduction they carefully defined what they meant by "original," and also noted some sixty-five places where they suspected the presence of early corruption prior to all surviving witnesses, acknowledging that in these cases emendation was likely necessary.[70]

In short, the shift from "original text" (however defined) to "initial text" involves a shift from an ultimate to a penultimate goal. It is a shift that has, as we have seen above, implications not merely for how we characterize the texts that editors produce, but also for how we envision the text-critical task itself.

6. Further Questions

We have already discussed above one question arising from this shift, that of the relationship between the initial text and the "source" text. Of course, this question in turn gives rise to others.[71] These include: Is the recovery of earlier forms even the proper concern of an editor? If it is, are we able to

---

69. Zuntz, *Text of the Epistles*, 274–83.

70. Westcott and Hort, *Introduction*, 288–310; 279–82 (for specific readings, see the *Appendix*); Zuntz, *Text of the Epistles*, 12.

71. This may be an appropriate point to note that the definition of "source" text given above—"the form of text in which an early Christian book first began to be copied and made available for circulation" (whenever and in whatever form that was for a particular document)—also leaves open or declines to address certain questions. It leaves open, e.g., the historical question of when a particular writing was composed (other than pointing to the earliest extant manuscript as a *terminous ante quem*), and declines to address, as prior to the competency of textual criticism, literary questions attending the composition of a document: if a Pauline letter, e.g., represents a compi-

recover an earlier form of the text, or has the textual tradition been so disrupted in the course of its early transmission that our earliest extant texts look nothing like the earliest form (however one may define it)? Should we even be concerned with recovering earlier forms? Let us speak briefly to each of these, in reverse order.

Should we even be concerned with recovering an "original text" (however one might define it)? This question has been raised—and seemingly answered with a strong no—by Parker: "The goal of textual criticism is not, and in the case of the New Testament cannot be, the restoration of the original text."[72] In the context in which this statement occurs, however, the first claim ("should not be") appears to carry an exhortative rather than declarative force. The second should likewise apparently be read in light of his earlier claim that "the restoration of the original text ... is unlikely ever to be achieved," for the arguments he presents—"our oldest extensive manuscripts" date from the end of the second century, "a period for which we have no manuscript attestation, and in which we know the greatest amount of change and variation to have arisen"—do not support his claim, but instead raise what he correctly identifies as "the central question": "the degree to which we can recover forms of the text older than the end of the second century."[73]

Parker himself is rather skeptical regarding such prospects ("At present, the best editors can hope to do is, where the manuscripts are available, to recreate forms of text that were current in the period 200–300 C.E."[74]),

---

lation of two or more separate documents, any such literary activity took place prior to the point at which the letter as we know it today began to be copied and circulated.

72. David C. Parker, "Textual Criticism and Theology," *ExpTim* 118.12 (Sept. 2007): 586; cf. 585 (the traditional goal of textual criticism "assumes that the restoration of an original text is both appropriate and possible. Both assumptions are dubious"); see also idem, "Through a Screen Darkly: Digital Texts and the New Testament," *JSNT* 25 (2003): 401 ("The biblical text, rather than being corrupted and needing to be restored ... is constantly under development, one might even say is becoming the text. In this light, the quest for the original text may be seen as a complete misunderstanding of what editors were really doing").

73. Parker, "Textual Criticism and Theology," 586.

74. Ibid. Furthermore, "since we do not absolutely know" which variant is "best" (his term), one ought therefore to treat all of them "as early forms of commentary" rather than privileging any one of them as "authorial" (Parker, *New Testament Manuscripts*, 184).

and he is not alone in his skepticism. Here we may note in particular the work of Helmut Koester and William Petersen.

In a frequently referenced essay, Koester begins by suggesting that "The assumption that the reconstruction of the best archetype for the manuscript tradition is more or less identical with the assumed autograph is precarious."[75] Then at the end of his study, he concludes:

> All the evidence presented here points to the fact that the text of the Synoptic Gospels was very unstable during the first and second centuries. With respect to Mark, one can be fairly certain that only its revised text has achieved canonical status, while the original text (attested only by Matthew and Luke) has not survived. With respect to Matthew and Luke, there is no guarantee that the archetypes of the manuscript tradition are identical with the original text of each gospel. … New Testament textual critics have been deluded by the hypothesis that the archetypes of the textual tradition which were fixed ca. 200 CE—and how many archetypes for each Gospel?—are (almost) identical with the autographs. This cannot be affirmed by any evidence. On the contrary, whatever evidence there is indicates that not only minor, but also substantial revisions of the original texts have occurred during the first hundred years of the transmission. The story of the text of the Gospel of Mark and the revisions of its text—documented by Matthew, Luke, and the *Secret Gospel of Mark*—illustrates this, as well as the harmonizations of Matthew and Luke in Justin and in other witnesses.[76]

In evaluating Koester's claims, we may begin with his assessment of Mark's Gospel. Here he offers two lines of evidence: (1) *Secret Mark's* revisions of (what Koester terms) "the original text of the Gospel of Mark" and (2) agreements of Matthew and Luke against Mark.[77] Regarding the first line

---

75. Helmut Koester, "The Text of the Synoptic Gospels in the Second Century," in *Gospel Traditions in the Second Century: Origins, Recensions, Text, and Transmission* (ed. W. L. Petersen; Notre Dame and London: University of Notre Dame Press, 1989), 19. See also idem, *Ancient Christian Gospels: Their History and Development* (London: SCM, 1990), and François Bovon, "The Synoptic Gospels and the Non-canonical Acts of the Apostles," in *Studies in Early Christianity* (Grand Rapids: Baker Academic, 2005), 209–25 (cf. esp. 210, 221; repr. from *HTR* 81 [1988]: 19–36).

76. Koester, "Text," 37.

77. The idea of using the agreements of Matthew and Luke against Mark to reconstruct an earlier version of Mark is not uncommon; see, e.g., William Sanday, who argued that "by far the greater number of the coincidences of Mt Lk against Mk are

of evidence, I remain unpersuaded that the letter attributed to Clement is anything other than a hoax or forgery.[78] But even if one were inclined to accept it as authentic, it is not at all clear that "Secret Mark" is part of the prehistory of canonical Mark (so Koester) rather than its post-history.[79] Regarding the second line of evidence, note that his argument takes for granted a certain view of Synoptic relationships—one widely held, to be sure, but nonetheless increasingly challenged. If one were to adopt instead, for instance, the view that Luke made use of Matthew, then both the agreement and evidence of Matthew + Luke against Mark would disappear. In short, for his claims about Mark, Koester offers essentially only a single line of evidence, one that is subject to its own challenges.

As for the Gospels of Matthew and Luke, Koester offers two considerations: (1) "There is no guarantee that the archetypes of the manuscript tradition are identical with the original text of each gospel" and (2) "The harmonizations of these two Gospels demonstrate that their text was not sacrosanct and that alterations could be expected." True enough, but neither counts as evidence for his claims about unreliability; indeed, he offers no evidence to support his claims. Instead his line of argument is by analogy: Mark was changed—a conclusion resting, as we have just noted, on a weak foundation—so Matthew and Luke must have been as well; or Justin utilized Matthew and Luke in creating a Gospel harmony, so that means the text of each was fluid. But using Matthew and Luke as sources to create a new document—a Gospel harmony—is not the same

---

due to the use by Mt Lk—not of an *Ur-Marcus* or older form of the Gospel, but—*of a recension of the text of Mk different from that from which all the extant MSS. of the Gospel are descended*" (William Sanday, "The Conditions under Which the Gospels Were Written, and Their Bearing upon Some Difficulties of the Synoptic Problem," in *Studies in the Synoptic Problem* (ed. W. Sanday; Oxford: Clarendon, 1911), 21, emphasis original).

78. Koester's attempt to salvage the textual evidence by claiming that "even if the letter of Clement of Alexandria should not be genuine … the gospel text quoted here is certainly genuine" ("Text," 34 n. 49) is unpersuasive.

79. So Scott G. Brown, "On the Composition History of the Longer ('Secret') Gospel of Mark," *JBL* 122 (2003): 89–110. For an overview and bibliography of the debate about "Secret Mark," consult Adele Yarbro Collins, *Mark: A Commentary* (Hermeneia; Minneapolis: Fortress, 2007), 484–93. For yet another view of Mark, see Christian-Bernard Amphoux, "Une édition «plurielle» de Marc," in *The New Testament Text in Early Christianity /Le text du Nouveau Testament au début du christianisme* (ed. C. -B. Amphoux and J. K. Elliott; Lausanne: Éditions du Zèbre, 2003), 69–80.

as significantly altering or revising a document and continuing to call it by the same name. For example (assuming *per exemplum* a common solution to the Synoptic problem), the authors of Matthew and Luke made heavy use of the Gospel of Mark to create new documents with different titles, rather than a revised form of Mark that continued to use the existing title (whatever that may have been).[80] Also, the way that Koester makes use of Matthew and Luke as witnesses to the "original text" of Mark effectively takes for granted that the text of each Gospel has been transmitted reliably enough that even minor details in each can be relied upon as evidence. He cannot have it both ways: if Matthew and Luke are accurate enough to use as evidence in detail for the text of Mark, he cannot claim that their texts were "very unstable" during the early centuries; or if they were that unstable, then they are unusable as evidence for the text of Mark. In short: on the one hand he offers two considerations (but no evidence) suggesting the textual tradition of Matthew and Luke is unreliable, but on the other hand, he works with them as if those two considerations are not operative and the texts are reliable in detail. Indeed, his own later work basically rejects his earlier claims, particularly with respect to Matthew.[81] Koester's claims are incommensurate with his evidence and arguments.

---

80. Even without titles, "To the ancient reader the Gospels of Matthew and Luke did not look like interpolated versions of the Gospel of Mark. The obviously different beginnings and endings of these Gospels were sufficient indication that they were distinct texts" (Frederik Wisse, "The Nature and Purpose of Redactional Changes in Early Christian Texts: The Canonical Gospels," in *Gospel Traditions in the Second Century: Origins, Recensions, Text, and Transmission* [ed. W. L. Petersen; Notre Dame: University of Notre Dame Press, 1989], 42).

81. He writes, "It still seems to be the most plausible assumption that the manuscript tradition of Matthew's Gospel has preserved its text more or less in its oldest form. To be sure, there are variations in the manuscript transmission. But unlike the Gospels of John and Mark, there are no indications, internal or external, that an originally Hebrew or Greek text of the Gospel of Matthew underwent substantial alteration before the emergence of the archetype(s) of the text upon which the extant manuscript tradition depends" (Koester, *Ancient Christian Gospels*, 318).

Like Koester, Petersen also focuses on the text of the Gospels, and expresses similar views,[82] though (as we shall see) he builds them on a different foundation.[83] He writes:

> To be brutally frank, we know next to nothing about the shape of the "autograph" gospels; indeed, it is questionable if one can even speak of such a thing. This leads to the inescapable conclusion that the text in our critical editions today is actually a text which dates from no earlier tha[n] about 180 c.e., at the earliest. Our critical editions do not present us with the text that was current in 150, 120, or 100—much less in 80 c.e.[84]

The conclusion, however, does not follow: If nothing is known about the early text of the Gospels, then how can it be determined that they do not match our critical texts? The only way we could know whether current critical editions do or do not match the early text is if we knew what the early text looked like—but that, according to Petersen, is precisely what is not known.

The evidence Petersen offers is no more convincing than his logic. He investigates Gospel citations in early writers such as Justin Martyr and the apostolic fathers, concerning which he offers this assessment:

---

82. See Petersen, "What Text," 136–51; idem, "The Genesis of the Gospels," in *New Testament Textual Criticism and Exegesis: Festschrift J. Delobel* (ed. A. Denaux; Leuven: Leuven University Press and Peeters, 2002), 33–65; idem, "Textual Traditions Examined: What the Text of the Apostolic Fathers Tells Us about the Text of the New Testament in the Second Century," in *The Reception of the New Testament in the Apostolic Fathers* (ed. A. Gregory and C. Tuckett; Oxford: Oxford University Press, 2005), 29–46; idem, "Patristic Biblical Quotations and Method: Four Changes to Lightfoot's Edition of Second Clement," *VC* 60 (2006): 389–419.

83. For a more extensive discussion and analysis of Petersen, see Michael W. Holmes, "Text and Transmission in the Second Century," in *The Textual Reliability of the New Testament: Bart Ehrman and Daniel Wallace in Dialogue* (ed. R. Stewart; Minneapolis: Fortress, 2011), 61–79; see also Larry W. Hurtado, "The New Testament Text in the Second Century: Text, Collections and Canon," in *Transmission and Reception: New Testament Text-Critical and Exegetical Studies* (ed. J. Childers and D. C. Parker; Piscataway, NJ: Gorgias Press, 2006), 14–19.

84. Petersen, "Genesis of the Gospels," 62; see also 53–54: "We know next to nothing of the text of the gospels in the first century, for we have no manuscript evidence and few (if any) Patristic writings." See also idem, *Tatian's Diatessaron: Its Creation, Dissemination, Significance, and History in Scholarship* (Leiden: Brill, 1994), 9–34.

in the overwhelming majority of cases, those passages in the Apostolic Fathers which offer recognizable parallels with our present-day New Testament display a text that is very different from what we now find in our modern critical editions of the New Testament.[85]

The problem here is that "recognizable parallels" are not the same as identifiable citations of specific Gospels. What Petersen has shown is that early Christian writers incorporated a wide range of diverse Gospel *traditions* in their writings—some traditions that would later become canonical, and others that would not—and he correctly observes that some of these Gospel *traditions* occur in forms that sometimes are rather different than the texts of Matthew, Mark, Luke, and John as we know them from the earliest extant manuscripts. But what he rather clearly has not demonstrated is that identifiable *texts* or *citations* of Matthew, Mark, Luke, and/or John in the late first or early second century were to any significant degree different from the texts of those same Gospels as they are known from ca. 180 C.E. and later. One example will illustrate the point; it involves a Gospel citation in Justin Martyr (*Dialogue* 101.2) that has parallels in Matthew, Mark, and Luke.[86] Though Justin does not identify his source(s), Petersen believes that the similarity of Justin's "there is one who is good" to the text of Matthew "shows that it is the Matthean version which is being cited," and therefore Justin preserves the earliest version of Matt 19:17, a version that includes the phrase "my father in heaven"—proof, in his opinion, that our critical text of the Gospels does not correspond to the early second century text of that Gospel.[87]

---

85. Petersen, "Textual Traditions Examined," 34 (emphasis original); see also 45–46.

86. The texts read as follows:

> Matt 19:17: "Teacher … Why do you ask me about what is good? *There is one who is good.*"
>
> Mark 10:18: "Good teacher … Why do you call me good? No one is good but God alone."
>
> Luke 18:19: "Good teacher … Why do you call me good? No one is good but God alone."
>
> The text of Justin Martyr runs like this:
>
> "Good teacher … Why do you call me good? *There is one who is good,* **my father in heaven.**"

87. Petersen, "What Text," 142–43.

But Petersen's identification of this as a citation of Matthew is surely debatable: the *two* preceding phrases, "good teacher" and "why do you call me good," reflect Mark and/or Luke, not Matthew. Furthermore, Justin is known to have used a harmonized collection of sayings of Jesus, one that was based on multiple sources in addition to Matthew, Mark, and Luke.[88] How does Petersen know that the phrase "my father in heaven" comes from the Gospel of Matthew and not one of Justin's other sources? He does not—but he makes an identification anyway, and builds a claim upon it.[89] In the absence, however, of reliable identifications of Gospel material, Petersen's claims regarding a substantial lack of congruence between the early texts and our earliest MSS lack a foundation.

Of course, demonstrating that the skepticism of a Koester or a Petersen is unwarranted with regard to Parker's "central question" (namely, "the degree to which we can recover forms of the text older than the end of the second century"[90]) does not settle the matter of the relationship between

---

88. On Justin's use of multiple sources, see Oskar Skarsaune, "Justin and His Bible," in *Justin Martyr and His Worlds* (ed. S. Parvis and P. Foster; Minneapolis: Fortress, 2007), 64–68; differently Theo K. Heckel, *Vom Evangelium des Markus zum viergestaltigen Evangelium* (WUNT 120; Tübingen: Mohr Siebeck, 1990), 326–27. On Justin's use of a harmonized sayings collection, see Arthur J. Bellinzoni, *The Sayings of Jesus in the Writings of Justin Martyr* (NovTSup 17; Leiden: Brill, 1967), 49–100; Leslie L. Kline, "Harmonized Sayings of Jesus in the Pseudo-Clementine Homilies and Justin Martyr," *ZNW* 66 (1975): 223–41; Koester, *Ancient Christian Gospels*, 360–402; William L. Petersen, "Textual Evidence of Tatian's Dependence upon Justin's ΑΠΟΜΝΗΜΟΝΕΥΜΑΤΑ," *NTS* 36 (1990): 512–34; Petersen, *Tatian's Diatessaron*, 27–29; Craig D. Allert, *Revelation, Truth, Canon and Interpretation: Studies in Justin Martyr's* Dialogue with Trypho (Leiden: Brill, 2002), 195–202; Graham N. Stanton, "Jesus Traditions and Gospels in Justin Martyr and Irenaeus," in *The Biblical Canons* (ed. J. -M. Auwers and H. J. de Jonge; Leuven: Leuven University Press, 2003), 353–70, esp. 364–65 (repr., *Jesus and Gospel* [Cambridge: Cambridge University Press, 2004], 92–109); differently (but unpersuasively) Georg Strecker, "Eine Evangelienharmonie bei Justin und Pseudoklemens?" *NTS* 24 (1978): 297–316. There is no indication that this harmonized sayings source was a complete Gospel or meant to replace earlier Gospels; see Graham N. Stanton, "The Fourfold Gospel," *NTS* 43 (1997): 329–35 (repr., *Jesus and Gospel*, 75–81), contra Koester, "Text of the Synoptic Gospels," 28–33.

89. For a more detailed discussion of these and other texts, see Joseph Verheyden, "Assessing Gospel Quotations in Justin Martyr," in *New Testament Textual Criticism and Exegesis: Festschrift J. Delobel* (ed. A. Denaux; Leuven: Leuven University Press and Peeters, 2002), 363–70.

90. Parker, "Textual Criticism and Theology," 586.

the earliest surviving manuscripts and earlier forms of text; it only leaves it open for further investigation.

Petersen himself suggests one promising way to undertake such an investigation: to take what we know about trends, patterns, and tendencies from a later period for which we have evidence, project them back into the earlier period for which we lack evidence, and see what they might suggest.[91] A wide range of evidence, observations, and considerations deserve to be taken into account; a partial list could include:[92]

- the observation that copying apparently is a more conservative type of activity than composition;[93]
- that existing documents appear to have been utilized as sources for new documents rather than revised and then circulated under the same name (e.g.—assuming popular solutions to the Synoptic problem for the sake of illustration—later Gospel writers made heavy use of Mark not to produce a revised version of Mark circulating under the same title, but to create new compositions with different titles[94]);

---

91. Petersen, "Genesis," 53–54: "We know next to nothing of the text of the gospels in the first century, for we have no manuscript evidence and few (if any) Patristic writings. Therefore, our only route of inquiry is to take what we have discovered thus far, from our study of the second century, project these trends and tendencies back into the first century, and see what they suggest"; see also Wisse, "Nature and Purpose," 47.

92. The following list offers a partial summary of the discussion (with documentation) in Holmes, "Text and Transmission in the Second Century," 74–79. See also Tommy Wasserman, "The Implications of Textual Criticism for Understanding the 'Original Text,'" in *Mark and Matthew: Text and Contexts* (ed. E. -M. Becker and A. Runesson; Tübingen: Mohr Siebeck, 2011), 77–96.

93. As Kim Haines-Eitzen has argued, "the scribes who copied Christian literature during the second and third centuries were not 'uncontrolled' nor were the texts that they (re)produced marked by 'wildness.' Rather, the (re)production of texts by early Christian scribes was bounded and constrained by the multifaceted and multilayered discursive practices of the second- and third-century church" (Kim Haines-Eitzen, *Guardians of Letters: Literacy, Power, and the Transmitters of Early Christian Literature* [New York: Oxford University Press, 2000], 106).

94. Two obvious exceptions, Marcion's treatment of Luke and the *Shepherd of Hermas* (which apparently circulated in two or more forms at one point in its history), exhibit precisely the kind of evidence notably absent in other cases.

- evidence (see above) that not all original readings appear to have survived;
- observable (and widely different) patterns of scribal habits, work styles, and patterns in the early papyri (some manuscripts preserve evidence of surprising carelessness, while others—one thinks of the remarkable relationship between P75 and Vaticanus, for example—raise the possibility of exceedingly faithful transmission at an early stage in the history of the transmission of a text);
- the relative absence of evidence that recensional activity (i.e., deliberate, extensive, and authoritative scholarly revision) has affected the text of the books of the New Testament to any appreciable extent after they began to be copied for circulation;
- the social context of early Christianity (including the use of early Christian texts in worship and liturgical settings);
- that apart from the endings of Romans and of the Gospel of Mark, nearly all variation affects a sentence or less of the text.[95]

In seeking to move from the time of the earliest extensive evidence (which dates from the late second to the late fourth centuries) back to the late first century,[96] it is clear that we are dealing with a situation characterized by a mixture of both fluidity and stability; the critical issue is the relationship between the two. Particularly in view of the last observation in the preceding list, it may be suggested that we are dealing with a situation characterized by a combination of macro-level stability (from the paragraph level up) and micro-level fluidity (from the sentence level down). Furthermore, even though we have very little physical evidence that can be securely dated any earlier than the end of the second century, it nonetheless provides, as Epp observes, a "close continuity with the remote past" that "is unusual in ancient text transmission"[97]—an important point not

---

95. I leave aside the *pericope adultera* (John 7:53–8:11): though some form of it may have been known to second-century figures such as Papias, it does not make an appearance in the manuscript tradition until ca. 400, in Codex Bezae.

96. Using the phrase "the late first century" as shorthand for "the time when the various documents that now comprise the New Testament began to be copied and circulate," whenever and in whatever form that was for a particular document.

97. Epp, "Are Early New Testament Manuscripts Truly Abundant," 105.

to be neglected as we continue to investigate the relationship between the earliest witnesses and earlier forms or stages of the texts they preserve.

It is not necessary, however, to resolve this question before taking up Parker's other concern, which in any case is more central to the present topic: whether the recovery of earlier forms ought even to be the concern of an editor. Parker offers a forthright opinion on the matter:

> The distance between the critical text and the beginning of the existence of this text is an important matter for consideration. ... Whether bridging this gap is the task of the critical editor is another matter, and wisdom inclines to the view that it is not. Rather, this gap is part of the study of the history of the text.[98]

This is a reasonable position, if only for pragmatic reasons. It is also a position with which other editors or editorial committees have differed, and because it involves a matter of opinion rather than evidence, it is a point on which editors will continue to differ—if only because it is part of their freedom as editors to decide how they wish to go about their business. There is little point in arguing this question one way or the other: agreement as to what our edited texts ought to represent is not the key issue. The more important point is whether an editor or committee of editors declares their understanding of what the text they have edited represents, and indicates the evidence, assumptions, and principles upon which that understanding is based. When editors share this information with their readers—as do, for example, Robinson and Pierpont, and the editors of the *ECM*—then readers may nonetheless use it fruitfully with understanding and appreciation, even if they disagree with the editorial perspective adopted by a particular edition. When nothing is said, however, about the goal or character of an edition, readers are disadvantaged by such silence. In short, those who use an edition of the text of the New Testament should not have to ask "What Text Is Being Edited?" Instead, one may suggest, it is the obligation of editors to answer that question.

---

98. Parker, *New Testament Manuscripts*, 180.

THE COHERENCE-BASED GENEALOGICAL METHOD: A NEW WAY TO RECONSTRUCT THE TEXT OF THE GREEK NEW TESTAMENT

Klaus Wachtel

1. MAXIMUM PARSIMONY AND THE TEXTUAL HISTORY OF THE NEW TESTAMENT

Shortly after Christmas 1998, the German news magazine *Der Spiegel* surprised us by announcing that a part of the approximately 5,500 Greek New Testament manuscripts written between the second century and modern times could now be brought into genealogical order, thanks to research done by evolutionary biologists.[1] The note in the *Spiegel* article was prompted by a collaboration between the Institute for Textual Research and Peter Robinson, a Chaucer editor and software developer, to apply phylogenetic techniques to the New Testament textual tradition. Robinson had previously applied to the prologue of Chaucer's "The Wife of Bath's Tale" a computer program called "SplitsTree," which was originally developed for evolutionary biology. Being an Anglicist, Robinson was part of the STEMMA project at the University of Cambridge's Department of Biochemistry, the aim of which was to test and refine the use of phylogenetic programs in studying the evolution of texts. In August 1998 Robinson and his colleagues had published a paper in *Nature* entitled "The Phylogeny of *The Canterbury Tales*"[2] that included a diagram showing the results of

---

1. "Ein Teil der rund 5000 griechischen Manuskripte aus der Zeit vom 2. Jahrhundert nach Christus bis zum Beginn der Neuzeit könnte dank der Evolutionsforscher endlich in einem Familienstammbaum geordnet werden" (*Der Spiegel* 53 [1998]: 151).

2. Adrian C. Barbrook, Christopher J. Howe, Norman Blake, and Peter Robinson, "The Phylogeny of *The Canterbury Tales*," *Nature* 394 (1998): 839.

a SplitsTree analysis of the manuscript tradition of the Prologue of "The Wife of Bath's Tale" in the form of a so-called "unrooted tree." This diagram brought known groupings of Chaucer manuscripts into genealogical relationship. The manuscripts were represented by terminal nodes at the end of bifurcating edges while the branching points (i.e., nonterminal nodes) represented common ancestors that are lost. Influenced by the success of this technique for a relatively small manuscript tradition, Robinson may have spoken a bit too optimistically about the potential for applying programs such as "SplitsTree" to the New Testament textual tradition.

The *Spiegel* article is characteristic of the belief that "real" science can solve problems that textual scholarship has wrestled with for decades and centuries if only it finds the right algorithm. At the Institute for Textual Research scepticism was strong, but the STEMMA results were intriguing. In 1999 we established contact with the STEMMA team. Matthew Spencer, a biologist who was then studying medieval texts for STEMMA, and I decided to investigate the genealogy of a group of manuscripts on the basis of full collations done at the Münster Institute for the *Editio Critica Maior* (*ECM*) of the Letter of James.[3] Spencer applied software developed for evolutionary biology, the cladistic Maximum Parsimony Method (MP), while I used Gerd Mink's Coherence-Based Genealogical Method (CBGM), which we employ at Münster to reconstruct the initial text for the *ECM*.[4] The results were published in 2002 in the online journal *TC: Journal of Biblical Textual Criticism*, under the title "The Greek Vorlage of the Syra Harclensis: A Comparative Study on Method in Exploring Textual Genealogy."[5] A

---

3. Barbara Aland, Kurt Aland, Gerd Mink, Holger Strutwolf, and Klaus Wachtel, eds., *Catholic Letters* (vol. 4 of *Novum Testamentum Graecum: Editio Critica Maior*; The Institute for New Testament Textual Research; Stuttgart: Deutsche Biblegesellschaft, 1997–2005).

4. "The first full presentation of the method was by Gerd Mink, "Problems of a Highly Contaminated Tradition: The New Testament—Stemmata of Variants as a Source of a Genealogy for Witnesses," in *Studies in Stemmatology II* (ed. P. van Reenen, A. den Hollander, and M. van Mulken; Amsterdam/Philadelphia: John Benjamins Publishing Company, 2004), 13–85. For a more recent account, see Gerd Mink, "Contamination, Coherence, and Coincidence in Textual Transmission," in *The Textual History of the Greek New Testament* (ed. K. Wachtel and M. W. Holmes; SBLTCS 8; Atlanta: Society of Biblical Literature, 2011), 141–216. A more general overview and additional literature is Gerd Mink, "The Coherence-Based Genealogical Method— What Is It About?" (http://www.uni-muenster.de/INTF/Genealogical_method.html).

5. Matthew Spencer, Klaus Wachtel, and Christopher J. Howe, "The Greek Vor-

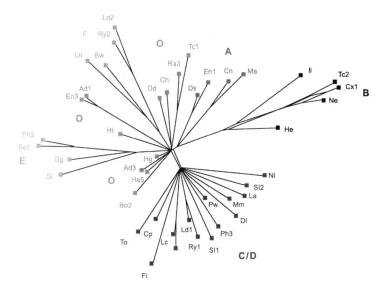

Fig. 1: "The Philogeny of *The Canterbury Tales*," *Nature* 394 (1998): 839. Courtesy of the Nature Publishing Group.

look back at the results from Spencer's and my contributions seems to be an effective way to show characteristic features of the Coherence-Based Genealogical Method.

Spencer produced the circular diagram shown in figure 2 to visualize the results of applying the MP method to the transmission of the Letter of James. It looks like a mandala, and one might guess that it shows all the strands of the transmission emanating from the center. However, this is not the case. As in the SplitsTree diagram above, there is no source indicated in this graph. It is all about finding the most parsimonious way to connect the terminating nodes, which represent extant Greek manuscripts, with internal nodes, which represent what philologists might call hyparchetypes.[6]

Our study focused on the genealogy of a group of manuscripts that is closely related to the text from which a translation into Syriac was done by Thomas of Harquel in 616.[7] I shall refer to these manuscripts as the

---

lage of the Syra Harclensis: A Comparative Study on Method in Exploring Textual Genealogy," *TC: A Journal of Biblical Textual Criticism* 7 (2002); online: http://purl .oclc.org/NET/TC/SWH2002.html.

6. Ibid., n. 5 par. 18.

7. Barbara Aland and Andreas Juckel, eds., *Die Großen Katholischen Briefe* (vol. 1

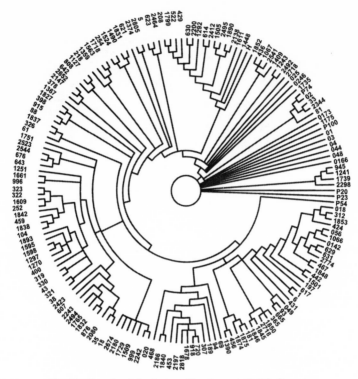

Fig. 2: Circular Maximum Parsimony (MP) diagram.

Harclensis group (HG) hereafter. Manuscripts which belong to or are closely related to the HG are displayed in red in the circular graph. Pairs of manuscripts most similar to each other are connected with their common source by short edges. For example, 206 and 1799 both derive from a lost text which is itself a descendant of another hyparchetype from which 522 is also descended. 630 and 2200 form a pair which is related to the manuscripts on its left by three internal nodes. The superordinate node and 1292 are connected by another internal node, and so on.

2. Coherence Method versus Maximum Parsimony

Let us now look at a diagram based on results from the CBGM as applied to the same data.

of *Das Neue Testament in syrischer Überlieferung*, ANTF 7; Berlin: de Gruyter 1986), 271–75; Spencer, Wachtel, and Howe, "The Greek Vorlage," 4–12.

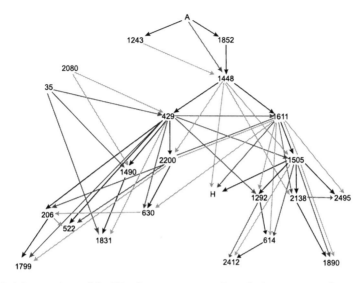

Fig. 3: Manuscripts of the Harclensis group, each with three potential ancestors.

Three fundamental differences distinguish the graph produced by the Coherence Method from the one produced by Maximum Parsimony:

- There is one source (or, if you like, one root) referred to as "A" which does not indicate a manuscript but the reconstructed *initial text.*
- There are no hyparchetypes, but both terminal and intermediary nodes represent *manuscript texts.*
- More than one edge may emanate from or point to a node, which reflects the fact that the manuscript tradition of the New Testament is highly contaminated.

Figure 4 shows the graph of manuscripts of the Harclensis group together with the upper part of the table on which it is based. It shows the three most closely related *potential ancestors* for each of the manuscripts. In the case of 206, for example, these are 429, 2200, and 630. The entries referring to the relationship of 206 and 429 show that they both cover a total of 761 variant passages in the letter of James and that they are equal in 742, or 98 percent, of these. 429 is most closely related to 206 because no other witness agrees with it at more variant passages. Of the remainder, 429 attests the priority reading in thirteen, and the secondary

ms 1	ms 2	Total	Equal	1<<2	1>>2
35	18	761	753 (99%)	5	3
35	2423	760	736 (97%)	11	9
35	617	761	734 (97%)	14	9
206	429	761	742 (98%)	13	4
206	2200	759	731 (96%)	14	10
206	630	760	728 (96%)	16	12
429	1448	760	716 (94%)	25	13
429	35	761	694 (91%)	29	28
429	2080	761	691 (91%)	31	29
522	429	758	728 (96%)	25	4
522	2200	757	718 (95%)	26	10
522	206	758	715 (94%)	25	14
614	1292	758	726 (96%)	18	13
614	1505	761	725 (95%)	21	13
614	1611	761	721 (95%)	23	15
630	2200	759	745 (98%)	7	6
630	429	760	743 (98%)	10	5
630	1611	760	708 (93%)	24	23
1243	A	741	686 (93%)	54	0
1243	1175	754	694 (92%)	29	28
1243	025	708	648 (92%)	29	26
1292	429	760	724 (95%)	22	10

Fig. 4: Ancestors and descendants—the data behind the diagram.

reading in four cases (1<<2: 13, 1>>2: 4). The preponderance of priority readings makes 429 a potential ancestor of 206. Because of similar proportions of 1<<2 and 1>>2, 2200 and 630 are potential ancestors, too. They follow after 429 because the "equal" values are lower. Thus the Coherence Method combines objective facts (the agreement values) with philological assessments to construct a graph illustrating the relationship of manuscript texts. The edges represent objective facts, and their direction depends on philologically reasoned decisions. While methods like Maximum Parsimony evaluate agreements and differences on a purely mathematical basis, the Coherence Method also processes philological statements on the genealogy of variants and derives statements on the relationships between extant manuscript texts from them. At the top of the resulting diagram there is a reconstruction of the *initial text* for which the *ECM* editors adopted the variant that best explains the emergence of the others at each variant passage.

Constructing a stemma is an advanced application of the CBGM. Let us now turn to more basic features and procedures of the method, and the philological context in which and for which it was developed: the *Editio Critica Maior* of the Greek New Testament.

3. The Coherence-Based Genealogical Method (CBGM)

3.1 Key Terms and Axioms

"Initial text" is a key term characteristic not only of the CBGM but of the theoretical concept behind it. We strive to reconstruct a form of the New Testament text that best explains the states of text that are preserved in the manuscripts, and hence comes as close as possible to the text of the authors. In terms of stemmatology, this means that our aim is a rooted tree. Edges in graphs drawn to visualize results of the CBGM will be directed.

Yet we are aware that our reconstruction has the status of a hypothesis. At most variant passages we are confident that the text we have reconstructed from the extant witnesses is in fact the text that stood at the beginning of the transmission. However, there are quite a few cases in the Catholic Letters where we left open the question whether the text printed as the primary line of the edition or one of the variants below is more likely to be the source of the other readings of the passage. Moreover, at one instance (2 Pet 3:10 οὐχ) the editors arrived at the conclusion that the initial reading of the passage was lost and a conjecture is needed.

One other term, "state of text," which was just mentioned in passing, needs explanation. The state of text in a manuscript has to be clearly distinguished from the manuscript as artifact with its paleographical and codicological features. The relationships analyzed by the CBGM are strictly those between states of text, not between manuscripts.

Then there are the terms "coherence" and "genealogy," of course. They occur in the basic axioms of the method. The first is:

All surviving witnesses are related to each other and there is coherence within the entire tradition.[8]

A study of test passages conducted at the Institute for New Testament Textual Research[9] showed that most extant manuscripts of the New Testa-

---

8. Mink, "Problems of a Highly Contaminated Tradition," 32 n. 4.
9. All continuous text manuscripts available were collated at 1,400 short passages throughout the New Testament. The results were published in the Text und Text-

ment agree at more than 90 percent of the passages where there are variants, as well as in the rest of the text that was transmitted without variation. For each state of text there are very similar states.

The test passages study selected 185 manuscripts of the Catholic Letters
to represent the textual history of the first millennium. A collation of these
manuscripts yielded 3046 variant passages. The lowest percentage of agreement between two manuscripts compared at these passages (excluding
small fragments) is 77.9 percent (1241–1838). Only thirty-nine pairs agree
at less than 80 percent of the passages. Most of the manuscripts selected for
the *ECM* agree with each other in more than 85 percent of cases. It has to
be stressed that our selection comprises only those manuscripts that differ
from the majority text in more than 10 percent of these passages.

This means that for each manuscript of the tradition we can nominate
others that agree closely with it. In fact, we found only three manuscripts
that agree with their closest potential ancestors at less than 90 percent, and
none have levels of agreement less than 87 percent.

One further indicator of coherence in general is the similarity of representatives of the Byzantine text with earlier text forms like 03 or 1739. If
we look at a table that lists the manuscripts that are most closely related to
our reconstruction of the initial text, we find three pure representatives of
the Byzantine text among the first ten manuscripts, and more follow not
much farther down.

There can be no doubt about the existence of coherence between the
states of text that have survived to our day. The high degree of coherence
can be explained only by the serious and mostly successful efforts of the
scribes to copy their exemplars as carefully as possible.

Nevertheless there are still more than a few variants, and there is contamination, and editors have to cope with them. Given the impressive evidence for coherence, the second axiom of the CBGM follows as a corollary:

> Contamination … emerges from those texts which were at the
> disposal of the scribe, i.e., texts in his direct environment, texts
> which are, for most part, closely related with each other.[10]

---

wert series: Kurt Aland et al., *Die Katholischen Briefe* (vol. 1 of *Text und Textwert
der griechischen Handschriften des Neuen Testaments*; Berlin: de Gruyter, 1987), *Die
Paulinischen Briefe* (vol. 2, 1991), *Die Apostelgeschichte* (vol. 3, 1993), *Die synoptischen
Evangelien* (vol. 4, 1998–1999), and *Das Johannesevangelium* (vol. 5, 2005).
    10. Mink, "Problems of a Highly Contaminated Tradition," 14 n. 4.

To explain in some detail how we can cope with both the variants and contamination making use of coherence, we have to start afresh from the third axiom of the CBGM:

> The genealogy of states of a text as preserved in the manuscripts can be inferred from genealogical assessment of the variants they exhibit.

3.2 The Usefulness of the CBGM in Editing the Greek New Testament

The CBGM is an instrument for the reconstruction of the *initial text*, the text form from which the manuscript transmission started. This reconstruction serves as the base text of the *Editio Critica Maior* (*ECM*), the central project of the Münster Institute for New Testament Textual Research. The edition entered the publication phase in 1997, with the first installment comprising the Letter of James. Since then, all the Catholic Letters have become available in the *Editio Critica Maior*.[11]

Figure 5 shows the structure of the edition. The primary line contains the reconstruction of or, to put it more pointedly, the hypothesis about the initial text that preceded the process of copying. Each word has an even number printed below it, while odd numbers are reserved for the spaces between words. Thus each word or passage and also each space between words can be identified by a precise numerical address.

An overview of the variants that relate to the primary line enables the reader to study the readings as such before he or she takes their witnesses into account. A numerical address is assigned to each passage of variation and a letter to each single reading. This combination makes it easy to identify the corresponding entry in the critical apparatus proper and, more importantly, to signify each combination of a variant with each of its witnesses as one set of data in our database.

The passage we are looking at is part of the description of a case of προσωπολημψία, *respect of persons. If you*, asks the author, *say to a man who wears fine clothing, Sit here in the good place*—here begins the sample text—σὺ κάθου ὧδε καλῶς, *and to the poor you say, You stand or sit there by my footstool*, καὶ τῷ πτωχῷ εἴπητε · σὺ στῆθι ἐκεῖ ἢ κάθου ὑπὸ τὸ ὑποπόδιόν

---

11. Ibid., 14 n. 3.

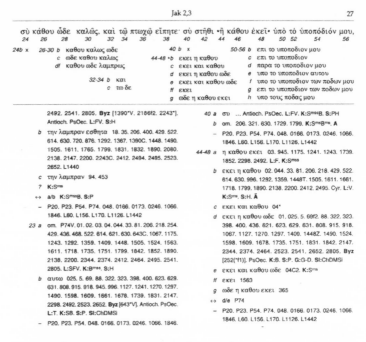

Fig. 5: Editio Critica Maior, sample page showing a part of Jas 2:3.

μου, *do you not*, he continues in verse 4, *make distinctions among your-selves, and become judges with evil thoughts?*

As stated above, the reconstruction of the initial text cannot be established at every place with the same degree of certainty. We use **bold dots** to indicate that the preponderance of arguments for the primary line text is only slight as compared with one or more variants placed in the apparatus. On the present page words 44–48 are marked by such dots. This is a passage where the editorial team opted for a reading different from the NA[27] text.

It is obvious that in all the variants at 44–48, the position and the kind of adverbs pose the problem. The bold dot marks reading *b* as a competitor with reading *a* for the distinction of being the initial reading. In *b* the adverb has a position that looks preferable stylistically, resulting in a smoother correspondence with the preceding κάθου ὧδε (words 26–28) and the following ἢ κάθου ὧδε ὑποπόδιόν μου. Hence it is more likely that *b* derives from *a* than vice versa. Reading *c* (*stand there and sit by my foot-stool*) does not make sense, but it has the local adverb in the same position as *b*. Thus it appears likely that ἤ was misread as καὶ compendium when *c* was copied from a text containing *b*. In reading *d*, the second ὧδε after the second κάθου interferes with the correspondence κάθου ὧδε—στῆθι ἐκεῖ that is the virtue of reading *b*. The second ὧδε may have been inserted to produce an additional correspondence στῆθι ἐκεῖ—κάθου ὧδε, possibly an unsuccessful attempt to improve the style. It appears likely that *b* represents an intermediate step between *a* and *d*, because the process would thus be split into two steps, the transposition of ἐκεῖ and the introduction of an additional local adverb. The καὶ in reading *e* is as awkward as that in reading *c*, and it is in fact the same reading in codex 04 that was extended by ὧδε in a correction. Reading *f* is marked as an error by an additional *f* (for the German *Fehler*). That it is an error becomes clear if we compare the reading of 1563 at the next passage of variation (50–56b) where it reads ἐπί τὸ ὑποπόδιόν μου, resulting in the request *Stand there on my footstool*. Finally, there is an interchange of the local adverbs in reading *g*.

These considerations can take the graphical form of a local stemma as in figure 6. The witnesses are not a part of the stemma of variants proper, but they are kept in this graph to illustrate the corresponding axiom of the CBGM according to which the genealogy of states of a text as preserved in the manuscripts can be inferred from genealogical assessment of the variants they exhibit.

Figure 6 shows the local stemma that was used in the process of collecting genealogical data for an assessment of the relationship between the

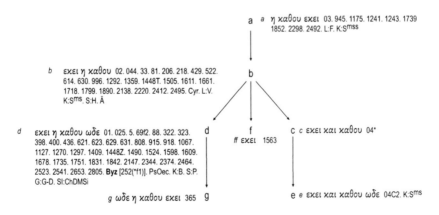

σὺ κάθου ὧδε καλῶς, καὶ τῷ πτωχῷ εἴπητε· σὺ στῆθι • ἤ κάθου ἐκεῖ • ὑπὸ τὸ ὑποπόδιόν μου,

a   *a* η καθου εκει 03. 945. 1175. 1241. 1243. 1739 1852. 2298. 2492. L:F. K:S^mss

b   εκει η καθου 02. 044. 33. 81. 206. 218. 429. 522. 614. 630. 996. 1292. 1359. 1448T. 1505. 1611. 1661. 1718. 1799. 1890. 2138. 2220. 2412. 2495. Cyr. L:V. K:S^ms. S:H. Ä

b

d   εκει η καθου ωδε 01. 025. 5. 69f2. 88. 322. 323. 398. 400. 436. 621. 623. 629. 631. 808. 915. 918. 1067. 1127. 1270. 1297. 1409. 1448Z. 1490. 1524. 1598. 1609. 1678. 1735. 1751. 1831. 1842. 2147. 2344. 2374. 2464. 2523. 2541. 2653. 2805. **Byz** [252(*f1)]. PsOec. K:B. S:P. G:G-D. Sl:ChDMSi

d   f   *c c* εκει και καθου 04*
ff εκει 1563

g ωδε η καθου εκει 365 g   *e e* εκει και καθου ωδε 04C2. K:S^ms

Fig. 6: Local stemma of variants at Jas 2:3/44–48.

witnesses. This passage counted as one instance where the witnesses of *a* have the prior variant compared to the witnesses of *b*. Compared to the witnesses of variant *d*, on the other hand, it counted as an instance of priority of the witnesses of *b*, and so on.

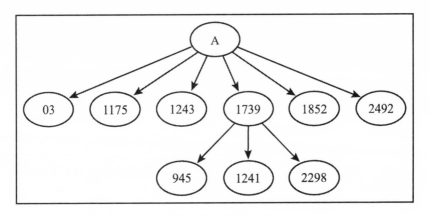

Fig. 7: Diagram of textual flow for Jas 2:3/44–48 a.

Whereas this passage is difficult to assess, as indicated by the bold dots, there are many more that do not pose a problem. Now that all the Catholic Letters have been edited we have a much larger basis for the deduction of tendencies than we had in the beginning. We can now review our previous assessments in the light of evidence from the 3046 variant passages in the entire corpus. The textual decision for variant *a* in the *ECM* was confirmed, but the relations we assumed between the readings require revision.[12]

The attestation of variant *a* is perfectly coherent in that all witnesses have either the reconstructed text "A" or 1739 as their most closely related potential ancestor.[13]

---

12. The "Genealogical Queries" application is online at http://intf.uni-muenster.de/cbgm/en.

13. "Genealogical Queries" (see n. 11) allows a user to assume that another variant besides *a* is the initial text. Setting *b* or *d* as initial here (with Connectivity set to "Average") would lead to the conclusion that the attestation of variant *a* was split into three strands which would have incorporated a change from *b* or *d* to *a* in their respective ancestries independently. But since *b* is the smoother reading and *d* can be

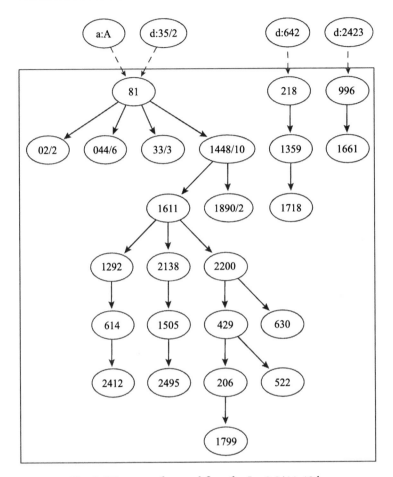

Fig. 8: Diagram of textual flow for Jas 2:3/44-48 b.

The potential ancestors that are most closely related to the key witnesses of variant *b* (i.e., 81, 218 and 996) attest variant *d* (35, 642 and 2423), with one important exception: "A," the reconstructed initial text. All potential ancestors of 04 (the only witness of variant *c*) support variant *a*, hence the arrow pointing to *c* in the local stemma should emanate from *a*. The attestation of variant *d*, the reading of the Byzantine text, is remarkably coherent, with 468 at its top. The potential ancestor most closely related to 468 is "A," followed by 04 with rank number 4 attesting variant *c*.

---

explained as an attempt at stylistic improvement, this interpretation of the evidence would be hard to defend.

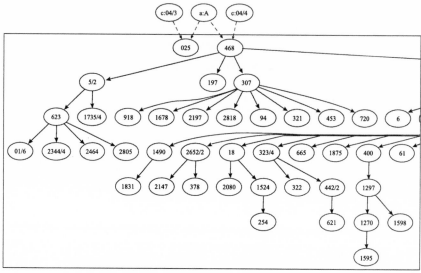

Fig 9: Diagram of textual flow for Jas 2:3/44–48 *d* (detail).

This leads to the conclusion that, in the light of our decisions at most other variant passages, the initially assumed dependence of variant *d* on *b* is rendered very unlikely. As a result, variants *b* and *d* should swap their positions in the local stemma, as shown in figure 10. However, the dependence of *g* on *d*, and of *f* on *b*, is confirmed.

4. The Current State of CBGM and Future Perspectives

Above all, the CBGM offers a means to the editor and textual scholar to keep track of his or her own assessments and decisions as to the genealogy of variants and the manuscript texts by which the New Testament writings were transmitted over nearly 1500 years. By examining the coherence of this transmission variant by variant and manuscript by manuscript, one can identify tendencies and strands from which a detailed and nuanced picture of the transmission emerges. Contamination cannot be reversed by these analyses; however, we can compensate for it by evaluating the directed textual flow yielded by summarizing the results from our text-critical work at every variant passage. What we gain is an external criterion for assessing textual variation that is far more discerning than the old text-type model.

σὺ κάθου ὧδε καλῶς, καὶ τῷ πτωχῷ εἴπητε· σὺ στῆθι • ἢ κάθου ἐκεῖ • ὑπὸ τὸ ὑποπόδιόν μου,

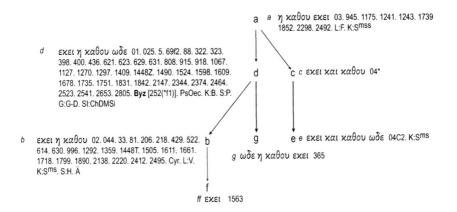

Fig. 10: Revised local stemma of variants at Jas 2:3/44–48.

An important feature of the CBGM is its iterative approach. We start from variant passages that do not pose serious textual problems, discover tendencies from them, and apply these to more complex cases. Regarding the Catholic Letters, we are now in the process of revising the local stemmata that were constructed in the course of our editorial work. We will very probably publish a second edition of the *ECM* of the Catholic Letters as a result. Gerd Mink is currently working at the final overall stemma of the manuscripts included in the apparatus. It will display the *stemmatic coherence* of the tradition. *Stemmatic coherence* is a feature of the optimal substemma for each state of text included, and subsequently of the overall stemma that comprises all optimal substemmata. A substemma is optimal if it contains only the witnesses necessary to explain the state of text in question, for example, a manuscript of the Harclensis group. The list of potential ancestors of 2495, for instance, shows that the only connection necessary in terms of stemmatic coherence comes from 1505. At all eight passages where 1505 and 2495 differ from each other, 1505 has the prior variant. In other areas of the graph showing three potential ancestors of each HG manuscript, the search for the optimal substemma is more interesting. Is it necessary, for example, to keep the line from 35, a pure form of the Byzantine text, to 429, or would the result be better if we took a connection of the fourth or fifth order into account? After optimizing the graph of textual flow by applying stemmatic coherence we will have a very effective tool for assessing the attestation of a variant in the light of all textual decisions taken so far. It is quite likely that the optimized means for assessing attestations may cast new doubt on cases that we had considered settled before.

The CBGM is a method that helps to control the subjective element in textual criticism, but it is clear that other scholars starting from different premises will come to different conclusions. Thus our most important task now is to put the CBGM online so that it can be used and tested by others. A pilot project by the title "Genealogical Queries" was launched in August 2008 (http://intf.uni-muenster.de/cbgm/en.html). So far its primary use is to document the work of the *ECM* editors because it presupposes their textual decisions. The next phase will be interactive, enabling users to make their own decisions and feed them back into the system.

Scribal Practices and the Transmission of Biblical Texts: New Insights from the Coherence-Based Genealogical Method

Holger Strutwolf

The most important task of textual criticism is to reconstruct the original text, or to be more modest: to establish a sound and well-argued hypothesis about the initial text of the transmission of a certain piece of literature that was handed down to posterity via manuscripts.[1] This reconstruction of the oldest form of the text is traditionally sought through internal and external criteria. In the history of New Testament textual criticism there was much debate about which kind of criteria should prevail: the argument of the better manuscript or the evaluation of the genealogy of readings? In this paper I want to argue for the inseparable union of both criteria.

---

1. This description of the central goal of textual criticism is no longer self-evident. While in the classical handbooks of the discipline there was a unanimous consensus in this question, in recent research it was challenged in many ways; see Eldon Jay Epp, "The Mulitivalence of the Term 'Original Text' in New Testament Textual Criticism," *HTR* 92 (1999): 245–81. Bart D. Ehrman ("The Text as Window: New Testament Manuscripts and the Social History of Early Christianity," in *The Text of the New Testament in Contemporary Research: Essays on the Status Quaestionis* [ed. B. D. Ehrman and M. W. Holmes; Grand Rapids: Eerdmans, 1995], 361 n. 1) seems to hold that there is an opposition between the task of reconstructing the "original text" and the research concerning the history of the text: "Given these historical concerns, there may indeed be scant reason to privilege the 'original' text over forms of the text that developed subsequently." But although the history of the text is a very important task for textual criticism and should be taken more seriously than it was in the past, the quest for the original text still remains the most important question, as every hypothesis concerning that history will also necessarily imply a hypothesis on the starting point of this historical development.

The reconstruction of the initial text and the examination of the history of the New Testament text are possible when we know the mechanisms and tendencies that led to a transformation of the text during the process of copying. The knowledge of these mechanisms and tendencies consisting of the typical behavior of scribes in copying their sources is traditionally laid down in the classical rules of textual criticism such as *lectio brevior potior, lectio difficilior potior,* and others. They claim to be based on the recognition that scribes normally tend to expand texts rather than to abbreviate them, and that they normally prefer clearer and stylistically better readings over difficult and odd ones. The first scholar who systematically dealt with these rules and thereby formed their canon was Johann Jakob Griesbach. After Johann A. Bengel,[2] who stated that all rules of internal textual criticism could be summarized in the one rule: *proclivi scriptioni praestat ardua* ("the difficult reading surpasses the easy one"), Griesbach formulated fifteen rules of inner textual criticism in the second edition of his Greek New Testament,[3] stating for example the famous *lectio brevior* rule in the following way:

> The shorter reading, if not wholly lacking the support of old and weighty witnesses, is to be preferred over the more verbose. For scribes were much more prone to add than to omit. They hardly ever leave out anything on purpose, but they added much.[4]

This statement surely sounds as if it were based on the knowledge of a vast number of collated manuscripts—and certainly Griesbach had much experience dealing with manuscripts and evaluating their different read-

---

2. *H ΚΑΙΝΗ ΔΙΑΘΗΚΗ. Novum Testamentum Graece ita adornatum ut textus probatarum editionum medullam margo variantium lectionum in suas classes distributarum, locumque parallelorum delectum apparatus subiunctus criseos sacrae Millianae praesertim compendium, limam, supplementum ac fructum exhibeat inserviente J.A.B.* (Tübingen, 1734), 433.

3. Johann Jakob Griesbach, ed., *Novum Testamentum Graece* (2nd ed.; London, 1796–1806).

4. *Brevior lectio, nisi testium vetustorum et gravium auctoritate penitus destituatur, praeferenda est verbosiori. Librarii enim multo proniores ad addendum fuerunt, quam ad omittendum.* (Johann Jakob Griesbach, ed., *Novum Testamentum Graece* [3rd ed.; Berlin: Laue, 1827], 1:lix). In the first edition of the Greek New Testament, the rule is formulated the following way: *Praeferatur lectio brevior....* (Johann Jakob Griesbach, ed., *Novum Testamentum Graece* [Halle, 1777], 1:xiv).

ings. But in the representation of his rules he is not arguing with manuscript evidence at all, so that the criticism of Royse seems to be true:

> Regrettably, though, most presentations of these canons are not—as far as one can tell from the exposition—based on the actual knowledge of documents of which Hort speaks, but rather appear to rest upon a priori reflections on how scribes behaved (or *must* have behaved).[5]

While these rules or notions of the typical behavior and habits of scribes very often were based on intuition, James Royse—following the traces of Colwell[6]—tries to put the study concerning scribal behavior on an empirical base by evaluating singular readings in papyri. Following Colwell, Royse assumes that "the singular readings of a manuscript are the textual creation of the scribe, and thus that an analysis of the patterns found within these singular readings will reveal the habits of the scribe."[7] So he explains that "Colwell's approach is reasonable and provides an objective way to isolate readings which are, most probably, scribally created."[8]

After listing the singular readings of the big old papyri and evaluating them, he comes to the astonishing conclusion that the common rule of *lectio brevior* must be abandoned, or even turned upside down: The observation that his lists of singular readings of the papyri 45, 46, 47, 66, 72, and 75 reveal "that all six of the papyri analysed here omit more often than they add" leads him to the conclusion that this rule "goes against the scribal activity evidenced in our papyri." As a result he can even enunciate a new rule contradicting the old one: "*lectio longior est potior*," that is, "A

---

5. James R. Royse, *Scribal Habits in Early Greek New Testament Papyri* (NTTSD 36; Leiden: Brill, 2008), 10.

6. Ernest Colwell, "The Greek New Testament with a Limited Critical Apparatus: Its Nature and Uses," in *Studies in New Testament and Early Christian Literature: Essays in Honor of Allen P. Wikgren* (ed. D. Aune; Leiden: Brill, 1972); idem, "The International Greek New Testament Project," *JBL* 87 (1968): 187–97; idem, "Method in Locating a Newly-Discovered Manuscript within the Manuscript Tradition of the Greek New Testament," in *Studia Evangelica: Papers Presented to the International Congress on "The Four Gospels in 1957" Held at Christ Church, Oxford 1957* (ed. K. Aland; Berlin: Akademie-Verlag, 1959), 757–77; Edgar J. Goodspeed and Ernest C. Colwell, *A Greek Papyrus Reader, with Vocabulary* (Chicago: University of Chicago Press, 1935).

7. Royse, *Scribal Habits*, 29.

8. Ibid., 42.

canon of transcriptional probability could ... be formulated as follows: In general the longer reading is to be preferred."[9]

As the discussion about the thesis of Royse and his followers went on, some objections were made which should be taken very seriously, in my opinion. One of these objections is that it is far from sure that the singular readings a manuscript contains really are the individual readings of the scribe who produced the manuscript. Since we only possess a small portion of the vast number of manuscripts that ever existed, in most cases we do not know the real ancestors of the manuscript in question. So the singular readings of a certain manuscript might have been invented by its scribe, but could also already have existed in the ancestor or even have been passed down through three or more generations of ancestors now lost.

This argument makes us aware that the category of singular readings is a very problematic one: Singular readings are those readings of a certain manuscript that have no support in the manuscript tradition—as far as our present knowledge of this tradition reaches. Many of the readings Colwell—using the edition of Konstantin von Tischendorf[10]—labeled as singular lost this status in Royse's study, because the increased information concerning the readings of a vast number of manuscripts not available in Colwell's time showed that many readings that were singular readings before now enjoyed support from other manuscripts.

By the way, some twelve of the singular readings of P72 listed by Royse have lost their status as singular readings when the *Editio Critica Maior* of the Catholic Epistles appeared.[11]

Jude 16	στομα	P72. 0142. 424C. 1409
1 Pet 1:6	πολλοις	P72. 398
1 Pet 1:12	υμιν	P72.996.1661.1729.2544

---

9. Ibid., 608.

10. Konstantin von Tischendorf, ed., *Novum Testamentum Graece* (Leipzig: Koehler, 1841; 16th ed., 1904).

11. Barbara Aland, Kurt Aland, Gerd Mink, Holger Strutwolf, and Klaus Wachtel, eds., *Catholic Letters* (vol. 4 of *Novum Testamentum Graecum: Editio Critica Maior*; 4 installments; The Institute for New Testament Textual Research; Stuttgart: Deutsche Bibelgesellschaft, 1997–2005): (1) *James* (1997; 2nd rev. impr., 1998); (2) *The Letters of Peter* (2000); (3) *The First Letter of John* (2003); (4) *The Second and Third Letter of John. The Letter of Jude* (2005).

1 Pet 1:24	οτι	P72. 181C
1 Pet 3:7	Τιμην απονεμοντες	P72. 1127
1 Pet 3:10	λαλειν	P72. 43. 330
1 Pet 5:1	θεου	P72. 1735
1 Pet 5:9	om. ω	P72. 93. 665T
2 Pet 1:4	Τιμια και μεγιστα ε πανγελματα ημιν	P72. 6
2 Pet 1:8	om. του αντε κυριου	P72. 1241
2 Pet 2:12	om. γεγενημενα	P72. 398. L:V
2 Pet 3:7	om. των	P72. 1409

The most interesting reading is 1 Pet 5:1/22–24b, presumed by Royse to be a theological change made by the scribe of P72. While according to the majority of manuscripts Peter calls himself the "witness of the sufferings of Christ" (μάρτυς τῶν τοῦ χριστοῦ παθημάτων), P72 reads "witness of the sufferings of God" (μάρτυς τῶν τοῦ θεοῦ παθημάτων), a variant that if considered an intentional and not incidental change would accent the divine nature of Christ, whose suffering in consequence would be the suffering of God. Such a high Christology that strongly stressed the divinity of Christ and therefore could speak of him as a suffering God certainly was not unusual theologically even in early Christianity. Already by the beginning or middle of the second century Ignatius of Antioch could plead with the Romans not to prevent his suffering and death in the Roman circus, imploring them, "Allow me to be an imitator of the Passion of my God" (ἐπιτρέψατέ μοι μιμητὴν εἶναι τοῦ πάθους τοῦ θεοῦ μου) (Ign. Rom. 6:3).

The theological character of this variant also seems to fit very well with the tendencies of P72 that can be traced in other parts of its text. In her presidential address at the SNTS meeting in Halle, Barbara Aland pointed out that this old papyrus from the third or fourth century created or handed down singular readings in three cases that emphasize the divine nature of Christ.[12]

---

12. Barbara Aland, "Welche Rolle spielen Textkritik und Textgeschichte für das Verständnis des Neuen Testaments?" Presidential address presented at the Sixtieth

In Jude 5b, P72 reads θεὸς χριστός, the "God Christ," instead of the simple name Δ|ησοῦς. In 2 Pet 1:2b, by the omission of a simple καὶ, it alters the meaning from "the knowledge of God and of Jesus our Lord" to "the knowledge of the God Jesus our Lord." In combination with these two instances of possible theological changes in P72, 1 Pet 5:1 may look like deliberate tampering with the text in order to strengthen its christological orthodoxy. But such a tendency would only be at work at these three places. In other passages of P72 where the same tendency could be expected to be at work, it has left no trace. So for example in 1 Pet 2:21 P72 is a reliable witness for the original wording χριστὸς ἔπαθεν ὑπὲρ ὑμῶν (Christ suffered for us) without any attempt to alter the text in favor of a high Christology. So I think it is also possible that the alteration from τοῦ χριστοῦ παθημάτων to τοῦ θεοῦ παθημάτων, like most of the other changes occurring in P72, happened by chance and have no deeper root in the theology of its scribe.

But there is still another—and I think even more fundamental—problem in the argument of Royse using the singular readings of certain early manuscripts not only to determine the special character of that manuscript and the individual scribal habits of its copyist, but also to reconsider and reformulate the rules of textual criticism. His argumentation for the reversing of the traditional rule of *lectio brevior est potior*—according to my point of view—depends on a category mistake. As we said, Royse tries to determine the way the scribes of the early papyri worked in copying the text of their model by evaluating the singular readings of the manuscripts they created in this act of copying. On the basis of this study of the singular readings, he comes to the conclusion that the scribes of these early papyri tended to omit far more than they added to the text. So he concludes that for the early papyri the rule of *lectio brevior* is proved to be wrong. Now a recent study by Juan Hernández Jr. on the scribal habits in the Apocalypse came to a similar result concerning the great uncials.[13] In his discussion of the singular readings of Codex Sinaiticus, Codex Alex-

Society for New Testament Studies Meeting, 2–6 August 2005, Halle (Saale); see also Marchant A. King, "Jude and 1 and 2 Peter: Notes on the Bodmer Manuscript," *Bibliotheca Sacra* 121:481 (1964): 57; Royse, *Scribal Habits*, 486–87; and Tobias Nicklas and Tommy Wassermann, "Theologische Linien im Codex Bodmer Miscellani?" in *New Testament Manuscripts: Their Texts and Their World* (vol. 2 of *Text and Editions for New Testament Study*; ed. T. J. Kraus and T. Nicklas; Leiden: Brill, 2006), 161–88.
    13. Juan Hernández, *Scribal Habits and Theological Influences in the Apocalypse:*

andrinus, and Codex Ephraemi Rescriptus, he shows that the scribes of these three manuscripts also omitted more often than they added to their texts. So the traditional view that the text of the New Testament is growing in the course of its transmission rather than shrinking would not be valid in the later times either. But here lies a problem revealing that this theory cannot be correct. For if we look at the material available now in the *Editio Critica Maior* of the Catholic Epistles we can make two interesting observations.

The first observation is that the vast majority of the omissions of single words or short expressions testified in the apparatus are singular readings or are supported by only a few manuscripts. This indicates clearly that the erroneous omission of words is the most frequent source of variation in the individual manuscripts.

The second interesting observation concerns the singular readings of late Byzantine manuscripts. If we apply the method of Royse to some Byzantine manuscripts which still have many singular readings, we come to the astonishing conclusion that even here the majority of the singular readings are omissions. A concrete example is Manuscript 2186: Nearly all of its singular readings consist of omissions.

SINGULAR READINGS OF 2186

Jude 8/6–8	om. και ουτοι	2186
Jude 5/4	om. δε	2186
2 John 12/6–8	γραφειν (om. υμιν)	2186
1 John 5:20/24–28	om. διανοιαν ινα γινωσκωμεν	2186
1 John 5:15/26–32	om. τα αιτηματα α ητηκαμεν	2186
1 John 5:2/28	om. και	2186
1 John 4:18/46–54	ου τετελειωται εν αγαπη	2186
1 John 3:19/4–20	om.	2186
1 John 3:6/2	Πας γαρ	2186

The Singular Readings of Sinaiticus, Alexandrinus and Ephraemi (Tübingen: Mohr Siebeck, 2006).

1 John 2:28/20–22	Παρρησιαν εχωμεν	2186
1 John 2:20/20	Απαντα	2186
1 Pet 4:17/46–52	Του θεου ευαγγελιω	2186
1 Pet 4:3/4	om. Γαρ	2186
1 Pet 3:14/2–8	αλλ ει πασχοιτε	2186
1 Pet 2:3/10	om. Ο	2186
1 Pet 1:3/18–20	om. Ιησου Χριστου	2186
1 Pet 1:2/20	om. Και	2186
Jas 1:11/34–46	om. και η ευπρεπεια του προσωπου αυτου απωλετο ουτος	2186

But that is the dilemma: if we look at the typical behavior of scribes from the viewpoint of the singular readings a single manuscript contains, we might get the impression that the text of the New Testament should be shrinking in the course of transmission. But the textual history as a whole shows us that in fact the text grew over time. If we compare the initial text of the transmission of the Greek New Testament with the majority text, we certainly find that this late text form is much longer than the initial text. "Text and Textwert" shows that there are far more additions than omissions in the Byzantine text as compared with earlier text forms.[14]

So we have to admit that the scribal habits that come into sight by using the singular readings are not representative for the textual flow of the whole transmission. So gathering the general rules of the overall transmission from the evaluation of singular readings of single manuscripts is a

---

14. See for example, *Text und Textwert IV: Das Matthäusevangelium. Bd. 2,2. Resultate der Kollation und Hauptliste sowie Ergänzungen* (ed. K. Witte et al.; ANTF 29; Berlin: de Gruyter, 1999), 2–138: If we count only the instances where the majority text differs from the older text (the so-called 1 readings), we come to the result that within the totality of forty-five places of variation there are twenty-six places where the Byzantine text has an addition, while there are only two cases where it has an omission. The other seventeen places are variant readings that do not affect the length of the text.

category mistake. The problem with the singular readings is that they are singular readings; they were not copied in the ongoing history of the text, either because the manuscripts containing them had no descendants or because the singular readings were silently corrected in the next generation of copying. If we now evaluate manuscripts by means of their individual readings, we take into account exactly those portions of their text that are of no relevance for the history of the text, or for the transmission of the text. To sum up the results of my observations, evaluating the singular readings of manuscripts might give us some interesting insights into the special character of individual pieces of transmission, but it cannot help us to determine the rules and tendencies that prevail in the general history of the textual transmission as a whole. So we have to distinguish between the behavior of individual scribes and the overall tendencies of the textual history in general.[15]

To verify, control, or improve the rules of inner textual criticism we have to establish the scribal habits of textual history in general. This can only be done by evaluating the whole manuscript transmission, that is, all the readings of every single manuscript. Since we have the full collation of the manuscripts of the Catholic Epistles in the *Editio Critica Maior* and can analyze the tradition using the new Coherence-Based Genealogical Method, for the first time we have the opportunity to reconstruct empirically the typical behavior of our transmission viewed as a continuous process.[16] We are able to determine for each manuscript text we are studying those states of text that are its ancestors and from which it received its text by reproducing or varying the readings of the ancestors. As we now know

---

15. See David C. Parker (*An Introduction to the New Testament Manuscripts and their Texts* [Cambridge: Cambridge University Press, 2008], 296): "But one has to distinguish between the habits of individual manuscripts and the habits of textual histories."

16. See Gerd Mink, "Eine umfassende Genealogie der neutestamentlichen Überlieferung," *NTS* 39 (1993): 481–99; idem, "Editing and Genealogical Studies: the New Testament," *Literary and Linguistic Computing* 15 (2000): 51–56; idem, "Was verändert sich in der Textkritik durch die Beachtung genealogischer Kohärenz?" in *Recent Developments in Textual Criticism: New Testament, Other Early Christian and Jewish Literature* (ed. W. Weren and D.-A. Koch; Assen: Van Gorcum, 2003), 39–68; idem, "Problems of a Highly Contaminated Tradition: The New Testament Stemmata of Variants as a Source of a Genealogy for Witnesses," in *Studies in Stemmatology II* (ed. P. v. Reenen et al.; Amsterdam: Benjamins, 2004), 13–85. The method can now also be used online: http://intf.uni-muenster.de/cbgm/en.

the textual character of the ancestors the scribe was probably copying, we can reconstruct the scribal habits much better than was possible before. This procedure often shows that the traditional view of what scribes are likely to do is proved to be wrong or is at least not always correct.

1. EXAMPLE 1: 1 PET 2:18/32

So we would normally expect it to be more likely that the more correct and stylistically better reading would be secondarily inserted by the scribes. But in many cases we see that this rule of thumb does not always work; 1 Pet 2:18/32 may serve as an example.

Οἱ οἰκέται ὑποτασσόμενοι ἐν παντὶ φόβῳ τοῖς δεσπόταις, οὐ μόνον τοῖς ἀγαθοῖς καὶ ἐπιεικέσιν ἀλλά; καὶ τοῖς σκολιοῖς.

om. καὶ P72. 69. 81. 614. 2464. K:S^MSS

Servants, be in subjection to your masters with all fear; not only to the good and gentle, but also to the froward.

Everyone knows from his or her primary course in Greek the formula οὐ μόνον ... ἀλλὰ καὶ. We have learned it in our vocabulary lessons, so that we would expect that the scribes would tend to expand a shorter οὐ μόνον ... ἀλλὰ to the better Greek οὐ μόνον ... ἀλλὰ καὶ than the other way around. But looking at the attestation of these variants, one finds that many ancestors of the manuscripts that read the shorter variant attest the longer reading.

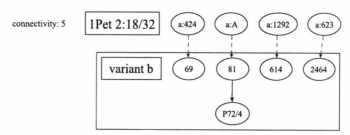

The diagram above shows that the omission of the word καὶ occurred several times independently. The first potential ancestor of Manuscript 69 is Manuscript 424. All the manuscripts that are close enough to 69 to be seriously taken into consideration if we look for the source of its readings are in the attestation of variant *a*. The first potential ancestor in the attestation of *b* would be Manuscript 81, but it is only the fifty-fourth potential ancestor and surely has nothing to do with Minuscule 69. So it is quite obvious that the text of Minuscule 69 depends on the text form of Minuscule 424. Quite a similar relation can be observed between 1292 and 614, between 623 and 2464, and between the initial text of the transmission and 81. Even P72 has its three closest potential ancestors in the attestation of *a*—and it is quite probable that it also created its reading out of the text of *a*.

Even if we presume that the omission was the original text—as is supposed in the following graph—the result concerning scribal behavior nearly remains the same:

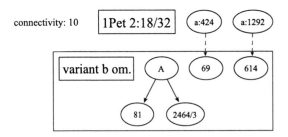

Even if the text without the particle καὶ were the original text, it is quite clear from this graph that in two cases the source of reading *b* was the longer text *a*—as can be seen in the case of 69 which altered the *a*-reading of its ancestor 424, and 614, which did the same with the text of its ancestor 1292.

This example can teach us two things: first, the involuntary omission of small words is one of the most important sources of variation in individual manuscripts, since the scribes were certainly not aiming at making the style of Peter rougher; second, on the other hand, this shorter reading they created did not prevail in the further course of transmission; rather, the manuscript that created the reading was also the last witness for it and did not transmit this reading to a following generation.

2. Example 2: Jas 2:13/8

ἡ γὰρ κρίσις ἀνέλεος τῷ μὴ ποιήσαντι ἔλεος· κατακαυχᾶται ἔλεος κρίσεως.

> For a merciless judgment is to him who does not show mercy,
> mercy will triumph over judgment.

Here the majority text is divided into reading *a*: ἀνέλεος and reading
b: ἀνέλεως. Both adjectives have the same meaning. The variant is only a
stylistic one. Both ἀνέλεως and ἀνέλεος are *hapax legomena* in New Testament Greek and in early Christian literature.

But in the context of Jas 2:13 where the word ἔλεος occurs twice, one
would expect a tendency of the scribes to alter from ἀνέλεως to ἀνέλεος.
Now let us see what really happened according to the evaluation of the
whole material using the Coherence-Based Genealogical Method (see the
diagram on p. 151).

What we see is a totally coherent attestation of the variant *b*. All the
witnesses of this attestation belong together. The reading *b*: ἀνίλεως was
"invented" only once and then copied without variation. So far the picture
appears as we would expect it. But what is the picture like if we look at the
attestation of the variant *b*, an assimilation to the context that should have
been created several times, if our conception of the influence of the imme-
diate context on the origin of variants were right?

If we look at the attestation of the variant *b*, we get a very similar picture as in the case of variant *a*: All the manuscripts that read variant *a* stay
together in perfect coherence.

The diagram on page 152 shows us that there are exceptions to the rule
and that alterations in the textual flow are influenced by the context. The
scribes normally transcribed what they read in their copy—the change,
although apparently tempting, was the exception to the rule and not the
rule itself.

3. EXAMPLE 3: JAS 2:13/20

With Colwell, Tune,[17] and Royse, we are used to thinking that scribal
errors have little chance to persist in the transmission that follows, because

---

17. Ernest C. Colwell and Ernst W. Tune, "The Quantitative Relationships
between MS Text-Types," in *Biblical and Patristic Studies* (ed. J. N. Birdsall; Freiburg:
Herder, 1963), 25–32; idem, "Method in Establishing Quantitative Relationships
between Text-Types of New Testament Manuscripts," in *Studies in Methodology in
Textual Criticism of the New Testament* (ed. E. C. Colwell; Leiden: Brill, 1969), 56–62;
idem, "Variant Readings: Classification and Use," *JBL* 83 (1964): 253–61.

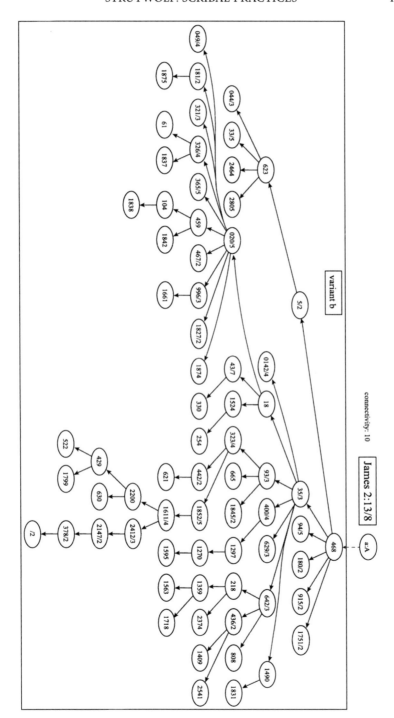

connectivity: 10　　James 2:13/8

variant a

they were readily corrected by later copyists.[18] And there are many cases where this rule proves to be true. I would even dare to say that most cases of an obvious scribal mistake or reading that later transcribers viewed as an error had little chance to survive. It was the professional task of the scribes or of the correctors who checked the manuscript when it left the desk of the copyist to correct obvious mistakes in the manuscripts. But there is no rule without exception, and the rules of textual criticism are not as universal as they might appear. In the verse we were just examining, we can find a striking example of a reading that is obviously wrong and was still copied in some manuscripts, and thus survived in the transmission.

In Jas 2:13/20 the majority of the manuscripts read: Κατακαυχᾶται ἔλεον κρίσεως. This is certainly not correct Greek, because the sentence requires a nominative case for the subject, and the word τὸ ἔλεον (does) exists neither in profane nor in New Testament Greek.

But if we look at the attestation of this variant we come to a very astonishing conclusion. The first graph establishing the relations of the witnesses of variant *a* to their potential ancestors still reveals a picture of transmission that meets our expectations (see diagram on p. 154).

As the graph shows, the false reading was in many instances altered in the direction of the correct *a*-reading; this happened many times, and it probably happened independently. But if we now take into account the graph mapping the relations within the attestation of the variant *b*, we get the picture represented on page 155.

This means that in the majority of cases the text containing a word that does not exist in Greek was faithfully copied from the exemplar. So the obvious mistake in the exemplar did not tempt the majority of the scribes to correct the mistake by an easy and nearby conjecture. The reason for this is open to discussion. In fact in many other cases the scribes were not scrupulous in emending the text if they found it to be obviously corrupt. So there must have been a reason why the scribes did not do what they normally would be expected to do. Maybe they did not find it to be as obviously wrong as we do today, since grammars and dictionaries tell us that the word τὸ ἔλεον does not exist in classical and koine Greek. But the average Greek scribes living in times when their spoken language was already on its way to modern Greek may have had another impression. Copying manuscripts day by day, they were used to coming across many

---

18. Royse, *Scribal Habits*, 35.

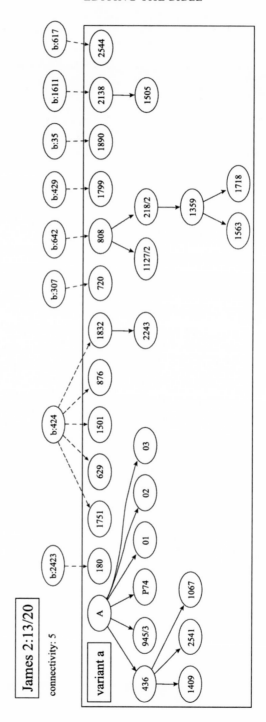

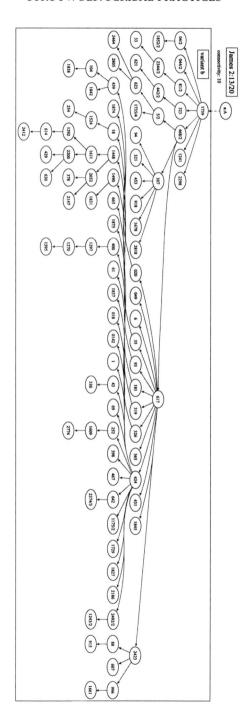

strange expressions in New Testament Greek, so they might not have been struck by the occurrence of a word like τὸ ἔλεον. Maybe we have to leave this question open.

But in any case this strange variant that became the majority text is another strong hint of what Kurt Aland called "tenacity of transmission,"[19] that the manuscript transmission of the New Testament is very conservative in keeping variants that once came into existence if they were not obviously wrong.

4. EXAMPLE 4: 2 PET 2:20/22–32

A last example may show that the traditional rule of *lectio brevior* is still functioning well. In 2 Pet 2:20 the reconstructed text reads: ἐν ἐπιγνώσει τοῦ •κυρίου ἡμῶν καὶ σωτῆρος Ἰησοῦ Χριστοῦ•. The editors had some doubt in this decision and thus marked the text of the variant with two dots. In the first apparatus the dot appears again preceding the variant *f*: •κυρίου καὶ σωτῆρος Ἰησοῦ Χριστοῦ. And if we look at the following graph showing the relation between the manuscript attesting variant *a* and *f*, we see that there is a strong argument that reading *f* may be the original one (see diagram on p. 157).

We see that the longer reading κυρίου ἡμῶν … certainly was developed several times out of reading *f* κυρίου. This shows that there is clearly movement from the shorter to the longer reading in this variation. If we opted for the shorter text as the original one, the case would become even clearer (see diagram on p. 158).

The attestation of variant *f*, the shorter reading, is in perfect coherence. All the manuscripts that are witnesses to this reading belong together. The shorter reading was never developed out of another reading. Therefore the rule of the shorter reading being the older one is in this case strongly confirmed.

5. EXAMPLE 5: 1 PET 5:1/22–24B

Let me return to the question of the theological tendency of P72 in the variant reading 1 Pet 5:1/22–24b. Above I have argued that the change τοῦ

---

19. Kurt Aland and Barbara Aland, *Der Text des Neuen Testaments: Einführung in die wissenschaftlichen Ausgaben sowie in Theorie und Praxis der modernen Textkritik* (2nd ed.; Stuttgart: Deutsche Bibelgesellschaft, 2006), 293–94 .

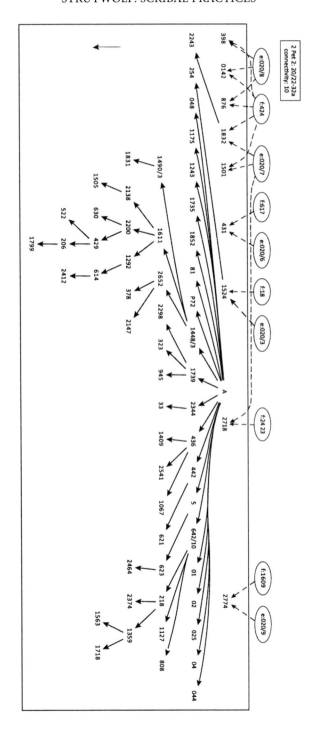

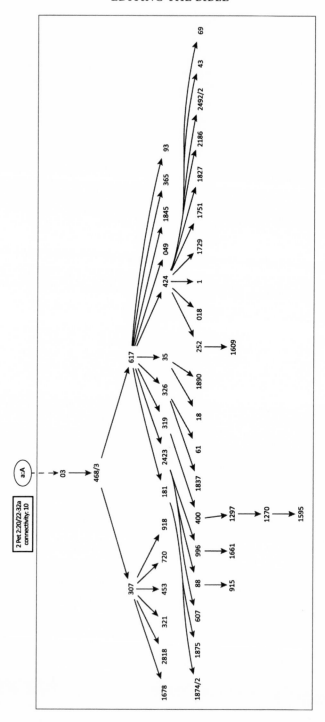

Χριστοῦ παθημάτων to τοῦ θεοῦ παθημάτων could also be due to accident. One argument for this could be that this alleged theological characteristic reading of P72 now has found new support in the manuscript 1735. This is a manuscript that is not very close to P72, only 80.5 percent agreement can be found between these two manuscripts in 1 Peter.

So one would argue that the reading did come into existence twice independently without direct contact, as shown in the following graph:

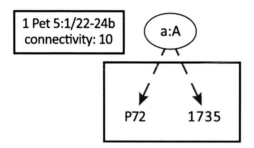

Since P72 and 1735 have nothing to do with each other, it is quite impossible that the reading found its way from the one manuscript to the other. And since 1735 is not known to have the same theological tendencies that P72 is presumed to have, it is quite obvious that the variant in 1735 did occur by chance. And what is possible in the case of 1735 should also be possible for P72.

In conclusion, using the Coherence-Based Genealogical Method in evaluating the scribal habits within the textual flow of the New Testament textual tradition, we found that the scribes did not always do what we expected them to do. I presented only a few examples in this paper, but I believe that the method I used has great potential to help us clarify the rules of internal textual criticism by combining them with the overall picture of the textual history we gain by using the Coherence-Based Genealogical Method. So the original text hypothesis, in combination with the picture of the textual history with which it is connected, may give us new insights into the rules of textual transmission and help us to clarify the rules of internal textual criticism.

This enterprise has only yet begun, but it can show the validity and the limits of the rules of internal criticism. In many cases the Coherence-Based Genealogical Method shows that these old rules are still functioning well, while in some instances they prove to be wrong. This means that the internal rules should not be isolated. They are only useful when they are employed within the framework of the external criteria, that is, if they are combined with our knowledge about the interrelation between the single manuscripts and about the history of the transmission as a whole.

"Knowledge of documents" surely has to "precede final judgement upon readings," as Hort claimed.[20] This knowledge of documents can now be refined by the Coherence-Based Genealogical Method. But it is also possible to use the same method to refine the criteria of internal criticism, as I have tried to show. I think judgment on readings must always be combined with the knowledge of the overall picture of transmission.

---

20. Brooke Foss Westcott and Fenton John Anthony Hort, eds., *The New Testament in the Original Greek*, vol. 1: *Text* (Cambridge: Macmillan, 1881), 543.

The New Testament in the Light of Book Publishing in Antiquity

David Trobisch

1. The Christian Bible as a Second-Century Publication

The student of the manuscript tradition of New Testament texts will discover that the extant manuscripts document a closed selection of twenty-seven writings, that the writings are arranged in the same sequence and grouped into four volumes, that they display uniform titles with very few variants, that they were produced almost exclusively using the form of the codex, and that they contain a unique system to mark sacred terms, the so-called *nomina sacra*.[1]

All of these elements—the notation of the *nomina sacra*, the codex form, the uniform arrangement and number of writings, the formulation of the titles, and the evidence indicating that the collection was called "New Testament" from the very beginning—indicate that the New Testament is a carefully edited publication; it is not the product of a gradual process which lasted for centuries.[2] These editorial features, which did not originate with the authors of the individual writings, serve to combine disparate material into a cohesive literary unit. Furthermore, these elements

---

1. David Trobisch, *The First Edition of the New Testament* (New York: Oxford University Press, 2000).

2. The assumption of gradual growth has dominated traditional studies of the history of the canon. These studies usually do not take the Greek manuscript evidence into account, but rely heavily on quotes from early Christian writers. See, for instance, Hans von Campenhausen, *Die Entstehung der christlichen Bibel* (BHT 39; Tübingen: Mohr Siebeck, 1968) = *The Formation of the Christian Bible* (Philadelphia: Fortress, 1972); Harry Y. Gamble, *The New Testament Canon: Its Making and Meaning* (Philadelphia: Fortress, 1985).

cannot be credited to several independently operating editors, but must be the work of a single editorial entity. In other words, the New Testament was edited and published by specific people at a very specific time and at a very specific place. Because the first documented readers of the New Testament are Irenaeus, Clement of Alexandria, Tatian, Tertullian, and Origen, all of whom wrote at the end of the second and the beginning of the third century, the New Testament must have been published before 180 C.E.[3] Seeking to understand and interpret the New Testament as a publication of the second century is a promising field of study. In the following I will touch on some aspects of ancient book publishing that seem of interest.

2. Aspects of Book Publishing in Antiquity

In the year 20 B.C.E. Horace published a collection of twenty of his letters in Rome. These letters were written as poems. The last letter of the collection was addressed to the book that Horace was just about to finish. In the very first sentence Horace mentions the address and the name of the publisher who would produce and distribute the letter collection: the Sosii brothers. Their business was located conveniently next to the temples of Janus and Vertumnus (*Ep.* 1.20):

> The bookshops by Janus' temple and that of Vertumnus—
> That's the direction you seem to be casting your eyes in,
> Hoping, no doubt, my book, to stand there on sale,
> Neatly scrubbed with the pumice of Sosii Brothers.[4]

---

3. Irenaeus uses the term *New Testament* repeatedly, but he does not use it in reference to the book; see W. C. van Unnik, "*Hē kainē diathēkē*—A Problem in the Early History of the Canon," *Studia Patristica* 4 (1961): 212–27, here 219–20; Adolf von Harnack, *Das Neue Testament um das Jahr 200* (Freiburg: Mohr, 1889), 42; Hermann-Josef Vogt, "Die Geltung des Alten Testaments bei Irenäus von Lyon," *Theologische Quartalschrift* 160 (Munich: Wewel, 1980): 17–28; Josef Hoh, *Die Lehre des Hl. Irenäus über das Neue Testament,* (Neutestamentliche Abhandlungen; 7 Münster: Aschendorffsche Verlagsbuchhandlung, 1919). Concerning the use of the term *New Testament* in Clement of Alexandria, *Stromata* 2.29.2–3, see Joseph Fischer, "Die Einheit der beiden Testamente bei Laktanz, Viktorin von Pettau und deren Quellen," *Münchener Theologische Zeitschrift* 1 (1950): 96–101, cf. 100; van Unnik, "*Hē kainē diathēkē*," 215. For Tertullian's use of the term *New Testament* in *Pud.* 1 and *Prax.* 15 and Origen's *Comm. Jo.* 5.8, see Trobisch, *First Edition*, 44.

4. Lord Dunsany and Michael Oakley, *The Collected Works of Horace* (London: Dent; New York: Dutton, 1961), 265.

Another Roman publisher of the first century B.C.E. whom we know by name was Atticus. He published the works of his close friend Cicero, and was also praised for his excellent editions of Plato, Aeschines, and Demosthenes.[5] In the first century C.E., Typhon published Quintilian's and Martial's works. Martial names Quintus Pollius Valerianus as his publisher.[6] Dorus and Polybius, a former slave of Emperor Claudius and a friend of the philosopher Seneca, were two other documented publishers at the time.[7] The oldest Christian publisher known by name was probably a certain Clement. In the *Shepherd of Hermas* 8.3, his duty is described as producing copies of the master manuscript and distributing those copies by sending them to other cities. In other words, his work was to "produce or release for distribution"— the definition of the word "publisher" in Webster's Collegiate Dictionary.

The value of a copy was entirely dependent on the quality of the master copy. A publisher had two possibilities for securing quality. For contemporary works, the publisher would cooperate closely with the author. But with older pieces of literature, the publisher would work with well known and highly recognized editors. Both publisher and author were interested in controlling the quality of the master copy. The correspondence between Cicero and his publisher Atticus gives us valuable insights into how far this cooperation sometimes reached. After Cicero had sent a master copy of his *Academica* to Atticus, he made substantial changes. Unfortunately, Atticus had already produced copies and was ready to distribute and sell the books. Atticus decided to destroy the finished copies; for him they had become worthless.[8] In another case Cicero confused the names of two comedy writers, Eupolis and Aristophanes. He felt so badly about this mistake that he not only asked Atticus to correct the master copy, but insisted that his publisher send scribes to the customers who had purchased the book to correct the mistake.[9]

---

5. Wilhelm Schubart, *Das Buch bei den Griechen und Römern* (2nd ed.; Berlin, Leipzig: de Gruyter, 1921), 154, 188.

6. Martial distinguishes between his publishers and the bookshops that carry his books. He mentions Atrectus and Secundus, who manage a store behind the Temple of Peace (Martial, *Epigrams* 1.117; 13.3).

7. Eduard Stemplinger, *Buchhandel im Altertum* (2nd ed.; Munich: Heimeran, 1933), 11.

8. Cicero, *Att.* 16.6.4; Schubart, *Das Buch bei den Griechen und Römern*, 151.

9. Cicero, *Att.* 12.6.3; Schubart, *Das Buch bei den Griechen und Römern*, 154. Martial (*Epigrams* 1.117) revises the master copy that he had submitted to his pub-

But how would a publisher successfully compete with other publishers when the works were written by authors who were no longer living? In this case the quality of the master copy was guaranteed by the person who edited the work. Atticus, for example, not only published the works of his friend Cicero, but very successfully produced and sold editions of Plato, Aeschines, and Demosthenes. For centuries the editions by Atticus were well known and in high demand.[10] Overall it was the claim that the master copy was authentic and without mistakes that guaranteed the copyright. If the master copy contained the author's handwriting, the value was enormous. Aulus Gellius reports that Plato paid a sum of 10,000 *denarii* for three books that had been copied by Philolaos; and Aristotle, he says, paid 18,000 *denarii* for books copied by the hand of Seusippos, the nephew of Plato. To put these prices into perspective, Martial mentions that one of his books sold for one *denarius*, another for five *denarii*.[11]

But an autograph does not always make a good master copy. It seems that Aristotle edited his own writings and authorized master copies for publication. Two hundred and fifty years after Aristotle's death, books surfaced in Rome that showed additions by Aristotle's hand in the margins. These manuscripts came from the library of Apellicon of Teos, which Sulla had stolen and carried off as war bounty. They were Aristotle's personal copies, from which he very likely read during his lectures, noting ideas in an abbreviated format that was difficult for anyone but the author to understand. The Roman publishers struggled to edit these books for publication, and in the end they produced a text full of repetitions and discrepancies. Nevertheless, these editions sold so well that they completely replaced the older versions, which had been edited by Aristotle himself.[12]

But how would a publisher secure the copyright? Horace's letter to his book ends with the following sentences (*Ep.* 1.20):

---

lisher. Cf. Plinius, *Ep.*, 5.10; in his letter to Sueton, Plinius writes about works being copied, widely read, and sold.

10. Schubart, *Das Buch bei den Griechen und Römern*, 154, 188.

11. Ibid., 188.

12. Dieter Georgi, "Die Aristoteles—und Theophrastausgabe des Andronikus von Rhodus: Ein Beitrag zur Kanonsproblematik," in *Konsequente Traditionsgeschichte*: *Festschrift für Klaus Baltzer zum 65. Geburtstag* (ed. Rüdiger Bartelmus et al.; OBO 126; Göttingen: Vandenhoeck & Ruprecht, 1993), 45–78, here 52.

Talk to people about me.... Say I was short in build,
Went grey early in life, was fond of the sunshine,
Was quick to get angry, though just as quickly appeased;
And if anyone happens to ask my age, you can tell them
I finished my four-and-fortieth December the year
That Lollius the consul got Lepidus named as his colleague.[13]

These words clearly identify the author of the book and give a date of publication, something everyone expects to find on the cover page of a publication.

The first century poet Martial begins his book of epigrams (1.2) with
the following note to the readers:

> You, who wish my poems should go with you wherever you go ... go
> and buy them! ... And so you may not fail to know where I am for sale,
> or wander aimlessly all over town, accept my guidance and you will find
> your way: Seek out Secundus, the freedman of learned Lucensis, behind
> the entrance to the Temple of Peace and the Forum of Pallas.[14]

Martial gives the name and the address of his publisher. In other places
he even mentions the price of the respective books. From the publisher's
perspective these comments by an author secure his copyright, because
the author endorses the publisher's master copy. Signals indicating that a
book was published from an autograph were important to book sellers and
readers alike. They were perceived as signs of high quality and most likely
justified a higher sales price.

3. Application to the New Testament

The New Testament contains features that link the publication to autographs. The *Third Letter of John*, of which Philipp Vielhauer wrote in his
Introduction to the New Testament, "This writing is a private letter—the
only real one in the NT,"[15] seems a rather trivial piece of communication. The letter writer complains to Gaius that some of his friends had

---

13. Horace, *Satires, Epistles and Ars poetica* (trans. H. Rushton Fairclough; LCL;
Cambridge: Harvard University Press, 1929).

14. Martial, *Epigrams* (trans. W. C. A. Ker; LCL; Cambridge: Harvard University
Press, 1919).

15. Philipp Vielhauer, *Geschichte der urchristlichen Literatur: Einleitung in das*

not been welcome by Gaius' congregation. He criticizes Diotrephes, one of the leaders of that congregation, and supports a certain Demetrius as a better leader. Equally, Paul's letter to Philemon seems to contain a rather insignificant message compared to Paul's letters to the Romans and to the Galatians and his Corinthian correspondence, which were published in the same volume. In the second century, however, Paul's letter to Philemon had the potential to promote the New Testament like few other New Testament writings. A potential reader was probably familiar with Bishop Polycarp's edition of the letters of Ignatius, which was published during the first decades of the second century, and in which a certain Onesimus is mentioned as being the bishop of Ephesus (Ignatius, *Eph.* 1.3ff.). This is the same Onesimus, a reader might conclude, about whom Paul talks in his letter to Philemon, the runaway slave who found grace in the eyes of his master Philemon through the intervention of the apostle Paul. The letter to Philemon, from a publisher's point of view, provided prominent support for this publication.

Paul's seemingly trivial remark at the end of Galatians ("See what large letters I make when I am writing in my own hand," Gal 6:11) tells the readers that the edition is based on autographs. Numerous letters of Paul (Romans, 1 Corinthians, Galatians, Philippians, 2 Thessalonians, Hebrews, Philemon) explicitly contain autographic subscriptions which convey to the reader that the publisher's master copy is based on originals. The end of 2 Thessalonians reads: "I, Paul, write this greeting with my own hand. This is the mark in every letter of mine: this is how I write (*houtōs graphō*)" (2 Thess 3:17). This passage suggests that the publishers based their edition exclusively on Pauline autographs: "This is the mark in *every* letter."

A copy of the Christian Bible came at a price. The title "New Testament," which seems to be transmitted in the manuscripts without significant variants, links the New Testament to the "Old Testament." Both collections were supposed to be read together. They formed one literary unit. The Old Testament presents itself as a Greek version of the Jewish Scriptures, closely related to the Septuagint, but not identical with it. The book of Daniel, for example, was taken from Theodotion's translation, and the introduction of *nomina sacra* clearly distinguishes the Christian Bible

---

Neue Testament, die Apokryphen und die Apostolischen Väter (2nd ed.; Berlin: de Gruyter, 1978), 477, my translation.

from contemporary Jewish Scriptures. The publication of the Old and the New Testaments as a literary venture was an ambitious project with significant production costs.

The New Testament itself conveys to its readers that religious literature does not come without a price. Acts 19:19 describes a revival in Ephesus: "A number of those who practiced magic collected their books and burned them publicly; when the value of these books was calculated, it was found to come to fifty thousand silver coins." In 1912 the German Bible Society published an annotated edition of Luther's German translation to celebrate the Society's one hundredth anniversary. The German editors commented on the passage as follows:

> They were so serious about their new Christian faith that they forwarded their books of magic and burned them, although their worth exceeded 35.000 German Marks. —It would be highly desirable for certain book distributors and modern authors to consider this option and to follow such a noble example.[16]

Bible Societies were aware of the costs involved and the price of Christian Bibles. The Christian Bible faced strong competition. Anyone who was interested in buying a book of the same general genre as the Christian Bible had several alternative publications to choose from. Competing with the "Old Testament" were the Septuagint and the edition of Theodotion of Ephesus mentioned above. Then there was the edition of Aquila, who according to legend was a distant relative of Emperor Hadrian and who became a Christian but then converted to Judaism.[17]

Competing with the New Testament was Marcion's Bible. Marcion, thought to be the son of a Pontic bishop, had moved to Rome sometime in the first half of the second century and had published a collection of Christian writings consisting of one Gospel and ten letters of Paul. From 135 C.E. on Valentinus, a representative of the Christian gnostic movement, lived in Rome. He is reported to have published a so-called *Gospel of Truth*. Sometime around or after 150 C.E., Tatian, a student of Justin, lived in Rome and had made a single Gospel out of the four canonical

---

16. *Stuttgarter Jubiläumsbibel mit erklärenden Anmerkungen* (Stuttgart: Privileg. Württembergische Bibelanstalt, 1912), my translation.

17. Henry Barclay Swete, *An Introduction to the Old Testament in Greek* (rev. R. R. Ottley; New York: Ktav, 1968), 49–50.

Gospels, the so-called *Diatessaron*. This edition became a strong competitor to the New Testament in the Syriac church. A well-informed Roman bookseller probably also kept copies of Papias's five-volume work in stock as well. Papias, bishop of Hierapolis, collected unpublished material on Jesus, because, as he said, "I am convinced, what you know from books is not nearly as helpful as what survived in the living oral tradition to this very day" (Eusebius, *Hist. eccl.* 3.39.4).

If the Old and New Testament had strong competitors during the middle of the second century, what distinguishes the edition of the two testaments from their competition? Whereas the New Testament writings carried the names of early followers of Jesus of Nazareth, the competing editions were published under the name of their editors: "the Seventy," Tatian, Valentinus, Marcion, Aquila, and Theodotion. By the end of the century, Tertullian, one of the first documented readers of the New Testament, sums up these authorial signals as he discusses Marcion's edition:

> So we must pull away at the rope of contention, swaying with equal effort to the one side or the other. I say that mine is true: Marcion makes that claim for his. I say that Marcion's is falsified: Marcion says the same of mine. Who shall decide between us? Only such a reckoning of dates, as will assume that authority belongs to that which is found to be older, and will prejudge as corrupt that which is convicted to having come later.[18]

Because the Christian Bible did not convey the name of its editor or editors, it conveyed to readers like Tertullian that it was older.

4. Contemporary Editions of the Christian Bible

The Christian Bible is probably the most heavily edited work of Western literary culture. There is not one sentence of the New Testament that has exactly the same wording in each of the manuscripts. The editorial problems that had to be solved in the second century were significant. I only touched on a few challenges: using the codex form, introducing the *nomina sacra*, organizing the books into volumes, designing the titles,

---

18. *Marc.* 4.4.1–2; Tertullian, *Adversus Marcionem* (ed. Ernest Evans; Oxford: Clarendon, 1972), 267; cf. 4.5.1; *Praescr.* 21–22; Irenaeus, *Haer.* 3.4.3; R. Joseph Hoffmann, *Marcion: On the Restitution of Christianity: An Essay on the Development of Radical Paulinist Theology in the Second Century* (Chico, Calif.: Scholars Press, 1984), 68.

signaling to the readers that the edition was based on autographs, and featuring authors over editors in order to be successful in the competitive religious market of the time.

A modern edition of the New Testament should reflect the Greek text of the first edition. Much critical work has been done in an attempt to establish the wording of the oldest documented text. In addition, a modern edition should reflect the redactional frame of this carefully designed work. With this goal in mind, I propose several changes.[19]

(1) Modern printed editions should preserve the four literary units of the New Testament: the Four-Gospel-Book, the *Praxapostolos*, the fourteen Letters of Paul and the Revelation of John, by noting them in the table of contents or giving them four separate title sheets. It seems especially important not to separate Acts from the General Letters, and to include the Letter to the Hebrews after 2 Thessalonians, where it is found in the vast majority of manuscripts before the eighth century.

(2) It seems appropriate to start out with the Four-Gospel-Book, followed by the *Praxapostolos* to honour the close connection between Luke and Acts, followed by the Letters of Paul and the Revelation of John with its concluding remarks (Rev 22:18–22). The present arrangement of inserting the Pauline letters between Acts and the Letter of James misrepresents the oldest manuscript tradition.

(3) Nothing could create a better sense for the whole of the Christian Bible than an edition of the Greek Old and New Testament following the same editorial guidelines, containing the same abbreviations, and using the same apparatus design and critical marks.

(4) Furthermore, it should be taken seriously that the Christian Old Testament differs from the Hebrew Bible and the Hellenistic-Jewish Septuagint. Often this difference is not addressed and not adequately reflected in today's academic practice. An obvious difference from the Hebrew Bible is that the Christian Old Testament contains more writings, which are included without negative bias. That the Old Testament is at best an edited version of the Septuagint, and differs from it in significant ways, was pointed out above. It is not my intention to reduce the academic and theological value of the Hebrew Bible for scholarly studies, but it must be acknowledged that the Masoretic edition does not represent the edition

---

19. See Trobisch, *First Edition*, 102–5.

used by early Christians.[20] The objective of scholarly engagement with religious traditions must be to understand and interpret the different editions in the context of the different faith communities and acknowledge the historical fact that the Jewish Scriptures have a twofold *Wirkungsgeschichte*, both Jewish and Christian.[21]

(5) Finally, for more than thirteen centuries, the *nomina sacra* formed a characteristic redactional element of the Christian Bible. I propose that modern editions should preserve this old tradition and represent the *nomina sacra*. They are a significant feature of the first edition of the Christian Bible and do not obstruct the reading process. At least the four generally noted terms: *kyrios*, *theos*, *iēsous*, and *christos* should be reintroduced into printed editions of the Greek text.

---

20. Saul Lieberman, *Hellenism in Jewish Palestine: Studies in the Literary Transmission, Beliefs and Manners of Palestine in the I Century B.C.E.–IV Century C.E.* (Texts and Studies of the Jewish Theological Seminary of America 18; New York: Jewish Theological Seminary, 1950).

21. Rolf Rendtorff, "Zur Bedeutung des Kanons für eine Theologie des Alten Testaments," in *"Wenn nicht jetzt, wann dann?" Aufsätze für Hans-Joachim Kraus zum 65. Geburtstag* (ed. H.-G. Geyer; Neukirchen-Vluyn: Neukirchner, 1983), 11.

Unseen Variants:
Conjectural Emendation and the New Testament

Ryan Wettlaufer

"Our vision is often more obstructed by what we think we know," wrote Krister Stendahl, "than by our lack of knowledge."[1] Textual critics working with the editorial difficulties of the New Testament text need to be reminded of this truth, especially in regard to the much-maligned method of conjectural emendation. Textual criticism is the scholarly art of recreating an earlier form of the text. Conjectural emendation is an advanced method of textual criticism that has been profitably employed for several centuries. Specifically, it is the act of restoring a given text at points where all extant manuscript evidence appears to be corrupt. The method could be classified into three types, depending on what type of corruption is being corrected. If a word or phrase has been omitted from all extant copies of the text, then conjectural emendation consists of adding it back in. Similarly, if a word or phrase has been added to all extant copies of the text, then conjectural emendation omits it. Finally, if a word has not been added or omitted but corrupted into a different word, conjectural emendation would repair it to its original state. An example of the first type could be 2 Pet 3:10, where it has been proposed that the negation οὐχ has been omitted in all extant Greek manuscripts from the phrase καὶ γῆ ... εὑρεθήσεται.[2] An example of the second type is 1 Cor 14:34–35, which many modern translations place in brackets to reflect the popular proposal that these verses are later additions to the text that have managed to secure

---

1. Krister Stendahl, *Paul among the Jews and Gentiles, and Other Essays* (Philadelphia: Fortress, 1976), 7.

2. The reading does survive in the Sahidic. Despite the absence of Greek witnesses, the committee will be including the reading in the next edition of the Nestle-Aland (28th) on the basis of conjectural arguments.

a place in all extant manuscripts.[3] An example of the third type could be Eph 1:11, where it has been proposed that the awkward ἐκληρώθημεν found in all extant manuscripts is actually a corruption of ἐπληρώθημεν. In all three of these operations the common aim of conjectural emendation is to offer a plausible correction at points where corruption appears to have overtaken all extant manuscripts of the New Testament.[4]

In the restoration of classical texts, conjectural emendation has long been assumed as a standard tool. Bruce Metzger himself confirms this when he refers to it as "a process which has so often been found essential in the restoration of the right text in classical authors."[5] This is further attested by many classics scholars. Martin West writes, "but the archetypal reading, reconstructed or extant, may be unsatisfactory. In that case, further conjecture is called for, just as it may be called for if there is complete agreement among the manuscripts."[6] Likewise, E. J. Kenney states that "if the ancient MSS do not provide the answer, recourse must be had to conjecture."[7] These writers merely echo the seminal introductory text of Paul Maas, who writes:

> In each individual case the original text either has or has not been transmitted. So our first task is to establish what *must* or *may* be regarded as transmitted—to make the recension (*recensio*); our next is to examine

---

3. The uncials D F G and some Old Latin manuscripts, while not omitting the text, do move it to the end of the chapter.

4. We should note, however, as was vocally protested by T. D. Barnes at the *Conference on Editorial Problems* at the University of Toronto (Toronto, 1–4 November 2007), that some textual critics, particularly in classical studies, have come to consider the correction of additions to be an exercise distinct and separate from conjectural emendation in general, and refer to this type simply as *interpolations*. While it should be elementary enough that the emending of interpolations is, if based on conjecture, obviously a form of conjectural emendation, it is nevertheless notable that in his seminal text Paul Maas is careful to organize the discussion of interpolations within the section on conjectural emendation. Further, in New Testament studies, the Nestle-Aland apparatus employs the abbreviation "*Cj.*," i.e., "*Conjecit,*" to indicate proposed emendations of all three types discussed here, including interpolations.

5. Bruce Metzger, *The Text of the New Testament* (New York: Oxford University Press, 1992), 185.

6. Martin West, *Textual Criticism and Editorial Technique Applicable to Greek and Latin Texts* (Stuttgart: Teubner, 1973), 53.

7. E. J. Kenney, *The Classical Text* (Berkeley: University of California Press, 1974), 35.

this tradition and discover whether it may be considered as giving the original (*examinatio*); if it proves not to give the original, we must try to reconstruct the original by conjecture (*divinatio*) or at least to isolate the corruption.[8]

Of course, even within classical text-critical studies there has been some question as to the place and propriety of conjectural emendation, but as West indicates these concerns have been easily laid to rest:

> In what circumstances is it legitimate to depart from the paradosis [the extant manuscripts], to entertain a conjecture? Many scholars would answer "only when it is clear that the paradosis cannot be right." Those are scholars who will dismiss a conjecture from consideration on the ground that it is "unnecessary." But it does not have to be "necessary" in order to be true; and what we should be concerned with is whether or nor [sic] it may be true.[9]

In the end, then, classical text criticism has had little problem seeing the value and virtue of conjectural emendation. As Maas neatly summarizes: "If the tradition proves to be corrupt, we must attempt to remedy it by conjecture (*divinatio*).... The typical conjecture consists in the removal of an anomaly."[10]

This practice can easily be demonstrated through even a cursory examination of the critical editions of classical texts. In his edition of Josephus for the Loeb Classical Library, for example, Henry St. John Thackeray comments on the text, "Each variant has to be considered on its merits; and there is considerable scope for conjectural emendation, on which many eminent scholars have exercised their ingenuity."[11] Similarly, in his Loeb edition of Clement of Alexandria, George William Butterworth feels free to mention without justification that "the text printed here is substantially that of [a previous] edition, though I have occasionally preferred the conjectures of other scholars."[12] In his enduring edition of the troublesome text of Euripides's *Bacchae*, it is interesting to note that E. R. Dodds evi-

---

8. Paul Maas, *Textual Criticism* (Oxford: Clarendon, 1958), 1.

9. West, *Textual Criticism*, 55.

10. Maas, *Textual Criticism*, 11.

11. Henry St. John Thackeray, *Josephus* (LCL), xviii.

12. George William Butterworth, *Clement of Alexandria* (LCL), xix.

dently assumed that the text-critical discussion would proceed on conjectural grounds, that is, without the benefit of "new evidence":

> In the field of language and textual criticism a twentieth-century editor is unlikely to better very substantially the work of Elmsely and Hermann, Paley and Sandys and Wecklein, except where he is lucky enough to be armed with new evidence: the solid scholars of the last century stated all the major linguistic and textual problems of the play, and brought most of them as near to a solution as they are likely to be brought in the absence of such evidence.[13]

Clearly textual critics of classical texts have long seen the value of conjectural emendation.

In times past, New Testament textual critics also recognized that value. As Jan Krans describes it, at one time conjectural emendation was simply one of the ways by which a text could be corrected:

> "Emendation" was not necessarily "conjectural," but simply meant the correction of ... the *editio princeps*. Critics emended, improved a previous edition with respect to details.... Emendation, the adoption of alternative readings, was done in two distinct ways, depending on the way these readings were found: they could either be derived from manuscripts or be arrived at through rational argument. Hence a distinction was made between *emendatio codicum ope* ("emendation by means of manuscripts") and *emendatio ingenii ope* ("emendation by means of reasoning").[14]

Not surprisingly, then, past New Testament scholars frequently made use of the method in their efforts to recover the text. As Krans further notes, "Throughout the centuries critics have made conjectures on the Greek text of the New Testament.... The total number of conjectures probably comes to several thousands."[15] Editors such as Erasmus and Bezae included many such conjectures in their published New Testaments,[16] while critics like William Bowyer published dedicated collections of conjectures.[17] Early

---

13. E. R. Dodds, *Euripedes Bacchae* (Oxford: Clarendon, 1960), v.

14. Jan Krans, *Beyond What Is Written: Erasmus and Beza as Conjectural Critics of the New Testament* (Leiden: Brill, 2006), 4.

15. Ibid., 2.

16. Krans's study is focused, in fact, entirely on the conjectures of these two editors.

17. William Bowyer, *Conjectures on the New Testament* (London: Nichols, 1782).

editions of the Nestle-Aland text still included several hundred conjectures.[18] If one thing could be said to have been conclusive then, it was that the technique of conjectural emendation was certainly no modern novelty or baseless amusement, but rather a method firmly rooted in history, proven in pedigree, and affirmed by the broader field of textual criticism.

It is all the more startling, then, that the vision of contemporary New Testament textual critics seems to be obstructed in this regard. Metzger dismissively writes, "Although several scholars during the eighteenth and nineteen [*sic*] centuries amused themselves in proposing thousands of conjectural emendations for various passages of the New Testament … the tendency in recent days has been to exercise much more caution in proposing or adopting such corrections."[19] Harold Greenlee echoes even more dimly:

> If examination of the available mss. fails to indicate satisfactorily the original text of a certain word or phrase, a scholar may resort to an "educated guess" known as conjectural emendation.... This tends to become what Kenyon has called "a process precarious in the extreme, and seldom allowing anyone but the guesser to feel confidence in the truth of its results."[20]

Finally, J. Keith Elliott explains:

> [There is] no need to resort to conjectural emendation, which often turns out to be a mere imaginative rewriting of the New Testament. Conjectural emendation of the New Testament was practiced in earlier periods, but few of these conjectures or guesses met with widespread scholarly acceptance. A decreasing number of some famous conjectures are still allowed to clutter unnecessarily the apparatus of the NA editions.[21]

---

18. The exact number depends how one counts, but at least 200. See Erroll F. Rhodes, "Conjectural Emendations in Modern Translations," in *New Testament Textual Criticism* (ed. E. J. Epp and G. D. Fee; Clarendon: Oxford, 1981), 361–74. It is interesting that the latest Nestle-Aland (27th) has reduced that number to 127. See also Bruce Metzger and Bart Ehrman, *The Text of the New Testament* (4th ed.; New York: Oxford University Press, 2005), 230.

19. Metzger, *Text of the New Testament* (1992), 287.

20. J. Harold Greenlee, *Introduction to New Testament Textual Criticism* (Grand Rapids: Eerdmans, 1964), 15.

21. J. Keith Elliott, "The Case for Thorough-Going Eclecticism," in *Rethinking New Testament Textual Criticism* (ed. D. A. Black; Grand Rapids: Baker, 2002), 120.

Unfortunately, these attitudes are not isolated but representative of a common reluctance among New Testament critics. Standard texts like the Alands' advise that "textual difficulties should not be solved by conjecture.... Such attempts amount to capitulation before the difficulties and are themselves violations of the text."[22] In general practice, while Elliott is correct that some conjectures still "clutter" the apparatus of the latest Nestle-Aland New Testament, it is noteworthy that none have made it into the body of the text.[23] More significantly, the conjectures that remain have been almost entirely ignored by modern English translations.[24]

Why have New Testament scholars so departed from the norm with such a rejection? What do they think they know that is blocking their vision? The answer is at least threefold: some misunderstand the nature of conjectural emendation in relation to the extant manuscript base; some misunderstand how faith should be allowed to influence textual criticism; and some misunderstand the purpose and goals of textual criticism.

The first is a common misunderstanding of how conjectural emendation works and how it relates to the extant manuscript base. Leading New Testament scholars can often be found arguing that the staggering size of the extant manuscript base somehow ensures that the correct reading has survived somewhere, thereby eliminating the need for conjectural emendation. Metzger, for example, writes that the need for conjectural emendation is "reduced to the smallest dimensions," because *the amount of evidence for the text of the New Testament*, whether derived from manuscripts, early versions, or patristic quotations, *is so much greater* than that available for any ancient classical author."[25] Likewise J. Harold Greenlee concludes, *"When a large number of mss. are available,* as in the case of the New Testament, conjecture is less often, if ever, necessary."[26] Finally, George D. Kilpatrick argues, "We may assume as a rule of thumb that at each point the true text has survived somewhere or other among our

---

22. Kurt Aland and Barbara Aland, *The Text of the New Testament* (trans. E. F. Rhodes; 2nd ed.; Grand Rapids: Eerdmans; Leiden: Brill, 1989), 280.

23. However, see n. 2 above regarding the pending 28th edition of the Nestle-Aland.

24. Rhodes, "Conjectural Emendations," 361–74. Rhodes finds one conjecture, that of Crell in Acts 16:12, which appears to have been adopted by some modern translations.

25. Metzger, *Text of the New Testament*, 185, emphasis added.

26. Greenlee, *Introduction*, 15, emphasis added.

manuscripts."[27] That such examples can be found in such a diverse body of respected scholars leads to the unfortunate implication that this misunderstanding is widespread in New Testament scholarship.

What can be said of this? Is conjectural emendation unnecessary because the correct reading has necessarily survived somewhere in such a glorious glut of manuscripts? It is true that modern text criticism is blessed with a vast wealth of manuscripts—some 5,700 of them dating from the second to fifteenth century. Numbers alone, however, are not enough to carry the argument: the history and nature of those manuscripts must be taken into account. As Westcott and Hort wrote, "all trustworthy restoration of corrupted texts is founded upon the study of their history, that is, of the relations of descent or affinity which connect several documents."[28] The history of the modern manuscript base begins bleakly in the second century when the text of the New Testament was at the mercy of a largely poor and lower class church that was therefore mostly bereft of professional scribes. Consequently it was this earliest period that was especially prone to corruption. Bart Ehrman writes, "Because the early Christian texts were not being copied by professional scribes, at least in the first two or three centuries of the church, but simply by educated members of the Christian congregations who could do the job and were willing to do so, we can expect that in the earliest copies, especially, mistakes were commonly made in transcription."[29] Unfortunately it is from this troublesome period that the least amount of manuscript evidence has survived. Precious few of the earliest papyri date from the period, and none of those contain any substantial amount of text or significant evidence of a continuous text-type. In other words, the best modern evidence dates almost exclusively from the time *after* the earliest period of significant corruption.[30] Léon

---

27. George D. Kilpatrick, "Conjectural Emendation in the New Testament," in *The Principles and Practice of New Testament Textual Criticism* (ed. J. K. Elliott; Leuven: Leuven University Press, 1990), 98.

28. Brooke Foss Westcott and Fenton John Anthony Hort, *Introduction to the New Testament in the Original Greek* (Eugene, Ore.: Wipf & Stock, 2003), 40.

29. Bart Ehrman, *Misquoting Jesus* (New York: Harper Collins, 2005), 51.

30. Some would give a more positive appraisal, of course, of the ability of the papyri to establish a New Testament text in the second century (see, e.g., summaries in Eldon Jay Epp, "The New Testament Papyrus Manuscripts in Historical Perspective," in *To Touch the Text: Biblical and Related Studies in Honor of Joseph A. Fitzmyer, S.J.* [ed. M. P. Horgan and P. J. Kobelski; New York: Crossroad, 1989], 261–88). Even if this is true, however, it would still be questionable whether the text they establish

Vaganay less dramatically concludes, "It must be borne in mind that in the very early period, in the second century for example, when the form of the text is not easy to determine, corruptions of the text were possible."[31] This surely qualifies as what Westcott and Hort called "an interval" which "divide[s] the autograph from the earliest point or points to which genealogy conducts us back," and consequently their conclusion is all the more accurate that "any interval implies the possibility of corruption, while every addition to the length of the interval increases the probability of corruption."[32] These earliest corruptions would necessarily be, of course, entirely outside of the modern manuscript database.

Thus the history of the manuscript tradition shows why the size of the extant base cannot be any guarantee of accuracy. The base may include many manuscripts but, as is universally agreed, it does not include the originals nor more than a fraction of all the copies that were ever made from the originals. Vast numbers of New Testament manuscripts have been eternally lost—especially from that earliest period—and since the transmission and survival of those that were not lost was completely random, modern scholarship simply has no way of knowing how accurately the body of extant manuscripts represent the whole. It is, as Kurt Aland admits:

> Like a child, who, having picked up stones or shells on the shore and brought them home, then seeks to determine from the collected specimens the kinds of stones or shells which can be found on that particular shore. This child might have had the good fortune to collect specimens of all the important kinds of stones or shells to be found on that shore, so that a thorough examination of this shore would merely add few and unimportant new kinds to those already known. It may be that, in NT

---

is more or less a correct text, deserving of acceptance. As Stanley Porter notes, that answer seems to be in the negative: "Even the more radically revised Nestle-Aland[26] (identical to the 27th edition) is only changed in 176 places, rejecting 980 possible places where the earliest papyri have another reading, including a number from 𝔓45, 𝔓46 and 𝔓66" (Stanley E. Porter, "Textual Criticism in the Light of Diverse Textual Evidence for the Greek New Testament: An Expanded Proposal," in *New Testament Manuscripts* [ed. T. J. Kraus and T. Nicklas; Leiden: Brill, 2006], 309–10).

31. Léon Vaganay, *An Introduction to New Testament Textual Criticism* (Cambridge: Cambridge University Press, 1991), 85.

32. Wescott and Hort, *New Testament*, 66.

textual research, we are in a position similar to that of this child. But who knows it with certainty and who can really take it for granted?[33]

To continue Aland's analogy, while it would be tempting to think that the more stones you gathered the better chance you had of accumulating a full cross-sampling of that shore, this is actually where the analogy breaks down. For the geological processes that deposit stones on a shore are actually more predictable than the happenstance and human error that sometimes dropped readings or whole manuscripts from the tradition of transmission. It was precisely to fight the temptation to equate numbers with accuracy that the discipline of textual criticism fought to secure its most hard-won principle: that manuscripts must be *weighed* not *counted*. In other words, the number of manuscripts that have survived does not count for much if the correct reading has not managed to survive among them. As Westcott and Hort noted, that is often a strong possibility: "Are there as a matter of fact places in which we are constrained by overwhelming evidence to recognise the existence of textual error in all extant documents? To this question we have no hesitation in replying in the affirmative."[34] For this reason the method of conjectural emendation seeks to look beyond the extant manuscript base and recover those readings which began with the original text but did not survive in any preserved manuscript: victims of total corruption of the manuscript base.

Points of complete textual corruption—or, as Westcott and Hort called them, "primitive errors"—can usually be identified on either transcriptional or intrinsic grounds. Transcriptional grounds refers to the inability of any of the extant readings at a given variation point to account satisfactorily for the rise of the others. Conjectural emendation at such points would consist of offering a new reading that both makes better sense of the text and better explains the origin of the other readings. "Intrinsic grounds" refers to points where the text is simply too divergent from either the contextual sense of the text or the author's style to be considered authentic. While such points may be found at existing variant units, logic dictates that they could also be found just as feasibly where there is no extant variation. That is, if the preserved text is truly unsatisfactory on

---

33. Kurt Aland, "The Significance of the Papyri for Progress in New Testament Research," in *The Bible in Modern Scholarship* (ed. J. P. Hyatt; New York: Abingdon, 1965), 330.

34. Westcott and Hort, *New Testament*, 279.

intrinsic grounds, then the lack of variation in extant manuscripts is no necessary obstacle to proposing a conjectural emendation. This is because inherent in the premise that the correct text has not survived in any extant manuscripts is the implication that the correct text has been supplanted in the extant manuscript base by an incorrect text, and if the correct text has been supplanted, then there is no reason that it could not have been completely supplanted so that no trace or variation of the conflict remains. In other words, a particular reading's dominance of the extant manuscript base does not necessarily imply its originality, even if that dominance is complete. As West writes, "Sometimes one sees a conjecture dismissed simply on the ground that all the manuscripts agree in a different reading. As if they could not agree in a false reading, and as if it were not in the very nature of a conjecture that it departs from them!"[35] Conjectural emendation, then, is unaffected by the size of the manuscript base for the simple reason that by its nature it looks outside of that base to find readings that have long been lost to it. It is this nature that seems to be misunderstood by many New Testament textual critics and keeps them from seeing the full value of conjectural emendation.

A second cause for the widespread rejection of conjectural emendation by New Testament critics is the residual influence of particular faith positions. The premise of conjectural emendation is that the correct reading has been entirely lost from the manuscript tradition, that the text is completely corrupt at that point. This is a supposition, however, that does not always sit comfortably with some theological doctrines of revelation, which often assume that God—having a vested interest in his own words, after all—would have exerted more of a protective influence over the sacred Scriptures. Other theologians have simply been overly hesitant to make changes with the divine text justified only by their own conjecture. Theodore Beza, no stranger to emendations himself,[36] nevertheless declared, "To me it has always been a matter of utmost scrupulousness not to change even a tittle in these holy books out of mere conjecture."[37]

A modern manifestation of this thinking can be found—albeit in an extreme form—in the King James Only movement. Its proponents not only believe that God took special steps to ensure the survival of the correct text, but also believe that the text so protected can be identified with

---

35. West, *Textual Criticism*, 59.

36. Krans, *Beyond What Is Written*, 195ff.

37. *Apud* Krans, *Beyond What Is Written*, 193.

the Elzevir's Textus Receptus, which underlies the King James Bible. One promoter has written at length:

> It would have been passing strange if God had guided His people in regard to the New Testament canon but had withheld from them His divine assistance in the matter of the New Testament text. This would mean that Bible believing Christians today could have no certainty concerning the New Testament text but would be obliged to rely on the hypotheses of modern, naturalistic critics. But God in His mercy did not leave His people to grope after the True New Testament Text. Through the leading of the Holy Spirit He guided them to preserve it during the manuscript period.... It is upon this *Textus Receptus* that the King James Version and the other classic Protestant translations are based.[38]

While this style of thinking appears to be confined to the remote extremes of conservative Christianity, its advocates are vocal enough that some scholars have felt compelled to issue treatments, such as D. A. Carson, who published *The King James Version Debate: A Plea for Realism*.[39]

Moderate theologies can also struggle with the basic tension between a text that is divinely inspired and a text that is entirely corrupt and in need of emendation. It is easy to assume that even if he left it to be retrieved by the human efforts of text criticism, at least God used *some* divine power to ensure that the true reading survived *somewhere* in the extant manuscripts. For example, describing his own development at Princeton Theological Seminary, Ehrman writes:

> This became a problem for my view of inspiration, for I came to realize that it would have been no more difficult for God to preserve the words of scripture than it would have been for him to inspire them in the first place. If he wanted his people to have his words, surely he would have given them to them (and possibly even given them the words in a language they could understand, rather than Greek and Hebrew). The fact that we don't have the words surely must show, I reasoned, that he did not preserve them for us. And if he didn't perform that miracle, there seemed to be no reason to think that he performed the earlier miracle of inspiring those words.[40]

---

38. Edward F. Hills, *The King James Version Defended!* (Des Moines, Iowa: Christian Research Press, 1973), 124.

39. D. A. Carson, *The King James Version Debate* (Grand Rapids: Baker, 1978).

40. Ehrman, *Misquoting Jesus*, 11.

Some scholars have dealt with these questions directly, such as Kilpatrick, who asked, "If 'some special Providence' has watched over the text of the NT to ensure that at every point the original form of our text has survived among some or the other witnesses ... we might wonder why this Providence has not exerted itself a little further to ensure that at each point of variation the original reading would be manifest and immediately demonstrable."[41] On the whole, however, surely such theological questions are best left for the theologians. Suffice it to say, with approximately 300,000 different variants[42] in the approximately 5,700 extant manuscripts, the evidence does not immediately suggest any special providential protection of the New Testament text.

A third cause for the abandonment of conjectural emendation by New Testament critics is a misunderstanding of the purpose of textual criticism and confusion regarding its goals. As Epp narrates, in times past many scholars simply assumed that the task of textual criticism was to recover the original text of the New Testament.[43] Indeed, when Westcott and Hort published their seminal edition in 1881, its title was the humble yet telling *The New Testament in the Original Greek*. In recent years, however, New Testament critics have begun to join their Hebrew Bible colleagues[44] in questioning the ideal of an original text as a valid goal for textual criticism.

This emerging trend, which David Parker has called "narrative textual criticism"[45] really began at least as early as 1904, when Kirsopp Lake connected the corruption of the text with the social and theological history of the church: "We need to know ... what the early Church thought

---

41. Kilpatrick, "Conjectural Emendation," 99.

42. Eldon Jay Epp, "Textual Criticism (NT)," *ABD* 6:415.

43. Eldon Jay Epp, "The Multivalence of the Term 'Original Text' in New Testament Textual Criticism," *HTR* 92 (1999): 248–54.

44. As Epp notes, Hebrew Bible scholars carried this line of thought much farther and much earlier than New Testament critics. This was likely by force of necessity, given the comparative size, antiquity, and conflated complexity of both the Hebrew Bible text and extant manuscript base. For discussion, see Emanuel Tov, *Textual Criticism of the Hebrew Bible* (Minneapolis: Fortress, 1992). Also note a recent presentation of this perspective in John Van Seters, *The Edited Bible: The Curious History of the "Editor" in Biblical Criticism* (Winona Lake, Ind.: Eisenbrauns, 2006).

45. David C. Parker, review of Bart Ehrman, *Orthodox Corruption of Scripture*, *JTS* 45 (1994): 704. Cited in Eldon Jay Epp, "The Oxyrhynchus New Testament Papyri: 'Not Without Honor Except in Their Hometown'?" *JBL* 123:1 (Spr., 2004): 9.

[a passage] meant and how it altered its wording in order to emphasize its meaning."[46] Ten years later J. Rendel Harris argued along similar lines when, in homage to Westcott and Hort, he offered the dictum that "knowledge ... of church history should precede final judgement as to readings."[47] It was not until 1993, however, that the idea of treating textual variants not as obstacles to the singular goal of restoring the original text but as windows into theological history began to get traction after the publication of Ehrman's *The Orthodox Corruption of Scripture*.[48] Shortly after this Parker published *The Living Text of the Gospels*, taking this idea to the next level.[49] Essentially he argued that using the variants of a text to reconstruct the history of those who copied that text is not only a possible goal for text criticism, but is in fact the best goal. Recovering the original text is, at least in some cases, a fruitless endeavor given the arguably equal strength (or perhaps equal weakness) of the variant options. Thus rather than seeking a single and static *original text*, textual critics are encouraged to seek the eponymous *living text*, which ebbed and flowed with the rise and fall of the early Christians whose text it was.

In his 2003 presidential address to the Society of Biblical literature, Epp gave his endorsement to the new narrative approach.[50] His own contribution, however, came four years earlier in the provocative article "The Multivalence of the Term 'Original Text' in New Testament Textual Criticism."[51] In that more philosophical discussion, Epp outlined some of the conceptual obstacles even to defining the "original text," let alone recovering it. First there are questions of preceding text forms. In composite documents like the synoptic Gospels, for example, which form of a given pericope counts as original? The version that was taken up by the first Gospel author, the version as it was redacted by a second Gospel author, or perhaps one of the versions that circulated prior to being used by any Gospel author? A second set of obstacles stem from what is tra-

---

46. *Apud* Eldon Jay Epp, "Issues in New Testament Textual Criticism," in *Rethinking New Testament Criticism* (ed. D. A. Black; Grand Rapids: Baker, 2002), 52. I am indebted to Epp's summary for much of the chronology of this section.

47. Epp, "Issues in New Testament Textual Criticism," 53.

48. Bart Ehrman, *The Orthodox Corruption of Scripture* (New York: Oxford, 1993).

49. David C. Parker, *The Living Text of the Gospels* (Cambridge: University of Cambridge, 1997).

50. Published as Epp, "Oxyrhynchus New Testament Papyri," 5–55.

51. Epp, "Multivalence of the Term," 245–81.

ditionally known as the autograph stage: the text as it existed during the composition process. Here too the definition of "original text" can be difficult to pinpoint. If the author dictated to an amanuensis, for example, what constitutes the original: the oral dictation, or whatever was written by the amanuensis? Or, if multiple copies were made so that the composition could be a circular letter, which one is the original? The first copy? The second? Finally, if the author or the amanuensis made a mistake in the composition, which is the original: the text that the author composed, or the nonexistent text that the author intended to compose? A third set of complexities is introduced by the question of canon: Is the original text that which the author wrote, or is it that which the church later ruled as canon? Should, for example, the *pericope adulterae* be accepted into the original text of John? A final group of obstacles comes from the interpretive life of the text, the text as it was read, used, and rewritten by a living church for their worship and theology. Corresponding with Parker's living text, this perspective asks why an initial form of a text should be given priority over a later form that was more meaningful to the people who used it. Cumulatively, these questions preclude for Epp any continued usage of a singular concept such as the traditional original text. He concludes that text criticism must "shed whatever remains of its innocence" by giving up the "myopic quest for a single original text."[52]

This nascent shift in the commonly accepted task of textual criticism carries necessary implications for the practice of conjectural emendation. When textual criticism had the straightforward goal of recovering a single original text, conjectural emendation was simply one way to attain that goal, one tool for removing the errors that had crept into that text. If that goal, however, is shown to be a chimera, then the rationale for conjectural emendation quickly becomes clouded in confusion. To what end would a scholar employ such a tool? What text would they be trying to emend? In a discipline like narrative textual criticism, where the task is to look forward to see how the church changed the text through their use of it, there appears to be little need for a technique that looks back to a text prior to the church's corruption of it. The popularity of conjectural emendation, therefore, seems unlikely to rise with the spread of this trend.

Krans, an accomplished student of conjectural emendation, has already begun to formulate an interesting response to this newest chal-

---

52. Ibid., 280.

lenge. In what we can perhaps call "narrative conjectural emendation," he suggests that historical conjectures can be studied and used as windows into the historical and theological history of the church in the same way that traditional manuscript variants can. In a detailed study of the conjectures of Desiderius Erasmus and Theodore Beza that does just that, he describes his approach:

> With the method adopted here, the present study takes part in the current paradigm shift in New Testament Textual Criticism. Manuscripts are no longer seen as mere sources for variant readings, but also as historical products that deserve to be studied as wholes. Moreover, variant readings as such no longer function as stepping stones towards the "original" text, to be disposed of once this (chimeric) goal has been attained, but they acquire historical importance as mirrors of scribal convictions and conventions. In line with this new paradigm, it is asked here whether a critic's conjectural emendations mirror particular ideas of the text, its interpretability and its status.[53]

Krans's proposal is both interesting and compelling, and he is surely correct that the essential act of conjectural emendation is not drastically dissimilar from that of the many scribes in centuries past who also sought to fix the text. In this way the conjectures of the modern academy really do become the textual variants of the Gutenberg age. The shortcoming of his response, however, is that while it successfully preserves a place in the new narrative paradigm for the *study* of conjectural emendation, it does little for the actual *practice* of it.

Is there anything then that can be said to this new perspective that does establish a basis for the practice of conjectural emendation? Ehrman has written that the latest developments "may be going too far,"[54] but how far should they go? Surely Epp is right to point out the concept of the original text is more vague and complex than traditionally assumed, and Parker and others are definitely correct to see value in the narrative history of textual variants. It goes too far, however, to suggest that the quest for an original text should be discarded completely, or that narrative textual criticism is the only viable future for the field. Whether it is fully recoverable or not, there will necessarily always be an original text, at least in the

---

53. Krans, *Beyond What Is Written*, 3.
54. Ehrman, *Misquoting Jesus*, 210.

strict sense of *origin*. Every text, though it may have been changed and developed into many subsequent text forms, had to begin somewhere, and as textual critics excavate through those layers they cannot help but move closer to that point of origin. As Ehrman writes:

> I do not mean to deny that there are difficulties that may be insurmountable in reconstructing the originals.... Even so—despite the imponderable difficulties—we do have manuscripts of every book of the New Testament; all of these manuscripts were copied from other, earlier manuscripts, which were themselves copied from earlier manuscripts, and the chain of transmission has to end *somewhere*, ultimately at a manuscript produced either by an author or by a secretarial scribe who was producing the "autograph"—the first in a long line of manuscripts that were copied for nearly fifteen centuries until the invention of printing. So at least it is not "non"-sense to talk about an original text.[55]

There is, therefore, a point of textual origin and a line of text forms descending from it. Using traditional methods to trace that descent and recover any earlier text form is thus a valid goal for textual criticism. If at any stage of that task a corruption can be identified through either reasoned argument or manuscript variation, then conjectural emendation can be used as a valid means of reverting that change. While it may be difficult to define which text form deserves the mantle "original," or even to identify which layer has been recovered, the resultant emended text will necessarily be an earlier form of it. The value or authority of that text form will necessarily be dependent on the purpose and perspective of the reader—whether, for example, they are motivated by religious doctrines of canon or a historical interest in the text form of, say, the fifth century. For those interested in narrative textual criticism, however, logic demands this task as a necessary prerequisite. Without first tracing the descent from some principal text form, the narrative paradigm collapses into hopeless circularity. It is simply impossible to investigate what the text was changed *to* without first establishing what it was changed *from*. Or in other words, we cannot discuss the theological or social significance of the new version of the text until we know how it differs from the old version. Thus, far from outgrowing the quest for the original text, the new text criticism depends on it more than ever, and inherent in that

---

55. Ibid., 200.

dependence is, as we have seen above, the inevitable need for the critical practice of conjectural emendation.

Now that we have surveyed three of the major reasons why New Testament textual critics reject conjectural emendation as a tool for editing the Bible, is there a good, solid example that demonstrates why they should instead accept it? Most discussions of conjectural emendation seem to focus on finding that one incontrovertible example that will compel universal assent. In fact, as Georg Luck has noted,[56] many critics of the method depend on this strategy, assuming that if they can refute that one supreme example, then they will have dismissed the entire method. This phenomenon can be seen, for example, in the general response to what was probably the most persuasive and impassioned advocacy for conjectural emendation so far, the 1974 article by John Strugnell, "A Plea For Conjectural Emendation in the New Testament."[57] In that paper, Strugnell surveyed both the historical attitudes about conjectural emendation and the theoretical foundations for it, and then concluded with a detailed proposal for a conjecture in 1 Cor 4:6. This final example was intended to settle the argument and secure the status of conjectural emendation as a valid critical technique, but instead it was this example which garnered Strugnell the most criticism and allowed many to discount much of the preceding work. Kilpatrick concluded his critique by saying, "This note of dissent having been sounded, we must acknowledge our indebtedness to Professor Strugnell's paper.... All he has to do now is to come up with some conjectures that we cannot gainsay."[58] So will this paper now offer that one incontestable example? Not even close! Instead, having discussed how modern scholarship misunderstands conjectural emendation, this paper will now offer an example of how that misunderstanding is affecting and undermining text-critical studies. As a conjecture, this example might not be ultimately compelling, but as a demonstration of the detriments of this misunderstanding, it is startling.

---

56. Georg Luck, "Conjectural Emendation in the Greek New Testament" (paper presented at the Conference on Greek Textual Criticism, Cáceres, Spain, June 2007), 3–4.

57. John Strugnell, "A Plea for Conjectural Emendation in the New Testament," *CBQ* 36 (1974): 543–58.

58. Kilpatrick, "Conjectural Emendation," 109.

At the turn of the last century, Louis Massebieau[59] and Friedrich Spitta,[60] though working independently,[61] both arrived at the same conclusion: that an earlier version of James existed as a Jewish composition, a collection of standard Jewish ethical instructions. Since early Christianity differed from Judaism primarily in orthodoxy rather than orthopraxy,[62] they reasoned, it was relatively easy for later Jewish Christians to adapt and edit the epistle, producing the edition we know today for Christian use. Their argument can be summarized in two steps: first, it proposes that on the basis of conjecture the text be emended at 1:1 and 2:1 to omit, as later interpolations, the lone pair of explicit references to Christ;[63] second, it notes that without those references the text is devoid of anything necessarily Christian and is in fact most naturally read as a Jewish work. Massebieau summarized, "One would search the epistle in vain for the least mention of the acts of the redemption drama: the incarnation of the Son of God, his expiatory sacrifice, his resurrection, his glorious advent."[64] The implications of this proposal would be manifold and multiple. For text critics it would provide an earlier form of the text. For New Testament interpreters it would give a more accurate context for many of James's instructions and sayings. For students of Christian origins it would paint

---

59. Louis Massebieau, "L'épître de Jacques est-elle l'œuvre d'un chrétien?" *RHR* 32 (1895): 249–83.

60. Friedrich Spitta, *Der Brief des Jakobus untersucht* (Göttingen: Vandenhoeck & Ruprecht, 1896).

61. Though it is Spitta who seems to earn the most mention in modern commentaries, it should be noted that Massebieau beat him to press by one year.

62. Indeed, Martin Dibelius writes that early Christianity looked to Judaism for its orthopraxy: "However, the ethical directives of Jesus—the only materials of their own with which the Christians could supply the need—by no means covered all the areas of life and culture for which decisions had to be made. Quite understandably the Christian churches availed themselves of the praxis of Diaspora Judaism, in this matter as in others. In its missionary activities, Judaism in the Diaspora had produced just what the young churches were lacking: ethical directives for new converts" (Martin Dibelius, *James* [Hermeneia; Philadelphia: Fortress, 1976], 3–4).

63. This conjecture is, in fact, not without textual support. Many commentators concede that the grammatical clumsiness of the extant version would be eliminated by the conjecture (e.g., Dibelius), and variants on 2:1 in the modern manuscript tradition demonstrate that the text has long been the cause of textual consternation.

64. "Or c'est vainement qu'on chercherait dans l'epitre la moindre mention d'un des actes du drame de la Redemption: incarnation du Fils de Dieu, son sacrifice expiatoire, sa resurrection, son glorieux avenement" (Massebieau, "L'épître," 253).

a picture of earliest Christianity as a big tent religion, more flexible and willing to adapt or assimilate than perhaps previously thought, or it might shed more light on early Jewish-Christian relations. For scholars of early Judaism it would give a welcome addition to the meager library from this period. Thus, while it is a provocative proposal, the potential benefits seem more than sufficient to warrant a thorough investigation.

A brief review of the evidence shows that the proposal is not immediately implausible. First, it concerns the Epistle of James which, of all the New Testament texts, probably bears the most potential for sound conjectural emendation. As is well documented,[65] James was initially not accepted in the western church, and the consequent obscurity meant that it was less copied and less preserved than other New Testament texts. In the modern manuscript database, genealogy conducts us only as far back as the fourth century texts of Vaticanus and Sinaiticus. There are two third-century papyri—P20 and P23—but these are both extremely lacunary.[66] In other words, for at least the first two centuries of the epistle's life—when untrained lay scribes were introducing some of the harshest corruptions—we have no direct textual evidence. Given this gap, it would not be irresponsible to assume that almost any reasonable conjecture of James could deserve serious study.

Second, exclusively Christian elements are scarce. Without the explicit Christ references of 1:1 and 2:1, there is very little that would immediately suggest a Christian provenance. As Luke Timothy Johnson admits, the epistle's "explicitly messianic character is more muted than any other canonical writing.... James makes no obvious use of any of the narrative traditions concerning Jesus. Most notably, he makes no mention of the death of Jesus."[67] Only a few potentially Christian references can be cobbled together. In 1:21 we find a reference to "the word implanted that is able to save your souls," which sounds like a clause that got lost on its way to John's Gospel. In 2:5 we find an apparently misplaced excerpt from the Sermon on the Mount wherein "the poor of this world" are called "heirs to the kingdom." In 2:7 there are echoes of Paul in the instruction to "not blaspheme the fair name by which you have been called," while in 4:15 the

---

65. See, for example, discussions in Peter Davids, *James* (NIGTC; Grand Rapids: Eerdmans, 1982), 59–61; and Dibelius, *James*, 57–61.

66. P20 contains 2:19–3:2 and 3:4–9, while P23 contains 1:10–12, 15–18.

67. Luke Timothy Johnson, *The Letter of James* (AB 37A; Garden City, N.Y.: Doubleday, 1995), 49.

text refers to the Lord's will in a way that Peter Davids thinks indicates a distinctively Christian theology.[68] There is a possible allusion to the saying of Jesus recorded in Matt 5:34 in James 5:12's "do not swear ... with any other oath, but let your yes be yes and your no, no," and in 5:14 the reader is instructed to call "the elders of the *church*," using the popular Christian term for the gathering of the faithful. Obviously many of these elements deserve a much fuller discussion, and after a thorough examination several might prove to be authentic Christian references. For the time being, however, the timidity of their testimony supports Massebieau and Spitta more than not.

Third, there appear to be many elements in James that would most naturally be read as expressions of Jewish faith. In 1:25 the person who intently studies "the perfect law" is commended—and as if that appraisal is not sufficiently positive, the next clause calls it "the law of liberty." In 2:2 a standard English translation talks about the person who "comes into your *assembly*," thereby obscuring the fact that the Greek text uses the much more recognizably Jewish term *synagōgē*. Furthermore, it is not just any *synagōgē*, but *your synagōgē*; the synagogue of the epistle's recipients. Similarly, in 2:21 the author makes a point of adding that Abraham was not just anyone's father, but "*our* father." A creedal reference to the Jewish *Shema* of Deut 6:4 is clearly found in 2:19, while an allusion to ritual washing is probably hiding in 4:8's "cleanse your hands, you sinners." Another curiously unchristian estimation of the law comes in 4:11, which commands readers not to judge or dismiss the law, but just to do it, while in 5:10 it is most interesting that when the author needs an ultimate example of pious suffering he looks not to the passion of the Christ but to the persecution of the prophets. Finally, while the phrase "in the name of the Lord," gives a Christian flavor to the instructions to "anoint the sick with oil" in 5:14, it is notable that the clause is in doubt, being absent from Codex Vaticanus. While individually many of these examples could be explained away and claimed as Christian—Matthew likewise, for example, has some high appraisals of the law,[69] and Paul also alludes to the Shema—what needs to be asked here is whether that is the most natural way to read the text as a whole, or if anyone would think to read the text that way if it had not been found in the New Testament?

---

68. Davids, *James*, 173.
69. Matt 5:17–20.

All this is *not* to say that Massebieau and Spitta were correct, but only that their proposal was not immediately implausible and deserved serious and sustained study. Has that been the case in the century since they first proposed this conjectural emendation? While some have engaged the question more intensively,[70] most appear simply to have dismissed the proposal out of hand. Davids, for example, proclaims without serious supporting argument that "Spitta and Meyer … claim that nothing Christian exists in this work other than minor Christian editing. We must firmly reject this claim."[71] Such unexamined rejection seems more often than not to be motivated by the same dim and dismissive view of conjectural emendation that we saw at the start of this paper. Davids continues, "This interpolation theory is normally used to support Jewish origin for the work, which is too much weight for such a tentative hypothesis to bear."[72] Dibelius similarly concludes, "But if the text can be understood as it stands, there is no necessity for the hypothesis of an interpolation which finds no support in the textual tradition, especially not if that hypothesis is then to be burdened with the weighty assertion that the entire document is of Jewish origin."[73] Finally, if there were any doubt, Joseph Mayor makes it clear that conjectural emendation is simply not a sound enough technique to support such serious claims: "If the Epistle is proved on other grounds to be pre-Christian, we should then be compelled to admit interpolation here, but not otherwise."[74]

We have already surveyed the major reasons why scholars reject conjectural emendation, but it is interesting to see those cases at work in specific arguments. Johnson, for example, typifies the common overreliance on the extant manuscript base when he writes:

> The suggestion has been advanced, after all, that James originated as a Jewish writing to the "to the twelve tribes of the dispersion" (1:1) and was later lightly baptized by the double interpolation of "Jesus Christ" in 1:1 and 2:1. The interpolation theory has no text-critical basis, since "Jesus Christ" is attested in all extant witnesses.[75]

---

70. E.g., Johnson, *James*; Joseph B. Mayor, *The Epistle of James* (Grand Rapids: Kregel, 1990).

71. Davids, *James*, 14.

72. Ibid., 106.

73. Dibelius, *James*, 127.

74. Mayor, *James*, cxcv.

75. Johnson, *James*, 48.

Ralph P. Martin similarly overstates, calling it "integral to the textual evidence," when he discusses the Christ reference in 2:1:

> The troublesome feature is that it is a genitive phrase coming in a series of such grammatical usages; this leads to one extreme conclusion that [it] is a later interpolation to give a Christian flavour to an otherwise Jewish document (so Spitta, Massebieau ...).[76]

Surprisingly, Dibelius's work appears to betray a basic misunderstanding of the potential impact of primitive corruption on the preserved text. In one case he writes, "The interpolation hypothesis recommended by Spitta and Massebieau can provide no proof for the resolution of this question. There is nothing at all in 1:1 to suggest deletion of 'and the Lord Jesus Christ.'"[77] In another case he argues, "Massebieau deletes only the words 'Jesus Christ' ... but there is no reason for doing this either, since the text which has been transmitted offers not the slightest problem."[78] Finally, the general contempt of conjectural emendation almost descends to ridicule when Davids, commenting on another text, writes, "Yet since it lacks manuscript evidence, it must remain a counsel of desperation for those who can accept no other solution."[79]

In the end, what can be said of all this? Massebieau and Spitta offered a reasonable proposal that deserved to be thoroughly investigated and extensively discussed. Instead, much of New Testament scholarship has rejected the idea out of hand. Given the examples above, one would be hard pressed to say that this was fueled by anything but a prejudicial bias against conjectural emendation that hinders some scholars from fairly considering any proposal that involves it. This bias, we have seen, is based on a misunderstanding of the nature and necessity of conjectural emendation. Whether that misunderstanding involves the power of the extant manuscripts, a theology of inspiration, or the goals of textual criticism itself, it should not be allowed to undermine the academic discussion any longer. Too many scholars have concluded in advance that conjectural emendation should not have a voice in the conversation, and that our quest for knowledge will go better without it. It is that very conclusion,

---

76. Ralph P. Martin, *James* (WBC; Waco, Tex.: Word, 1988), 60.
77. Dibelius, *James*, 22.
78. Ibid., 66.
79. Davids, *James*, 123.

however, that claim of what we think we already know, as Stendahl put it, that is obstructing our view. It is time to clear our vision.

Bibliography

Abegg, Martin, Peter Flint, and Eugene Ulrich, eds. *The Dead Sea Scrolls Bible*. San Francisco: HarperSanFrancisco, 2002.

Aejmelaeus, Anneli. "Septuagintal Translation Techniques—A Solution to the Problem of the Tabernacle Account." Pages 116–30 in *On the Trail of Septuagint Translators: Collected Essays*. Edited by Anneli Aejmelaeus. Kampen: Kok Pharos, 1993.

———. "What Can We Know about the Hebrew *Vorlage* of the Septuagint." Pages 77–115 in *On the Trail of Septuagint Translators: Collected Essays*. Edited by Anneli Aejmelaeus. Kampen: Kok Pharos, 1993.

Aland, Barbara, "Der textkritische und textgeschichtliche Nutzen früher Papyri, demonstriert am Johannesevangelium." Pages 19–38 in *Recent Developments in Textual Criticism*. Edited by W. Weren and D.-A. Koch. Assen: Van Gorcum, 2003.

———. "Welche Rolle spielen Textkritik und Textgeschichte für das Verständnis des Neuen Testaments?" Presidential address presented at the Sixtieth Society for New Testament Studies Meeting. 2–6 August, Halle (Saale).

Aland, Barbara, Kurt Aland, Gerd Mink, Holger Strutwolf, and Klaus Wachtel, eds., *Catholic Letters*. Vol. 4 of *Novum Testamentum Graecum: Editio Critica Maior*. The Institute for New Testament Textual Research. Stuttgart: Deutsche Biblegesellschaft, 1997–2005: (1) *James* (1997). (2) *The Letters of Peter* (2000); (3) *The First Letter of John* (2003); (4) *The Second and Third Letter of John. The Letter of Jude* (2005).

Aland, Barbara, and Andreas Juckel. *Das Neue Testament in syrischer Überlieferung. II. Die paulinischen Briefe. Teil 3: 1./2. Thessalonicherbrief, 1./2. Timotheusbrief, Titusbrief, Philemonischer und Hebräerbrief*. ANTF 32. Berlin: de Gruyter, 2002.

Aland, Kurt, ed. *Die alten Übersetzungen des Neuen Testaments, die Kirchenväterzitate und Lektionare*. Berlin: de Gruyter, 1972.

———. "Die Bedeutung des P75 für den Text des Neuen Testaments. Ein Beitrag zur Frage der 'Western Non-interplorations.'" Pages 155–72 in *Studien zur Überlieferung des Neuen Testaments und seines Textes*. ANTF 2. Berlin: de Gruyter, 1967.

———, ed. *The Greek New Testament*. 3rd ed. Stuttgart: United Bible Societies, 1983.

———. "Neue neutestamentliche Papyri." *NTS* 3 (1957): 261–65.

———. "Neue neutestamentliche Papryi II." *NTS* 12 (1965–1966): 193–210.

———. "Der neue 'Standard-Text' in seinem Verhältnis zu den frühen Papyri und Majuskeln." Pages 257–75 in *New Testament Textual Criticism: Its Significance for*

Exegesis: Essays in Honour of Bruce M. Metzger. Edited by E. J. Epp and G. D. Fee. Oxford: Clarendon, 1981.

———. "Novi Testamenti graeci editio maior critica: Der gegenwärtige Stand der Arbeit an einer neuen grossen kritischen Ausgabe des Neuen Testamentes." *NTS* 16 (1969–1970): 163–77.

———. "The Significance of the Papyri for Progress in New Testament Research." Pages 325–46 in *The Bible in Modern Scholarship: Papers Read at the 100th Meeting of the Society of Biblical Literature, December 28–30, 1964.* Edited by J. Philip Hyatt. Nashville: Abingdon, 1965.

Aland, Kurt, and Barbara Aland, *Der Text des Neuen Testaments.* Stuttgart: Deutsche Bibelgesellschaft, 1982; 2nd ed., 1989.

———. *The Text of the New Testament.* Translated by E. F. Rhodes. Grand Rapids: Eerdmans; Leiden: Brill, 1987; 2nd ed., 1989.

———, eds. *Text und Textwert der griechischen Handschriften des Neuen Testaments.* ANTF 9–11, 16–21, 26–31, 35–36. Berlin: de Gruyter, 1987–2005. Vol. 1: *Die Katholischen Briefe* (1987); vol. 2: *Die Paulinischen Briefe* (1991); vol. 3: *Die Apostelgeschichte* (1993), vol. 4: *Die Synoptischen Evangelien* (1998–1999), vol. 5: *Das Johannesevangelium* (2005).

———. *Text und Textwert der griechischen Handschriften des Neuen Testaments 4: Die Synoptischen Evangelien. Das Matthäusevangelium 2.2: Resultate der Kollation und Hauptliste sowie Ergänzungen.* In collaboration with Klaus Wachtel and Klaus Witte. ANTF 29. Berlin: de Gruyter, 1999; repr. 2003.

Aland, Kurt, et al. *Novum Testamentum Graece.* 26th ed. Stuttgart: Deutsche Bibelgesellschaft, 1979.

Aland, Kurt, Matthew Black, Carlo M. Martini, Bruce M. Metzger, and Allen Wikgren, eds. *The Greek New Testament.* 2nd ed. New York: United Bible Societies, 1968.

Albrektson, Bertil. "Reflections on the Emergence of a Standard Text of the Hebrew Bible." Pages 49–65 in *Congress Volume Göttingen.* VTSup 29. Leiden: Brill, 1978.

Allen, Thomas W. *Homer: The Origins and Transmission.* Oxford: Clarendon, 1924.

Allert, Craig D. *Revelation, Truth, Canon and Interpretation: Studies in Justin Martyr's Dialogue with Trypho.* VCSup 64. Leiden: Brill, 2002.

Amir, Y. "Philo and the Bible." *SPhilo* 2 (1973): 1–8.

Amphoux, C. -B. "Une édition «plurielle» de Marc." Pages 69–80 in *The New Testament Text in Early Christianity/Le text du Nouveau Testament au début du christianisme.* Edited by C. -B. Amphoux and J. K. Elliott. Lausanne: Éditions du Zèbre, 2003.

Attridge, Harold W. *A Commentary on the Epistle to the Hebrews.* Hermeneia. Philadelphia: Fortress, 1989.

Barbrook, A. C., C. J. Howe, N. Blake, and P. Robinson, "The Phylogeny of The Canterbury Tales." *Nature* 394 (1998): 839.

Bardtke, Hans. *Biblia Hebraica Stuttgartensia 11: Liber Psalmorum.* Stuttgart: Württembergische Bibelanstalt, 1969.

Bellinzoni, Arthur J. *The Sayings of Jesus in the Writings of Justin Martyr.* NovTSup 17. Leiden: Brill, 1967.

Bengel, Johann Albrecht. *H KAINH ΔIAΘHKH. Novum Testamentum Graece ita adornatum ut textus probatarum editionum medullam margo variantium lectionum in suas classes distributarum, locumque parallelorum delectum apparatus subiunctus criseos sacrae Millianae praesertim compendium, limam, supplementum ac fructum exhibeat inserviente J.A.B.* Tübingen, 1734.

Biblia Hebraica Quinta 18: General Introduction and Megilloth. Edited by A. Schenker. Stuttgart: Deutsche Bibelgesellschaft, 2004.

Black, Matthew. "Review: The Greek New Testament. United Bible Societies." *SJT* 19 (1966): 486–88.

Blenkinsopp, Joseph. *Isaiah 1–39: A New Translation with Introduction and Commentary.* AB. New York: Doubleday, 2000.

Bovon, François. "The Synoptic Gospels and the Non-canonical Acts of the Apostles." Pages 209–25 in idem, *Studies in Early Christianity.* Grand Rapids: Baker Academic, 2005.

Bowyer, William. *Conjectures on the New Testament.* London: Nichols, 1782.

Brooke, Alan E., and Norman McLean, eds. *The Old Testament in Greek according to the Text of Codex Vaticanus, Supplemented from Other Uncial Manuscripts, with a Critical Apparatus Containing the Variants of the Chief Ancient Authorities for the Text of the Septuagint.* Volume 1: *The Octateuch*, part 4: *Joshua, Judges and Ruth.* Cambridge: Cambridge University Press, 1917.

Brown, Scott G. "On the Composition History of the Longer ("Secret") Gospel of Mark." *JBL* 122 (2003): 89–110.

Bultmann, Rudolf K. *The History of the Synoptic Tradition.* Translated by John Marsh. Oxford: Basil Blackwell, 1963.

Burrows, Millar, with John C. Trever and William H. Brownlee, eds., *The Isaiah Manuscript and the Habakkuk Commentary.* Vol. 1 of *The Dead Sea Scrolls of St. Mark's Monastery.* New Haven: American Schools of Oriental Research, 1950.

Carson, D. A. *The King James Version Debate.* Grand Rapids: Baker, 1978.

Clark, Elizabeth A. *History, Theory, Text: Historians and the Linguistic Turn.* Cambridge: Harvard University Press, 2004.

Collins, Adela Yarbro. *Mark: A Commentary.* Hermeneia. Minneapolis: Fortress, 2007.

Colwell, Ernest C. "The Genealogical Method: Its Achievements and Its Limitations." Pages 63–83 in idem, *Studies in Methodology in Textual Criticism of the New Testament.* NTTS 9. Leiden: Brill, 1969.

———. "The Greek New Testament with a Limited Critical Apparatus: Its Nature and Uses." Pages 31–40 in *Studies in New Testament and Early Christian literature: Essays in Honor of Allen P. Wikgren.* Edited by D. Aune. NovTSup 33. Leiden: Brill, 1972.

———. "The International Greek New Testament Project." *JBL* 87 (1968): 187–97.

———. "Method in Evaluating Scribal Habits: A Study of P45, P66, P75." Pages 106–24 in idem, *Studies in Methodology in Textual Criticism of the New Testament.* NTTS 9. Leiden: Brill, 1969.

———. "Method in Locating a Newly-Discovered Manuscript within the Manuscript Tradition of the Greek New Testament." Pages 757–77 in *Studia Evangelica: Papers presented to the International Congress on "The Four Gospels in 1957" Held at Christ Church, Oxford 1957*. Edited by K. Aland. Berlin: Akademie-Verlag, 1959.

———. "Scribal Habits in Early Papyri: A Study in the Corruption of the Text." Pages 370–89 in *The Bible in Modern Scholarship: Papers Read at the 100th Meeting of the Society of Biblical Literature, December 28–30, 1964*. Edited by J. Philip Hyatt. Nashville: Abingdon, 1965.

Conzelmann, Hans. *The Theology of St. Luke*. Translated by Geoffrey Buswell. New York: Harper & Row, 1960.

Crüsemann, Frank. *The Torah: Theology and History of Old Testament Law*. Edinburgh: T&T Clark; Minneapolis: Augsburg Fortress, 1996.

Dahl, Nils A. "Wellhausen on the New Testament." *Semeia* 25 (1982): 89–110.

Davids, Peter H. *The Epistle of James: A Commentary on the Greek Text*. NIGTC. Grand Rapids: Eerdmans, 1982.

De Troyer, Kristin. "From Leviticus to Joshua: The Old Greek Text in Light of Two LXX Manuscripts from the Schøyen Collection." *Journal for Ancient Judaism* 2 (2011): 29–78.

———. "The Hebrew Text behind the Greek Text of the Pentateuch." In *Proceedings from the IOSCS Meeting in Helsinki 2010*. Edited by M. Peters. SBLSCS. Atlanta: Society of Biblical Literature, forthcoming.

———. "Joshua." Pages 79–145 + plates XVI–XXVII in *Papyri Graecae Schøyen* I. Edited by R. Pintaudi. Papyrologica Florentina 35; Manuscripts in the Schøyen Collection, Greek Papyri 5. Firenze: Gonnelli, 2005.

———. "Leviticus." Pages 1–68 + plates I–XVI in *Papyri Graecae Schøyen* II. Edited by D. Minutoli and R. Pintaudi. Papyrologica Florentina 40; Manuscripts in the Schøyen Collection, Greek Papyri 5.3. Firenze: Gonnelli, 2010.

———. "Which Text Are We Using for Our Studies of Dtr?" in *Proceedings of the IOSOT Meeting in Helsinki 2010*. Edited by M. Nissinen, forthcoming.

Debel, H. "Greek 'Variant Literary Editions' to the Hebrew Bible?" *JSJ* 41 (2010): 161–90.

Dibelius, Martin. *James: A Commentary on the Epistle of James*. Revised by Heinrich Greeven. Translated by Michael A. Williams. Hermeneia. Philadelphia: Fortress, 1976.

Dodds, E. R. *Euripides Bacchae*. 2nd. ed. Oxford Classical Texts. Oxford: Clarendon, 1960.

Dunsany, Lord, and Michael Oakley, trans. *The Collected Works of Horace*. London: Dent; New York: Dutton, 1961.

Ehrman, Bart D. *Misquoting Jesus*. New York: Harper Collins, 2005.

———. *The Orthodox Corruption of Scripture: The Effect of Early Christological Controversies on the Text of the New Testament*. New York: Oxford University Press, 1993.

———. "The Text as Window: New Testament Manuscripts and the Social History of Early Christianity." Pages 361–79 in *The Text of the New Testament in Contemporary Research: Essays on the Status Quaestiones. A Volume in Honor of Bruce M. Metzger*. Edited by Bart D. Ehrman and Michael W. Holmes. SD 46. Grand Rapids: Eerdmans, 1995.

Ehrman, Bart D., and Michael W. Holmes, eds. *The Text of the New Testament in Contemporary Research: Essays on the Status Quaestiones. A Volume in Honor of Bruce M. Metzger.* SD 46. Grand Rapids: Eerdmans, 1995.

Elliger, Karl. *Das Buch der zwölf Kleinen Propheten II: Die Propheten Nahum, Habakuk, Zephanja, Haggai, Sacharja, Maleachi.* ATD 25. Göttingen: Vandenhoeck & Ruprecht, 1949; 6th ed., 1967.

Elliott, J. Keith. "Absent Witnesses? The Critical Apparatus to the Greek New Testament and the Apostolic Fathers." Pages 47–58 in *The Reception of the New Testament in the Apostolic Fathers.* Edited by A. F. Gregory and C. M. Tuckett. Oxford: Oxford University Press, 2005.

———. *A Bibliography of Greek New Testament Manuscripts.* 2nd ed. SNTSMS 109. Cambridge: Cambridge University Press, 2000.

———. "The Case for Thorough-Going Eclecticism." Pages 101–24 in *Rethinking New Testament Textual Criticism.* Edited by D. A. Black. Grand Rapids: Baker, 2002.

———. "Four New Papyri Containing the Fourth Gospel and Their Relevance for the Apparatus Criticus." *JTS* 59 (2008): 674–78.

———. "The Nature of the Evidence Available for Reconstructing the Text of the New Testament in the Second Century." Pages 9–18 in *The New Testament Text in Early Christianity: Proceedings of the Lille Colloquium, July 2000.* Edited by C. -B. Amphoux and J. K. Elliott. HTB 6. Lausanne: Éditions du Zèbre, 2003.

———. "Thoroughgoing Eclecticism in New Testament Textual Criticism." Pages 321–35 in *The Text of the New Testament in Contemporary Research: Essays on the Status Quaestionis.* Edited by Bart D. Ehrman and Michael W. Holmes. SD 46. Grand Rapids: Eerdmans, 1995.

Elliott, J. Keith, Christian Amphoux, and Jean-Claude Haelewyck. "The *Marc Multilingue* Project." *Filología Neotestamentaria* 15 (2002): 3–17.

Emonds, Hilarius. *Zweite Auflage im Altertum.* Leipzig: Harrassowitz, 1941.

Epp, Eldon J. "Are Early New Testament Manuscripts Truly Abundant?" Pages 77–117 and 395–99 in *Israel's God and Rebecca's Children: Christology and Community in Early Judaism and Christianity.* Edited by D. B. Capes et al. Waco, Tex.: Baylor University Press, 2007.

———. "The Eclectic Method in New Testament Textual Criticism: Solution or Symptom?" *HTR* 69 (1976): 211–57.

———. "Issues in New Testament Textual Criticism." Pages 17–76 in *Rethinking New Testament Criticism.* Edited by D. A. Black. Grand Rapids: Baker, 2002.

———. "It's All about Variants: A Variant-Conscious Approach to New Testament Textual Criticism." *HTR* 100 (2007): 275–308.

———. "The Multivalence of the Term 'Original Text' in New Testament Textual Criticism." *HTR* 92 (1999): 245–81.

———. "New Testament Papyri and the Transmission of the New Testament." Pages 315–31 in *Oxyrhynchus: A City and its Texts.* Edited by A. K. Bowman et al. GRM 93. London: Egypt Exploration Society, 2007.

———. "The New Testament Papyrus Manuscripts in Historical Perspective." Pages 261–88 in *To Touch the Text.* Edited by M. P. Horgan and P. J. Kobelski. New York: Crossroad, 1989.

———. "The Oxyrhynchus New Testament Papyri: 'Not without Honor Except in Their Hometown'?" *JBL* 123 (2004): 5–55.

———. "The Papyrus Manuscripts of the New Testament." Pages 3–21 in *The Text of the New Testament in Contemporary Research: Essays on the Status Quaestiones.* Edited by Bart D. Ehrman and Michael W. Holmes. SD 46. Grand Rapids: Eerdmans, 1995.

———. "The Significance of the Papyri for Determining the Nature of the New Testament Text in the Second Century: A Dynamic View of Textual Transmission." Pages 71–103 in *Gospel Traditions in the Second Century: Origins, Recensions, Text, and Transmission.* Edited by W. L. Petersen. CJA 3. Notre Dame: University of Notre Dame Press, 1989.

———. "Textual Criticism (NT)." *ABD* 6:412–35.

———. "Textual Criticism in the Exegesis of the New Testament, with an Excursus on Canon." Pages 45–97 in *Handbook to Exegesis of the New Testament.* Edited by S. E. Porter. NTTS 25. Leiden: Brill, 1997.

Epp, Eldon J., and Gordon D. Fee. *Studies in the Theory and Method of New Testament Textual Criticism.* SD 45. Grand Rapids: Eerdmans, 1993.

Erasmus, Desiderius, ed. *Nouum Instrumentu[m] Omne.* Basil: In aedibus Ioannis Frobenij Hammelburgensis, 1516.

Eshel, Ester. "Book of Leviticus." Pages 488–93 in vol. 1 of *Encyclopedia of the Dead Sea Scrolls.* Edited by Lawrence H. Schiffman and James C. VanderKam. 2 vols. Oxford: Oxford University Press, 2000.

Feldman, Louis H. "Josephus's Biblical Paraphrase as a Commentary on Contemporary Issues." Pages 124–201 in *Interpretation of Scripture in Early Judaism and Christianity.* Edited by C. A. Evans. Sheffield: Sheffield Academic Press, 2000.

———. *Josephus's Interpretation of the Bible.* Berkeley: University of California Press, 1998.

Fernández Marcos, Natalio. *The Septuagint in Context: Introduction to the Greek Versions of the Bible.* Translated by W. G. E. Watson. Leiden: Brill, 2000.

Fischer, Joseph. "Die Einheit der beiden Testamente bei Laktanz, Viktorin von Pettau und deren Quellen." *Münchener Theologische Zeitschrift* 1 (1950): 96–101.

Fishbane, Michael. *Biblical Interpretation in Ancient Israel.* Oxford: Clarendon, 1985.

Freedman, David Noel, and Kenneth A. Mathews. *The Paleo-Hebrew Leviticus Scroll (11QpaleoLev).* Winona Lake, Ind.: ASOR/Eisenbrauns, 1985.

Gamble, Harry Y. *Books and Readers in the Early Church: A History of Early Christian Texts.* New Haven: Yale University Press, 1995.

Georgi, Dieter. "Die Aristoteles—und Theophrastausgabe des Andronikus von Rhodus: Ein Beitrag zur Kanonsproblematik." Pages 45–78 in *Konsequente Traditionsgeschichte: Festschrift für Klaus Baltzer zum 65. Geburtstag.* Edited by R. Bartelmus et al. OBO 126. Göttingen: Vandenhoeck & Ruprecht, 1993.

Gerstenberger, Erhard. *Leviticus: A Commentary.* OTL. Louisville: Westminster John Knox, 1996.

Ginsburg, Christian D. *Introduction to the Massoretico-Critical Edition of the Hebrew Bible, with a Prolegomenon by Harry M. Orlinsky. The Masoretic Text: A Critical Evaluation.* New York: Ktav, 1966.

Giuliani, Luigi, Herman Brinkman, Geert Lernout, and Marita Mathijsen, eds. *Texts in Multiple Versions: Histories of Editions.* Amsterdam: Rodopi, 2006.

Gooding, D. W. *The Account of the Tabernacle.* Cambridge: Cambridge University Press, 1959.

Goodspeed, Edgar J., and Ernest C. Colwell. *A Greek Papyrus Reader with Vocabulary.* Chicago: University of Chicago Press, 1935.

Goshen-Gottstein, Moshe H. "Editions of the Hebrew Bible—Past and Future." Pages 221–42 in *"Sha'arei Talmon": Studies in the Bible, Qumran, and the Ancient Near East Presented to Shemaryahu Talmon.* Edited by Michael Fishbane and Emanuel Tov, with the assistance of Weston W. Fields. Winona Lake, Ind.: Eisenbrauns, 1992.

———. *The Hebrew University Bible, The Book of Isaiah.* Jerusalem: Magnes, 1995.

Goshen-Gottstein, Moshe H., and Shemaryahu Talmon. *The Hebrew University Bible, The Book of Ezekiel.* Jerusalem: Magnes, 2004.

Grafton, Anthony. *Defenders of the Text: The Traditions of Scholarship in an Age of Science, 1450-1800.* Cambridge: Harvard University Press, 1991.

Griesbach, Johann Jakob, ed. *Novum Testamentum Graece.* 2nd ed. London, 1796–1806.

———, ed. *Novum Testamentum Graece.* 3rd ed. Berlin: Laue, 1827.

Greenlee, J. Harold. *Introduction to New Testament Textual Criticism.* Grand Rapids: Eerdmans, 1964.

Greenspoon, Leonard J. *Textual Studies in the Book of Joshua.* HSM 28. Chico, Calif.: Scholars Press, 1983.

Greg, Walter W. "The Rationale of Copy-Text." *Studies in Bibliography* 3 (1950–51): 19–36.

Grigely, Joseph. "The Textual Event." Pages 194–225 in *Textual Editing and Criticism: An Introduction.* Edited by E. Kelemen. New York: Norton, 2009.

Haines-Eitzen, Kim. *Guardians of Letters: Literacy, Power, and the Transmitters of Early Christian Literature.* Oxford: Oxford University Press, 2000.

Harlé, Paul, and Didier Pralon. *La Bible d'Alexandrie: Le Lévitique.* Paris: Cerf, 1988.

Harnack, Adolf von. *Das Neue Testament um das Jahr 200: Theodor Zahn's Geschichte des neutestamentlichen Kanons.* Freiburg: Mohr, 1889.

———. "Zur Textkritik und Christologie der Schriften des Johannes." Pages 105–52 in vol. 1 of *Studien zur Geschichte des Neuen Testaments und der Alten Kirche.* Arbeiten zur Kirchengeschichte 19. Berlin: de Gruyter, 1931.

Hecht, Richard D. "Preliminary Issues in the Analysis of Philo's De Specialibus Legibus." *SPhilo* 5 (1978): 1–56.

Heckel, Theo K. *Vom Evangelium des Markus zum viergestaltigen Evangelium.* WUNT 120. Tübingen: Mohr Siebeck, 1990.

Hendel, Ron S. "Oxford Hebrew Bible: Sample of Genesis 1:1–13." Online: ohb.berkeley.edu/samples.htm.

———. "The Oxford Hebrew Bible: Prologue to a New Critical Edition." *VT* 58 (2008): 324–51.

———. "Plural Texts and Literary Criticism: For Instance, 1 Sam 17." *Textus* 23 (2007): 97–114.

———. *The Text of Genesis 1–11: Textual Studies and Critical Edition.* New York: Oxford University Press, 1998.

Hernández, Juan. *Scribal Habits and Theological Influences in the Apocalypse: The Singular Readings of Sinaiticus, Alexandrinus and Ephraemi.* Tübingen: Mohr Siebeck, 2006.

Hills, Edward F. *The King James Version Defended!* Des Moines, Iowa: Christian Research Press, 1973.

Hoffmann, R. Joseph. *Marcion: On the Restitution of Christianity: An Essay on the Development of Radical Paulinist Theology in the Second Century.* Chico, Calif.: Scholars Press, 1984.

Hoh, Josef. *Die Lehre des Hl. Irenäus über das Neue Testament.* Neutestamentliche Abhandlungen 7. Münster: Aschendorff, 1919.

Holmes, Michael W. "The Case for Reasoned Eclecticism." Pages 77–100 in *Rethinking New Testament Textual Criticism.* Edited by D. A. Black. Grand Rapids: Baker, 2002.

———. "Codex Bezae as a Recension of the Gospels." Pages 123–60 in *Codex Bezae: Studies from the Lunel Colloquium June 1994.* Edited by D. C. Parker and C.-B. Amphoux. Leiden: Brill, 1996.

———. "Reasoned Eclecticism." Pages 336–60 in *The Text of the New Testament in Contemporary Research: Essays on the Status Quaestionis.* Edited by Bart D. Ehrman and Michael W. Holmes. SD 46. Grand Rapids: Eerdmans, 1995.

———. "Text and Transmission in the Second Century." Pages 61–79 in *The Textual Reliability of the New Testament: Bart Ehrman and Daniel Wallace in Dialogue.* Edited by R. Stewart. Minneapolis: Fortress, 2011.

———. "Working with an Open Textual Tradition: Challenges in Theory and Practice." Pages 65–78 in *The Textual History of the Greek New Testament: Changing Views in Contemporary Research.* Edited by Klaus Wachtel and Michael W. Holmes. Atlanta: Society of Biblical Literature, 2011.

Hurtado, Larry W. "The New Testament Text in the Second Century: Text, Collections and Canon." Pages 14–19 in *Transmission and Reception: New Testament Text-Critical and Exegetical Studies.* Edited by J. Childers and D. C. Parker. Piscataway, N.J.: Gorgias, 2006.

———. "P52 (P. Rylands Gk. 457) and the Nomina Sacra: Method and Probability." *TynBull* 54 (2003): 1–14.

Janko, Richard. *Books 13–16.* Vol. 4 of *The Iliad: A Commentary.* Cambridge: Cambridge University Press, 1992.

Johnson, Luke Timothy. *The Letter of James: A New Translation with Introduction and Commentary.* AB 37A. Garden City, N.Y.: Doubleday, 1995.

Joosten, Jan. "A Note on the Text of Deuteronomy xxxii 8." *VT* 57 (2007): 548–55.

Kahle, Paul. *The Cairo Geniza.* 2nd ed. Oxford: Basil Blackwell, 1959.

Kenyon, Frederic G. *The Chester Beatty Biblical Papyri I: General Introduction.* London: Walker, 1933.

———. *The Chester Beatty Biblical Papyri II: The Gospels and Acts. 1. Text.* London: Walker, 1933.

———. *The Chester Beatty Biblical Papyri III: Pauline Epistles and Revelation. 1. Text.* London: Walker, 1934.

Kilpatrick, G. D. "Conjectural Emendation in the New Testament." Pages 98–109 in *The Principles and Practice of New Testament Textual Criticism.* Edited by J. K. Elliott. Leuven: Leuven University Press, 1990.

King, Marchant A. "Notes on the Bodmer Manuscript, Jude and 1 and 2 Peter." *Bibliotheca Sacra* 121 (1964): 54-57.

Klein, Ralph W. "Archaic Chronologies and the Textual History of the Old Testament." *HTR* 67 (1974): 255–63.

Kline, Leslie L. "Harmonized Sayings of Jesus in the Pseudo-Clementine Homilies and Justin Martyr." *ZNW* 66 (1975): 223–41.

Kloha, Jeffrey. "1 Corinthians 6:5: A Proposal." *NovT* 46 (2004): 132–42.

Knohl, Israel. *The Sanctuary of Silence: The Priestly Torah and the Holiness School.* Minneapolis: Fortress, 1995.

Koch, Klaus. *The Growth of the Biblical Tradition: The Form-Critical Method.* Translated by S. M. Cupitt. New York: Charles Scribner's Sons, 1969.

Koester, Helmut. *Ancient Christian Gospels: Their History and Development.* London: SCM, 1990.,

———. "The Text of the Synoptic Gospels in the Second Century." Pages 19–37 in *Gospel Traditions in the Second Century: Origins, Recensions, Text, and Transmission.* Edited by W. L. Petersen. Notre Dame: University of Notre Dame Press, 1989.

Kooij, Arie van der. "The Textual Criticism of the Hebrew Bible before and after the Qumran Discoveries." Pages 167–77 in *The Bible as Book: The Hebrew Bible and the Judaean Desert Discoveries.* Edited by E. D. Herbert and E. Tov. London: British Library, 2002.

Krans, Jan. *Beyond What Is Written: Erasmus and Beza as Conjectural Critics of the New Testament.* NTTS 35. Leiden: Brill, 2006.

Kraus, Thomas J. *Ad fontes: Original Manuscripts and Their Significance for Studying Early Christianity: Selected Essays.* TENTS 3. Leiden: Brill, 2007.

———. " 'Pergament oder Papyrus?': Anmerkungen zur Signifikanz des Beschreibstoffes die der Behandlung von Manuskripten." *NTS* 49 (2003): 425–32.

Kuenen, Abraham. *An Historico-Critical Inquiry into the Origin and Composition of the Hexateuch.* London: Macmillan, 1886.

Lange, Armin. *Die Handschriften biblischer Bücher von Qumran und den anderen Fundorten.* Vol. 1 of *Handbuch der Textfunde vom Toten Meer.* Tübingen: Mohr Siebeck, 2009.

Lieberman, Saul. *Greek in Jewish Palestine: Studies in the Life and Manners of Jewish Palestine in the II–III Centuries.* 2nd ed. New York: Jewish Seminary of America, 1965.

———. *Hellenism in Jewish Palestine: Studies in the Literary Transmission, Beliefs and Manners of Palestine in the I Century B.C.E.–IV Century C.E.* Texts and Studies of the Jewish Theological Seminary of America 18. New York: Jewish Theological Seminary of America, 1950.

Luck, Georg. "Conjectural Emendation in The Greek New Testament." Paper presented at the Conference on Greek Textual Criticism, Cáceres, Spain, June 2007.

Maas, Paul. *Textual Criticism*. Oxford: Clarendon, 1958.

Mack, Burton L. "Exegetical Traditions of Alexandrian Judaism: A Program for Analysis of the Philonic Corpus." *SPhilo* 3 (1974–1975): 71–112.

Marcus, David. *Biblia Hebraica Quinta 20: Ezra and Nehemiah*. Stuttgart: Deutsche Bibelgesellschaft, 2006.

Martin, Michael W. "Defending the 'Western Non-interpolations': The Case for an Anti-separationist *Tendenz* in the Longer Alexandrian Readings." *JBL* 124 (2005): 269–94.

Martin, Ralph P. *James*. WBC 48. Waco, Tex.: Word, 1988.

Marxsen, Willi. *Mark the Evangelist: Studies on the Redaction History of the Gospel*. Translated by Roy A. Harrisville. Nashville: Abingdon, 1969.

Mason, Steve. "Josephus on Canon and Scriptures." Pages 217–35 in vol. 1.1 of *Hebrew Bible/Old Testament: The History of Its Interpretation*. Göttingen: Vandenhoeck & Ruprecht, 1996.

Massebieau, Louis. "L'Épître de Jacques est-elle l'oeuvre d'un chrétien?" *RHR* 31–32 (1895): 249–83.

Mathews, K. A. "The Leviticus Scrolls (11QPaleLev) and the Text of the Hebrew Bible." *CBQ* 48 (1986): 171–207.

Mayor, Joseph B. *The Epistle of St. James: The Greek Text with Introduction, Notes and Comments*. London: Macmillan, 1892; 3rd ed., 1910.

McCarthy, C. *Biblia Hebraica Quinta 5: Deuteronomy*. Stuttgart: Deutsche Bibelgesellschaft, 2007.

McDonald, Lee Martin, and James A. Sanders, eds. *The Canon Debate*. Peabody, Mass.: Hendrikson, 2002.

McGann, Jerome J. *A Critique of Modern Textual Criticism*. Chicago: University of Chicago Press, 1983.

McKane, William. *Selected Christian Hebraists*. Cambridge: Cambridge University Press, 1989.

Metso, Sarianna, and Eugene Ulrich. "The Old Greek Translation of Leviticus." Pages 247–68 in *The Book of Leviticus: Composition and Reception*. Edited by R. Rendtdorff and R. Kugler. Formation and Interpretation of Old Testament Literature. VTSup 93. Leiden: Brill, 2003.

Metzger, Bruce M. *The Early Versions of the New Testament: Their Origin, Transmission, and Limitations*. Oxford: Clarendon, 1977.

———. *The Text of the New Testament: Its Transmission, Corruption, and Restoration*. 2nd ed. New York: Oxford University Press, 1968.

———. *The Text of the New Testament*. 3rd ed. New York: Oxford University Press, 1992.

———. *A Textual Commentary on the Greek New Testament*. London: United Bible Societies, 1971; corr. ed., 1975; 2nd ed., 1994.

Metzger, Bruce M., and Bart D. Ehrman, *The Text of the New Testament*. 4th ed. New York: Oxford University Press, 2005.

Milgrom, Jacob. *Leviticus 1–16: A New Translation with Introduction and Commentary.* AB. New York: Doubleday, 1991.

Mink, Gerhard. "Editing and Genealogical Studies: the New Testament." *Literary and Linguistic Computing* 15 (2000): 51–56.

———. "Problems of a Highly Contaminated Tradition, the New Testament: Stemmata of Variants as a Source of a Genealogy for Witnesses." Pages 13–85 in *Studies in Stemmatology II.* Edited by P. van Reenen, A. den Hollander, and M. van Mulken. Amsterdam: Benjamins, 2004.

———. "Eine umfassende Genealogie der neutestamentlichen Überlieferung." *NTS* 39 (1993): 481–99.

———. "Was verändert sich in der Textkritik durch die Beachtung genealogischer Kohärenz?" Pages 39–68 in *Recent Developments in Textual Criticism: New Testament, Other Early Christian and Jewish Literature.* Edited by W. Weren and D.-A. Koch. Assen: Van Gorcum, 2003.

Mullen, Roderic L., Simon Crisp, and David C. Parker. *The Gospel according to John in the Byzantine Tradition.* United Bible Societies. Stuttgart: Deutsche Bibelgesellschaft, 2007.

Mülke, Markus. *Der Autor und sein Text: Die Verfälschung des Originals im Urteil antiker Autoren.* Untersuchungen zur antiken Literatur und Geschichte 93. Berlin: de Gruyter, 2007.

Najman, Hindy. *Seconding Sinai: The Development of Mosaic Discourse in Second Temple Judaism.* JSJSup 77. Leiden: Brill, 2003.

———. "Torah of Moses: Pseudonymous Attribution in Second Temple Writings." Pages 202–16 in *The Interpretation of Scripture in Early Judaism and Christianity: Studies in Language and Tradition.* Edited by C. A. Evans. JSPSup 33. SSEJC 7. Sheffield: Sheffield Academic Press, 2000.

Nestle, Eberhard, Kurt Aland, and Barbara Aland, eds. *Novum testamentum graece.* 27th ed. Stuttgart: Deutsche Bibelstiftung, 1999.

Nestle, Eberhard, *Novum Testamentum Graece cum apparatu critico ex editionibus et libris manuscriptis collecto.* Stuttgart: Privilegierte Württembergische Bibelanstalt, 1898[1], 1899[2], 1901[3], 1903[4], 1904[5], 1906[6], 1908[7], 1910[8], 1912[9], 1914[10], 1920[11], 1923[12], 1927[13], 1930[14], 1932[15], 1936[16], 1941[17], 1948[18], 1949[19], 1950[20], 1952[21], 1956[22], 1957[23], 1960[24], 1963[25].

Nicklas, Tobias, and Tommy Wassermann, "Theologische Linien im Codex Bodmer Miscellani?" Pages 161–88 in *New Testament Manuscripts: Their Texts and Their World.* Edited by T. J. Kraus and T. Nicklas. TENTS 2. Leiden: Brill, 2006.

Nodet, Étienne. "Josephus and the Pentateuch." *JSJ* 28 (1997): 154–94.

Noth, Martin. *A History of Pentateuchal Traditions.* Englewood Cliffs, N.J.: Prentice-Hall, 1972.

———. "Überlieferungsgeschichtliche Studien." *Schriften der Königsberger Gelehrten Gesellschaft. Geisteswissenschaftliche Klasse* 18 (1943): 43–266.

Parker, David C. *An Introduction to the New Testament Manuscripts and Their Texts.* Cambridge: Cambridge University Press, 2008.

———. *The Living Text of the Gospels.* Cambridge: Cambridge University Press, 1997.

———. "The Majuscule Manuscripts of the New Testament." Pages 22–42 in *The Text of the New Testament in Contemporary Research: Essays on the Status Quaestiones.* Edited by Bart D. Ehrman and Michael W. Holmes. SD 46. Grand Rapids: Eerdmans, 1995.

———. "Manuscripts of John's Gospel with Hermeneiai." Pages 48–68 in *Transmission and Reception: New Testament Text-Critical and Exegetical Studies.* Edited by J. W. Childers and D. C. Parker. Texts and Studies 3/4. Piscataway, N.J.: Gorgias, 2006.

———. "Textual Criticism and Theology." *ExpTim* 118 (2007): 583–89.

———. "Through a Screen Darkly: Digital Texts and the New Testament." *JSNT* 25 (2003): 395–411.

Patterson, Lee. "The Logic of Textual Criticism and the Way of Genius." Pages 55–91 in *Textual Criticism and Literary Interpretation.* Edited by J. J. McGann. Chicago: University of Chicago Press, 1985.

Petersen, William L. "The Genesis of the Gospels." Pages 33–65 in *New Testament Textual Criticism and Exegesis: Festschrift J. Delobel.* Edited by A. Denaux. Leuven: Leuven University Press and Peeters, 2002.

———. "Patristic Biblical Quotations and Method: Four Changes to Lightfoot's Edition of Second Clement." *VC* 60 (2006): 389–419.

———. *Tatian's Diatessaron: Its Creation, Dissemination, Significance, and History in Scholarship.* Leiden: Brill, 1994.

———. "Textual Evidence of Tatian's Dependence upon Justin's ΑΠΟΜΝΗΜΟΝΕΥΜΑΤΑ." *NTS* 36 (1990): 512–34.

———. "Textual Traditions Examined: What the Text of the Apostolic Fathers Tells Us about the Text of the New Testament in the Second Century." Pages 29–46 in *The Reception of the New Testament in the Apostolic Fathers.* Edited by A. Gregory and C. Tuckett. Oxford: Oxford University Press, 2005.

———. "What Text Can New Testament Textual Criticism Ultimately Reach?" Pages 136–52 in *New Testament Textual Criticism, Exegesis, and Early Church History.* Edited by B. Aland and J. Delobel. CBET 7. Kampen: Kok Pharos, 1994.

Pfeiffer, Robert H. *Introduction to the Old Testament.* New York: Harper & Brothers, 1941.

Porter, Stanley E. "Textual Criticism in the Light of Diverse Textual Evidence for the Greek New Testament: An Expanded Proposal." Pages 305–37 in *New Testament Manuscripts: Their Texts and Their World.* Edited by T. J. Kraus and T. Nicklas. TENTS 2. Leiden: Brill, 2006.

Rabin, Chaim, Shemaryahu Talmon, and Emanuel Tov. *The Hebrew University Bible, The Book of Jeremiah.* Jerusalem: Magnes, 1997.

Rad, Gerhard von. *Das formgeschichtliche Problem des Hexateuch.* BWANT 4. Stuttgart: Kohlhammer, 1938.

———. "The Form-Critical Problem of the Hexateuch." Pages 1–78 in *The Problem of the Hexateuch and Other Essays.* Edinburgh: Oliver & Boyd, 1966.

Reinhartz, Adele. "Philo's *Exposition of the Law* and Social History: Methodological Considerations." Pages 6–21 in *Society of Biblical Literature 1993 Annual Meeting Seminar Papers.* Edited by E. H. Lowering. Atlanta: Scholars Press, 1993.

Rendtorff, Rolf. "Zur Bedeutung des Kanons für eine Theologie des Alten Testaments." Pages 3–11 in *"Wenn nicht jetzt, wann dann?": Festschrift für Hans-Joachim Kraus.* Edited by H. G. Geyer. Neukirchen-Vluyn: Neukirchner, 1983.

Rhodes, Erroll F. "Conjectural Emendations in Modern Translations." Pages 361–74 in *New Testament Textual Criticism.* Edited by E. J. Epp and G. D. Fee. Oxford: Clarendon, 1981.

Richards, E. Randolph. *The Secretary in the Letters of Paul.* WUNT 42. Tübingen: Mohr Siebeck, 1991.

Rico, Francisco. "Scholarly Editions and Real Readers." *Variants* 5 (2006): 1–13.

Robinson, Maurice A., and William G. Pierpont, *The New Testament in the Original Greek according to the Byzantine/Majority Textform.* Atlanta: Original Word, 1991.

Rofé, Alexander. "Abraham Kuenen's Contribution to the Study of the Pentateuch: A View from Israel." Pages 105–12 in *Abraham Kuenen (1828–1891): His Major Contributions to the Study of the Old Testament.* Edited by P. B. Dirksen and A. van der Kooij. OtSt 29. Leiden: Brill, 1993.

Royse, James R. *Scribal Habits in Early Greek New Testament Papyri.* NTTSD 36. Leiden: Brill, 2008.

Runia, David T. *Exegesis and Philosophy: Studies on Philo of Alexandria.* Hampshire, U.K.: Variorum, 1990.

Sanday, William. "The Conditions under Which the Gospels Were Written, and Their Bearing upon Some Difficulties of the Synoptic Problem." Pages 1–26 in *Studies in the Synoptic Problem.* Edited by William Sanday. Oxford: Clarendon, 1911.

Sanders, James A. "The Hebrew University Bible and Biblia Hebraica Quinta." *JBL* 118 (1999): 518–26.

Sanders, Paul. *The Provenance of Deuteronomy 32.* OtSt 37. Leiden: Brill, 1996.

Schenker, Adrian. "Eine Neuausgabe der Biblia Hebraica." *ZAH* 9 (1996): 58–61.

Schubart, Wilhelm. *Das Buch bei den Griechen und Römern.* 2nd ed. Berlin: de Gruyter, 1921.

Segal, Michael. "4QReworked Pentateuch or 4QPentateuch?" Pages 391–99 in *The Dead Sea Scrolls: Fifty Years after Their Discovery.* Edited by L. H. Schiffman, E. Tov., and J. C. VanderKam, with G. Marquis. Jerusalem: Israel Exploration Society/The Shrine of the Book, Israel Museum, 2000.

Shillingsburg, Peter L. "Text as Matter, Concept, and Action." *Studies in Bibliography* 44 (1991): 31–82.

Skarsaune, Oskar. "Justin and His Bible." Pages 64–68in *Justin Martyr and His Worlds.* Edited by S. Parvis and P. Foster. Minneapolis: Fortress, 2007.

Skehan, Patrick. "A Fragment of the 'Song of Moses' (Deut. 32) from Qumran." *BASOR* 136 (1954): 12–15.

———. "The Qumran Manuscripts and Textual Criticism." Pages 148–60in *Volume de congrès, Strasbourg 1956.* VTSup 4. Leiden: Brill, 1957.

Soisalon-Soininen, Ilmari. *Der Character der asterisierten Zusätze in der Septuaginta.* Suomalaisen Tiedeakatemian Toimituksia/Annales Academiae Scientiarum Fennicae, Series B 114. Helsinki: Suomalainen Tiedeakatemia, 1959.

Spencer, Matthew, Klaus Wachtel, and Christopher J. Howe. "The Greek Vorlage of the Syra Harclensis: A Comparative Study on Method in Exploring Textual Genealogy." *TC: A Journal of Biblical Textual Criticism* 7 (2002). Online: http://purl.oclc.org/NET/TC/SWH2002.html.

Spitta, Friedrich. "Der Brief des Jakobus." Pages 1–239 in vol. 2 of *Zur Geschichte und Litteratur des Urchristentums*. Göttingen: Vandenhoeck & Ruprecht, 1896.

Stanton, Graham N. *Jesus and Gospel*. Cambridge: Cambridge University Press, 2004.

———. "Jesus Traditions and Gospels in Justin Martyr and Irenaeus." Pages 353–70 in *The Biblical Canons*. Edited by J.-M. Auwers and H. J. de Jonge. Leuven: Leuven University Press, 2003.

———. "The Fourfold Gospel." *NTS* 43 (1997): 329–35.

Steck, Odil H. *Old Testament Exegesis: A Guide to the Methodology*. Atlanta: Scholars Press, 1995.

Stemplinger, Eduard. *Buchhandel im Altertum*. 2nd ed. Munich: Heimeran, 1933.

Stendahl, Krister. *Paul among Jews and Gentiles, and Other Essays*. Philadelphia: Fortress, 1976.

Stephanus, Robert, Joseph Scaligerus, and Isaac Casavbonus, eds. *Novi Testamenti, Libri Omnes Recens Nunc Editi Cum Notis et Animadversionibus Doctissimorum, Praesertim Vero*. Variae item lectiones ex antiquissimis exemplaribus & celeberrimis bibliothecis, desumptae. London: Richard Wittaker, 1633.

Strecker, Georg. "Eine Evangelienharmonie bei Justin und Pseudoklemens?" *NTS* 24 (1978): 297–316.

Strugnell, John. "A Plea for Conjectural Emendation in the New Testament, with a Coda on 1 Cor 4:6." *CBQ* 36 (1974): 543–58.

Stuttgarter Jubiläumsbibel mit erklärenden Anmerkungen. Stuttgart: Württembergische Bibelanstalt, 1912.

Swete, Henry Barclay. *An Introduction to the Old Testament in Greek*. Cambridge: Cambridge University Press, 1900. Revised by R. R. Ottley. New York: Ktav, 1968.

Talmon, Shemaryahu. "The Textual Study of the Bible—A New Outlook." Pages 321–400 in *Qumran and the History of the Biblical Text*. Edited by Frank Moore Cross and Shemaryahu Talmon. Cambridge: Harvard University Press, 1975.

Tanselle, G. Thomas. "Classical, Biblical, and Medieval Textual Criticism and Modern Editing." *Studies in Bibliography* 36 (1983): 21–68.

———. "Editing without a Copy-Text." *Studies in Bibliography* 47 (1994): 1–22.

———. *Textual Criticism and Scholarly Editing*. Charlottesville: University Press of Virginia, 1990.

Tischendorf, Constantin von, ed. *Novum Testamentum Graece*. Leipzig: Koehler, 1841; 16th ed., 1904.

Toorn, Karel van der. *Scribal Culture and the Making of the Hebrew Bible*. Cambridge: Harvard University Press, 2007.

Tov, Emanuel. "The Biblical Texts from the Judaean Desert—An Overview and Analysis of the Published Texts." Pages 139–66 in *The Bible as Book: The Hebrew Bible and the Judaean Desert Discoveries*. Edited by E. D. Herbert and E. Tov. London: British Library, 2002.

——. *The Greek and Hebrew Bible: Collected Essays on the Septuagint.* VTSup 72. Leiden: Brill, 1999.

——. "The Growth of the Book of Joshua in the Light of the Evidence of the LXX Translation." *Scripta Hierosolymitana* 31 (1986): 321–39.

——. *Hebrew Bible, Greek Bible, and Qumran: Collected Essays.* TSAJ 121. Tübingen: Mohr Siebeck, 2008.

——. "Hebrew Scripture Editions: Philosophy and Praxis." Pages 281–312 in *From 4QMMT to Resurrection: Mélanges qumraniens en hommage à Émile Puech.* Edited by F. García Martínez et al. STDJ 61. Leiden: Brill, 2006.

——. "The Many Forms of Scripture: Reflections in Light of the LXX and 4QReworked Pentateuch." Pages 11–28 in *From Qumran to Aleppo: A Discussion with Emanuel Tov about the Textual History of Jewish Scriptures in Honor of His 65th Birthday.* Edited by A. Lange, M. Weigold, and J. Zsengellér. Göttingen: Vandenhoeck & Ruprecht, 2009.

——. "The Nature of the Large-Scale Differences between the LXX and MT S T V, Compared with Similar Evidence in Other Sources." Pages 121–44 in *The Earliest Text of the Hebrew Bible: The Relationship between the Masoretic Text and the Hebrew Base of the Septuagint Reconsidered.* Edited by A. Schenker. SBLSCS 52. Atlanta: Scholars Press, 2003.

——. *Scribal Practices and Approaches Reflected in the Texts Found in the Judean Desert.* STDJ 54. Leiden: Brill, 2004.

——. "Scribal Practices Reflected in the Texts from the Judaean Desert." Pages 403–29 in vol. 1 of *The Dead Sea Scrolls after Fifty Years: A Comprehensive Assessment.* Edited by P. W. Flint and J. C. VanderKam. Leiden: Brill, 1998.

——. "Some Thoughts about the Diffusion of Biblical Manuscripts in Antiquity." Pages 151–72 in *The Dead Sea Scrolls: Transmission of Traditions and Production of Texts.* Edited by S. Metso, H. Najman, and E. Schuller. Leiden: Brill, 2010.

——. *Textual Criticism of the Hebrew Bible.* 2nd ed. Minneapolis: Fortress, 2001.

Tov, Emanuel, and Sidnie White. "364–367. 4QReworked Pentateuch[b–e]." Pages 187–351 in *Qumran Cave 4.VIII: Parabiblical Texts, Part 1.* Edited by H. Attridge et al., in consultation with J. C. VanderKam. DJD 13. Oxford: Clarendon, 1994.

Trebolle Barrera, Julio. "Textual Variants in 4QJudg[a] and the Textual and Editorial History of the Book of Judges." *RevQ* 14 (1989): 229–45.

Trobisch, David. *Die Entstehung der Paulusbriefsammlung.* Freiburg: Universitätsverlag, 1989.

——. *The First Edition of the New Testament.* Oxford: Oxford University Press, 2000.

Tuckett, Christopher M. "P52 and Nomina Sacra." *NTS* 47 (2001): 544–48.

Ulrich, Eugene. "4QLev-Num[a]" and "4QLev[b]." Pages 153–87 in *Qumran Cave 4.VII: Genesis to Numbers.* Edited by Ulrich Eugene and Frank Moore Cross. DJD 12. Oxford: Clarendon, 1994.

——. "The Bible in the Making: The Scriptures at Qumran." Pages 77–93 in *The Community of the Renewed Covenant: The Notre Dame Symposium on the Dead Sea Scrolls.* Edited by Eugene Ulrich and James C. VanderKam. Notre Dame, Ind.: University of Notre Dame Press, 1994.

------. *The Dead Sea Scrolls and the Origins of the Bible.* Grand Rapids: Eerdmans, 1999.

------. "The Developmental Composition of the Book of Isaiah: Light from 1QIsa^a on Additions in the MT." *DSD* 8 (2001): 288–305.

------. "Double Literary Editions of Biblical Narratives and Reflections on Determining the Form to be Translated." Pages 101–16 in *Perspectives on the Hebrew Bible: Essays in Honor of Walter J. Harrelson.* Edited by J. L. Crenshaw. Macon, Ga.: Mercer University Press, 1988.

------. "From Literature to Scripture: Reflections on the Growth of a Text's Authoritativeness." *DSD* 10 (2003): 3–25.

------. "Multiple Literary Editions: Reflections toward a Theory of the History of the Biblical Text." Pages 78–105 in *Current Research and Technological Developments on the Dead Sea Scrolls: Conference on the Texts from the Judean Desert, Jerusalem, 30 April 1995.* Edited by D. W. Parry and S. D. Ricks. STDJ 20. Leiden: Brill, 1994.

------. "Pluriformity in the Biblical Text, Text Groups, and Questions of Canon." Pages 23–41 in *The Madrid Qumran Congress: Proceedings of the International Congress on the Dead Sea Scrolls, Madrid 18–21 March 1991.* Edited by J. C. Trebolle Barrera and L. Vegas Montaner. STDJ 11. Leiden: Brill, 1992.

------. "The Qumran Fragments of Joshua: Which Puzzle Are They Part of and Where Do They Fit?" Pages 159–94 in *Septuagint, Scrolls and Cognate Writings: Papers Presented to the International Symposium on the Septuagint and Its Relation to the Dead Sea Scrolls and Other Writings.* Edited by G. J. Brooke and B. Lindars. SBLSCS 33. Atlanta: Scholars Press, 1992.

------. "Qumran Witness to the Developmental Growth of the Prophetic Books." Pages 263–74 in *With Wisdom as a Robe: Qumran and Other Jewish Studies in Honour of Ida Fröhlich.* Edited by K. Daniel Dobos and M. Köszeghy. Hebrew Bible Monographs 21. Sheffield: Sheffield Phoenix, 2009.

------. "The Scrolls and the Biblical Text." Pages 79–100 in vol. 1 of *The Dead Sea Scrolls after Fifty Years: A Comprehensive Assessment.* Edited by P. W. Flint and J. C. VanderKam. Leiden: Brill, 1998.

------. "Our Sharper Focus on the Bible and Theology Thanks to the Dead Sea Scrolls." *CBQ* 66 (2004): 1–24.

Unnik, W. C. van. "*Hē kainē diathēkē*—A Problem in the Early History of the Canon." *Studia Patristica* 4 (1961): 212–27.

Urbina, Eduardo, Richard Furuta, Carlos Monroy, Neal Audenauert, Jie Deng, and Erika Pasquel. "The *Electronic Variorum Edition of 'Don Quixote'* at the Cervantes Project." Pages 205–19 in *Framing the Quixote, 1605–2005.* Edited by A. F. Sherman Jr. Provo: Brigham Young University, 2007.

Vaganay, Léon. *An Introduction to New Testament Textual Criticism.* Cambridge: Cambridge University Press, 1991.

------. *An Introduction to the Textual Criticism of the New Testament.* Translated by B. V. Miller. St. Louis: Herder, 1937.

Van Seters, John. *The Edited Bible: The Curious History of the "Editor" in Biblical Criticism.* Winona Lake, Ind.: Eisenbrauns, 2006.

———. "The Role of the Scribe in the Making of the Hebrew Bible." *JANER* 8 (2008): 99–129.

Verheyden, Josef. "Assessing Gospel Quotations in Justin Martyr." Pages 363–70 in *New Testament Textual Criticism and Exegesis: Festschrift J. Delobel.* Edited by A. Denaux. Leuven: Leuven University Press and Peeters, 2002.

Vielhauer, Philipp. *Geschichte der urchristlichen Literatur: Einleitung in das Neue Testament, die Apokryphen und die Apostolischen Väter.* 2nd ed. Berlin: de Gruyter, 1978.

Vogt, Hermann-Josef. "Die Geltung des Alten Testaments bei Irenäus von Lyon." *Theologische Quartalschrift* 160 (1980): 17–28.

Waard, Jan de. *Biblia Hebraica Quinta 17: Proverbs.* Stuttgart: Deutsche Bibelgesellschaft, 2007.

Wachtel, Klaus, and D. C. Parker. "The Joint IGNTP/INTF Editio Critica Maior of the Gospel of John: Its Goals and Their Significance for New Testament Scholarship." Online: http://epapers.bham.ac.uk/754/1/2005_SNTS_WachtelParker.pdf.

Wasserman, Tommy. "The Implications of Textual Criticism for Understanding the 'Original Text.'" Pages 77–96 in *Mark and Matthew: Text and Contexts.* Edited by Eve-Marie Becker and Anders Runesson. WUNT 271. Tübingen: Mohr Siebeck, 2011.

———. "P78 (P. Oxy XXXIV 2684): The Epistle of Jude on an Amulet?" Pages 137–60 in *New Testament Manuscripts: Their Texts and Their World.* Edited by T. J. Kraus and T. Nicklas. TENTS 2. Leiden: Brill, 2006.

———. "Papyrus 72 and the Bodmer Miscellaneous Codex." *NTS* 51 (2005): 137–54.

Weis, Richard D. "*Biblica Hebraica Quinta* and the Making of Critical Editions of the Hebrew Bible." *TC: A Journal of Biblical Textual Criticism* 7 (2002). Online: http://purl.org/TC.

Wellhausen, Julius. *Prolegomena to the History of Ancient Israel.* 1885. New York: Meridian, 1957.

West, Martin L. *Textual Criticism and Editorial Technique Applicable to Greek and Latin Texts.* Stuttgart: Teubner, 1973.

———. "The Textual Criticism and Editing of Homer." Pages 94–110 in *Editing Texts = Texte edieren.* Edited by G. W. Most. Aporemata 2. Göttingen: Vandenhoeck & Ruprecht, 1998.

Westcott, Brooke Foss, and Fenton John Anthony Hort, eds. *The New Testament in the Original Greek.* Vol. 1: *Text.* London: Macmillan, 1881; 2nd ed., 1896.

Westcott, Brooke Foss, and Fenton John Anthony Hort. *The New Testament in the Original Greek.* Vol. 2: *Introduction [and] Appendix.* London: Macmillan, 1896.

Wevers, John W. *Notes on the Greek Text of Leviticus.* Atlanta: Scholars Press, 1997.

———. *Text History of the Greek Leviticus.* MSU 19. Göttingen: Vandenhoeck & Ruprecht, 1986.

White Crawford, Sidnie, Jan Joosten, and Eugene Ulrich. "Sample Editions of the Oxford Hebrew Bible: Deuteronomy 32:1–9. 1 Kings 11:1–8, and Jeremiah 27:1–10 (34 G)." *VT* 58 (2008): 352–66.

Whitman, Cedric H. *Homer and the Homeric Tradition.* Cambridge: Harvard University Press, 1958.

Williamson, Hugh G. M. "Do We Need a New Bible? Reflections on the Proposed Oxford Hebrew Bible." *Bib* 90 (2009): 153–75.

Wisse, Fredrick. "The Nature and Purpose of Redactional Changes in Early Christian Texts: The Canonical Gospels." Pages 39–53 in *Gospel Traditions in the Second Century: Origins, Recensions, Text, and Transmission*. Edited by W. L. Petersen. Notre Dame: University of Notre Dame Press, 1989.

Wolf, F. A. *Prolegomena to Homer*. Translated by Anthony Grafton, Glenn W. Most, and James E. G. Zetzel. Princeton: Princeton University Press, 1985.

Zuntz, Günther. *The Text of the Epistles: A Disquistion Upon the Corpus Paulinum*. Schweich Lectures of the British Academy 1946. London: Published for the British Academy by Oxford University Press, 1953.

CONTRIBUTORS

Kristin De Troyer is Professor of Hebrew Bible/Old Testament at the University of St Andrews, Scotland.

Michael W. Holmes is University Professor of Biblical Studies and Early Christianity at Bethel University.

John S. Kloppenborg is Professor of Christian Origins in the Department for the Study of Religion at the University of Toronto.

Sarianna Metso is Associate Professor of Hebrew Bible, Dead Sea Scrolls, and Second Temple Judaism in the Departments of Historical Studies and Near and Middle Eastern Civilizations at the University of Toronto.

Judith H. Newman is Associate Professor of Hebrew Bible, Old Testament, and Early Judaism in the Department for the Study of Religion and Emmanuel College of Victoria University in the University of Toronto.

Holger Strutwolf is Professor and Director of the Institut für neutestamentliche Textforschung at the Westfälische Wilhelms-Universität Münster.

Eibert Tigchelaar is Research Professor in the Faculty of Theology and Religious Studies at the University of Leuven.

David Trobisch is Professor of New Testament at Bangor Theological Seminary.

Eugene Ulrich is the John A. O'Brien Professor of Theology at the University of Notre Dame.

John Van Seters is University Distinguished Professor Emeritus, University of North Carolina at Chapel Hill.

Klaus Wachtel is Research Associate in the Institut für neutestamentliche Textforschung at the Westfälische Wilhelms-Universität Münster.

Ryan Wettlaufer is Lecturer of New Testament in St. Michael's College at the University of Toronto.

INDEX OF PRIMARY SOURCES

Genesis

1:1–13	46
5	30–31
5:3–32 (SP)	30
11	30–31
11:10–32	31
12–22	26
12:1–3	26–27
12:10–19	26–27
14	26
15	26–27
16	26–27
18	26
18:1	28 n. 4
21	26–27
22	26–27
24:3	27
26:3–4	27
26:24	27
27:28–29	27
28:13–16	27
30:27	27
30:36	33
31:10–13	33
31:24	33 n. 13
31:29	33 n. 13
39:5	27
41:1–7	33 n. 13
41:17–24	33 n. 13

Exodus

3:6	27
3:16–18	27
4:5	27
12:32	27
20:17	32
25–31	31
32:7–14	27
35–39 (LXX)	31
35–40	89

Leviticus

1–7	72
1:17	69
10:10	76 n. 18
11:28	84–85
17–26	72
18:19	77 n. 19
19:17	76 n. 18
19:17–18	76 n. 18
19:19	77 n. 19
20:27	76 n. 18
21:17–21	77 n. 18
22:13	77 n. 19
22:16	76 n. 18
22:21–23	77 n. 18
25:9	77 n. 18
25:13	77 n. 18
25:31	85
27:29	77 n. 18

Numbers

| 14:1–19 | 27 |

Deuteronomy

5:10	46 n. 22
6:4	190
22	46 n. 21
22:15	46 n. 22
22:27	46 n. 22

Deuteronomy (*cont.*)		2 Kings	
22:28	46 n. 22	1:1–6	50 n. 33
22:29	46 n. 22		
24:14	46 n. 22	Isaiah	
27:1–3	34	13–23	29
27:4	35	24–27	29
32	46, 56 n. 59, 57		
32:1–9	46, 56	Jeremiah	
32:5a	57	7	29 n. 6
32:6	57	8	29 n. 6
32:8	46	10	29 n. 6
32:15	46	27:1–10	50
32:43	46 n. 22		
33	46	Ezekiel	
33:8	46 n. 22	36–40	36
34:1b–5a	27		
34:6	27	Daniel	
34:10	27	1–4 (LXX)	88
		4–6	48–49
Joshua			
4	34	Nehemiah	
5	34	10:35	33 n. 14
6	34	13:31	33 n. 14
10:11b	83		
10:23	84	NEW TESTAMENT	
Judges		Matthew	
6:2–6	35	5:17–20	190 n. 69
6:7–10	35	5:34	190
		19:17	118
1 Samuel			
1–2	49 n. 30	Mark	
16–18	49 n. 28	10:18	118 n. 86
17–18	48, 49 n. 30, 88 n. 30		
17:11	42 n. 6	Luke	
17:32–37	42 n. 6	18:19	118 n. 86
		22:43–44	6
1 Kings			
11	51	John	
11:1	51 n. 37, 57 n. 61, 59	7:53–8:11	6, 121 n. 95
11:1–2	59 n. 66		
11:1–8	50, 58	Acts	
11:8	59	16:12	167
		19:19	167

1 Corinthians
   4:6 — 187
   6:5 — 111–12
   14:34–35 — 171

Galatians
   6:11 — 166

Ephesians
   1:11 — 172

2 Thessalonians
   3:17 — 166

James
   1:11 — 146
   1:20 — 103
   2:3 — 132–37
   2:13 — 149–50, 153
   5:12 — 190

1 Peter
   1:2 — 146
   1:3 — 146
   1:6 — 142
   1:12 — 142
   1:24 — 142
   2:3 — 146
   2:18 — 148
   2:21 — 144
   3:7 — 143
   3:10 — 143
   3:14 — 146
   4:3 — 146
   4:17 — 146
   5:1 — 143–44, 157
   5:9 — 143
   5:22–24b — 143

2 Peter
   1:2b — 144
   1:4 — 143
   1:8 — 143
   2:12 — 143
   2:20 — 156

   3:7 — 143
   3:10 — 111, 129, 171

1 John
   2:20 — 145
   2:28 — 145
   3:6 — 145
   3:19 — 145
   4:18 — 145
   5:2 — 145
   5:7–8 — 6
   5:15 — 145
   5:20 — 145

2 John
   12 — 145

Jude
   5 — 145
   5b — 144
   8 — 145
   16 — 142

Revelation
   22:18–22 — 169

DEAD SEA SCROLLS

CD (Damascus Document)
   6:14–21 — 76 n. 18
   9:1 — 77 n. 18
   9:2–4 — 76 n. 18
   12:1b–2a — 77 n. 18

1QS (Rule of the Community)
   5:14–15 — 76 n. 18
   5:24–6:1 — 76 n. 18

1QSa (Rule of the Congregation)
   1:5–9 — 77 n. 18

1Q3 (paleoLev)
   frgs. 1–7, 22–24 — 78

4Q28 (4QD^f)		393	143
5 I, 18–19	77 n. 18	398	142
		424	148, 149
4Q364 (4QRP^b)		424C	142
frg. 4b–e II, 21–26	33 n. 13	429	127, 128, 137
		468	135
4Q365 (4QRPc)		522	126
frg. 23, 5–11	33 n. 13	614	148, 149
		623	149
Schøyen Papyri		630	126–128
		642	135
2648	81, 83	665T	143
2649	81	761	127
4611	67 n. 2	996	135, 142
		0142	142
New Testament Manuscripts		1127	143
(manuscripts listed in the		1241	143
diagrams are not noted)		1292	126
		1292	149
P20	132, 189	1409	142
P23	132, 189	1409	143
P45	141	1505	137
P46	6, 112, 141	1661	142
P47	141	1729	142
P52	91 n. 1	1739	134
P54	132	1735	143
P66	141	1735	159
P72	141–44, 148–49, 156, 159	1799	126
P74	132	2200	126–128
P75	121, 141	2186	145
P90	91 n. 1	2423	135
P98	91 n. 1	2495	137
P104	91 n. 1	2544	142
		2464	148, 149
04	135	K:SMSS	148
6	143	L:V	143
35	135		
43	143	Apostolic Fathers	
69	148, 149		
81	135, 148, 149	Ignatius, *To the Ephesians*	
93	143	1.3ff.	166
181C	143		
206	126–27, 129	Ignatius, *To the Romans*	
218	135	6.3	143
330	143		

Shepherd of Hermas, *Vision*
8.3   163

CLASSICAL AND ANCIENT CHRISTIAN
WRITINGS

Cicero, *Epistulae ad Atticum*
12.6.3   163 n. 9
16.6.4   163 n. 8

Clement of Alexandria, *Stromata*
2.29.2–3   162 n. 3

Eusebius, *Historia ecclesiastica*
3.39.4   168

Horace, *Epistulae*
1.20   162, 164

Irenaeus, *Adversus haereses*
3.4.3   168 n. 18

Josephus, *Antiquities*
5.20   34
5.45–57   34

Josephus, *Vita*
416–418   77 n. 21

Justin Martyr, *Dialogus cum Tryphone*
101.2   118

Martial, *Epigrammata*
1.117   163 n. 9

Origen, *In Joannem*
5.8   162 n. 3

Philo, *De Specialibus Legibus*
1.129–130   77 n. 19
3.32–33   77 n. 19
4.203   77 n. 19

Pliny the Younger, *Epistulae*
5.10   164 n. 9

Tertullian, *Adversus Marcionem*
4.4.1–2   168 n. 18

Tertullian, *Adversus Praxean*
15   162 n. 3

Tertullian, *De praescriptione haereticorum*
21–22   168 n. 18

Tertullian, *De pudicitia*
1   162 n. 3

Index of Modern Authors

Abegg, Martin, Jr. 76 n. 17
Aejmelaeus, Anneli 31 n. 10, 74 n. 14
Aland, Barbara 93 n. 9, 98 nn. 19–23, 99 n. 25–27, 103 n. 41, 106 n. 49, 109 n. 58, n. 63, 124 n. 3, 125 n. 7, 142 n. 11, 143, 156 n. 19, 176 n. 22
Aland, Kurt 92 n. 4–5, 93 n. 9, 95 n. 12, n. 14, 98–100, 103 n. 41,106 n. 49, 109 n. 58, n. 63, 124 n. 3, 130 n. 9, 141 n. 6, 142 n. 11, 156 n. 19, 176 n. 22, 179 n. 33
Albrektson, Bertil 21 n. 34
Allen, Thomas W. 18 n. 27
Allert, Craig D. 119 n. 88
Amir, Yehoshua 77 n. 19
Amphoux, Christian 91 n. 1, 107 n. 54, 115 n. 79
Attridge, Harold W. 33 n. 12
Audenauert, Neal 65 n. 84
Aune, David E. 141 n. 6
Auwers, Jean-Marie 119 n. 88
Barbrook, Adrian C. 123 n. 2
Bardtke, H. 45 n. 19
Barrera, J. Trebolle 35 n. 17, 48 n. 26
Bartelmus, Rüdiger 164 n. 12
Becker, Eve-Marie 120 n. 92
Bellinzoni, Arthur J. 119 n. 88
Bengel, Johann Albrecht 140 n. 2
Birdsall, J. Neville 150 n. 17
Black, David Alan 92 n. 3, 175 n. 21, 183 n. 46
Black, John Sutherland 14 n. 14
Black, Matthew 92 n. 4
Blake, Norman 123 n. 2
Blenkinsopp, Joseph 29 n. 7

Boer, Piet A. H. de 62 n. 75
Bovon, François 114 n. 75
Bowers, Fredson 56 n. 55
Bowyer, William 174 n. 17
Brinkman, Herman 49 n. 28
Brooke, A. E. 83 n. 10, 84 n. 14
Brooke, George J. 84 n. 13
Brown, Scott G. 115 n. 79
Brownlee, William H. 45 n. 17
Bultmann, Rudolf 15 n. 19
Burrows, Millar 45 n. 17
Butterworth, G. W. 173 n. 12
Campenhausen, Hans von 161 n. 2
Capes, David B. 91 n. 1
Carson, Donald A. 181 n. 39
Cavallo, Guglielmo 81 n. 1
Childers, Jeff W. 117 n. 83
Clark, Elizabeth A. 110 n. 64
Collins, Adela Yarbro 115 n. 79
Colwell, Ernest C. 109 n. 62, 141 n.6, 150 n. 17
Conzelmann, Hans 16 n. 21
Crawford, Sidnie White 33 n. 12, 42 n. 6, 50 n. 33, 56 n. 58, 57 n. 62
Crisp, Simon 104 n. 44
Cross, Frank Moore 10 n. 4, 61 n. 72, 69 n. 5
Crenshaw, James L. 47 n. 26
Crüsemann, Frank 72 n. 9
Dahl, Nils A. 15 n. 18, 106 n. 51
Davids, Peter 189 n. 65, 190 n. 68, 191 n. 71, 192 n. 79
Debel, Hans 47 n. 25
Delobel, Joël 106 n. 49
Denaux, Adelbert 117 n. 82, 119 n. 89

Deng, Jie 65 n. 84

Dibelius, Martin 188 n. 62–63, 189 n. 65, 191 n. 73, 192 n. 77–78

Dodds, E. R. 174 n. 13

Dunsany, Lord 162 n. 4

Ehrman, Bart D. 92 n. 3, 109 n. 63, 139 n. 1, 175 n. 18, 177, 181, 182 n. 45, 183 n. 48, 185–86

Elliger, Kurt 43 n. 11, 62 n. 75

Elliott, James Keith 91 n. 1, 109 n. 63, 115 n. 79, 175 n. 21, 177 n. 27

Emonds, Hilarius 108 n. 55

Enzies, Allen 14 n. 14

Epp, Eldon Jay 91 n. 1, 98 n. 23, 106 nn. 50–51, 121 n. 97, 139 n. 1, 175 n. 18, 177 n. 30, 182 nn. 42–44, 183 nn. 46–47, 50–51, 184 n. 52

Eshel, Esther 69 n. 5

Evans, Craig A. 71 n. 8, 77 n. 20,

Evans, Ernest 168 n. 18

Fee, Gordon D. 98 n. 23, 175 n. 18

Feldman, Louis H. 77 n. 20

Fernández Marcos, Natalio 82 n. 3

Fields, Weston W. 41 n. 1

Fischer, Joseph 162 n. 3

Fishbane, Michael 15 n. 17, 41 n. 1

Flint, Peter W. 76 n. 17, 89 n. 39

Foster, Paul 119 n. 88

Freedman, David N. 70 n. 7, 73 n. 12

Furuta, Richard 65 n. 84

Gamble, Harry Y. 106 n. 51, 107 nn. 52 and 54, 161 n. 2

García Martínez, Florentino 41 n. 1

Georgi, Dieter 164 n. 12

Gooding, David W. 32 n. 10

Ginsburg, Christian D. 9 n. 2

Goodspeed, Edgar J. 141 n. 6

Goshen-Gottstein, Moshe H. 38, 41 nn. 1 and 3, 43 n. 9, n. 13, 45 n. 20, 49 n. 31

Grafton, Anthony 13 n. 12

Greenlee, Harold 175 n. 20, 76 n. 26

Greenspoon, Leonard J. 83 n. 12, 84 n. 13

Greg, Walter W. 53 nn. 45–8, 56 n. 55, 58 n. 63

Gregory, Andrew F. 117 n. 82

Griesbach, Johann Jakob 140 n. 3, 4

Grigely, Joseph 110 n. 64

Giuliani, Luigi 49 n. 28

Haines-Eitzen, Kim 120 n. 93

Harlé, Paul 75 n. 15

Harnack, Adolf von 162 n. 3

Hecht, Richard D. 77 n. 19

Heckel, Theo K. 119 n. 88

Hendel, Ronald S. 31 n. 9, 42 nn. 5–7, 44 n. 15, 46 n. 24, 48 n. 26, 50 n. 32, n. 34, n. 36, 53 n. 44, 56 n. 56, 58 n. 63, 61

Herbert, Edward D. 43 n. 8

Hernández, Juan, Jr. 144 n. 13

Hills, Edward F. 181 n. 38

Hoffmann, Joseph 168 n. 18

Hoh, Josef 162 n. 3

Hollander, August den 101 n. 34, 124 n. 4

Holmes, Michael W. 91 n. 2, 92 n. 3, 106 n. 49, 107 n. 54, 109 n. 63, 117 n. 83, 120 n. 92, 124 n. 4, 139 n. 1

Horgan, Maurya P. 177 n. 30

Hort, Fenton John Anthony 96 n. 16, 98 n. 23, 109 n. 60, n. 62, 111 n. 68, 112 n. 70, 160 n. 20, 177 n. 28, 178 n. 32, 179 n. 35

Howe, Christopher J. 123 n. 2, 124 n. 5, 126 n. 7

Hurtado, Larry W. 117 n. 83

Hyatt, J. Philip 179 n. 33

Janko, Richard 19 n. 27

Johnson, Luke Timothy 189 n. 67, 191 n. 70, 75

Jonge, Henk Jan de 119 n. 88

Joosten, Jan 42 n. 6, 46 n. 24, 51 n. 37

Juckel, Andreas 125 n. 7

Kahle, Paul E. 10 n. 2, 43 n. 11

Kelemen, Erick 110 n. 64

Kenney, Edward J. 9 n. 1, 12 n. 10

Kenyon, Frederick G. 175

Ker, Walter Charles Alan 165 n. 14

Kilpatrick, George D. 177 n. 27, 182 n. 41, 187 n. 58

King, Marchant A. 144 n. 12
Kittel, Rudolf 43 n. 11
Klein, Ralph W. 31 n. 8
Kline, Leslie L. 119 n. 88
Kloha, Jeffrey 111 n. 67
Knohl, Israel 72 n. 9
Kobelski, Paul J. 177 n. 30
Koch, Dietrich-Alex 147 n. 16
Koch, Klaus 16 n. 23
Koester, Helmut 114 nn. 75–76, 115 n. 78, 116 n. 81, 119 n. 88
Kooij, Arie van der 14 n. 16, 43 n. 8
Krans, Jan 174 nn. 14–16, 179 n. 36, n. 37, 185 n. 53
Kraus, Thomas J. 144 n. 12, 178 n. 30
Kuenen, Abraham 14 n. 16
Kugler, Robert 69 n. 6
Lange, Armin 33 n. 11, 47 n. 25, 86 n. 23
Lernout, Geert 49 n. 28
Lieberman, Saul 18 n. 26, 170 n. 20
Lindars, Barnabas 84 n. 13
Lowering, Jr. Eugene H. 77 n. 19
Luck, Georg 187 n. 56
Maas, Paul 108 n. 56, 172 n. 4, 73 nn. 8 and 10
Mack, Burton L. 77 n. 19
Marcus, David 42 n. 4
Marquis, G. 33 n. 11
Martin, Ralph P. 192 n. 76
Martini, Carlo Maria 92 n. 4
Marxsen, Willi 16 n. 21–22
Mason, Steve 77 n. 20
Massebieau, Louis 188 n. 59
Mathews, Kenneth A. 69 n. 5, 70 n. 7, 73 n. 12
Mathijsen, Marita 49 n. 28
Mayor, Joseph B. 191 n. 74
McDonald, Lee Martin 71 n. 8
McGann, Jerome J. 48 n. 27, 105 n. 47
McKane, William 11 n. 8, 12 n. 11
McLean, Norman 83 n. 10, 84 n. 14
Metso, Sarianna 51 n. 40, 69 n. 6
Metzger, Bruce M. 9 n. 1, 92 n. 4, 95 n. 15, 96 n. 16, 172 n. 5, 175 nn. 18–19, 76 n. 25

Milgrom, Jacob 72 n. 9
Miller, B. V. 106 n. 48
Mink, Gerd 93 n. 9, 101 n. 34, 124 n. 4, 129 n. 8, 130 n. 10, 142 n. 11, 147 n. 16
Minutoli, D. 81 n. 1
Monroy, Carlos 65 n. 84
Most, Glenn W. 13 n. 12, 62 n. 76
Mülke, Markus 108 n. 55
Mulken, Margot van 101 n. 34, 124 n. 4
Mullen, Roderic L. 104 n. 44
Naeh, Shlomo 41 n. 3
Najman, Hindy 51 n. 40, 71 n. 8
Nicklas, Tobias 144 n. 12, 178 n. 30
Nodet, Étienne 77 n. 20
Noth, Martin 15 n. 20, 27 n. 3
Oakley, Michael 162 n. 4
Orlinsky, Harry M. 9 n. 2, 10 n. 3
Ottley, R. R. 167 n. 17
Parker, David C. 102 n. 37, 104 n. 44, 105 n. 46, 107 n. 54, 110 n. 65, 113 nn. 72–74, 117 n. 83, 119 n. 90, 122 n. 98, 147 n. 15, 182 n. 45, 183 n. 49
Parry, Donald W. 48 n. 26, 68 n. 4
Parvis, Sara 119 n. 88
Pasquel, Erika 65 n. 84
Patterson, Lee 105 n. 47
Peters, M. 85 n. 17
Petersen, William L. 106 n. 49, 114 n. 75, 116 n. 80, 117 nn. 82–84, 118 nn. 85, 87, 119 n. 88, 120 n. 91
Pheiffer, Robert H. 20 n. 32
Pierpont, William G. 93 n. 6, n. 8, 94 nn. 10–11
Pintaudi, Rosario 81 n. 1
Piquer Otero, Andrés 50 n. 33
Porter, Stanley E. 106 n. 50, 178 n. 30
Pralon, Didier 75 n. 15
Rabin, Chaim 41 n. 3
Rad, Gerhard von 15 n. 20
Reenen, Pieter van 101 n. 34, 124 n. 4, 147 n. 16
Reinhartz, Adele 77 n. 19
Rendtdorff, Rolf 69 n. 6
Rhodes, Erroll F. 98 n. 19, 175 n. 18, 176 n. 22, n. 24

Richards, E. Randolph 107 n. 52

Ricks, Stephen D. 48 n. 26, 68 n. 4

Rico, Francisco 60 n. 68

Robinson, Maurice A. 93 n. 6, n. 8, 94 n. 10

Robinson, Peter 123 n. 2

Rofé, Alexander 14 n. 16

Rosenblum, Joseph 53 n. 45

Royse, James Ronald 141 nn. 5 and 7, 143–44 n. 12, 153 n. 18

Rudolph, Wilhelm 43 n. 11

Runesson, Anders 120 n. 92

Runia, David T. 77 n. 19

Rushton, Fairclough 165 n. 13

Sanday, William 114 n. 77, 115 n. 77

Sanders, James A. 42 n. 7, 71 n. 8

Sanders, Paul 56 n. 59

Schenker, Adrian 42 n. 4, n. 7, 52 n. 42

Schiffman, Lawrence H. 33 n. 11, 69 n. 5

Schubart, Wilhem 163 n. 5, n. 8–9, 164 n. 10

Schuller, Eileen 51 n. 40

Segal, Michael 33 n. 11, 41 n. 3

Sherman, Alvin F. 65 n. 84

Shillingsburg, Peter L. 49 n. 29

Skarsaune, Oskar 119 n. 88

Skehan, Patrick W. 46 n. 23

Smith, W. Robertson 14 n. 14

Soisalon-Soininen, Ilmari 83 n. 9, 84 n. 16

Spencer, Matthew 124 n. 5, 125 nn. 5–6, 126 n. 7

Spitta, Friedrich 188 nn. 60–61

Stanton, Graham N. 119 n. 88

Steck, Odil H. 16 n. 23

Stemplinger, Eduard 163 n. 7

Stendahl, Krister 171 n. 1

Stewart, Robert 117 n. 83

Strecker, Georg 119 n. 88

Strugnell, John 187 n. 57

Strutwolf, Holger 93 n. 9, 124 n. 3, 142 n. 11

Swete, Henry Barclay 167 n. 17

Talmon, Shemaryahu 10 n. 4, 41 n. 3, 45 n. 20, 49 n. 31

Tanselle, G. Thomas 54 nn. 49–50, 56 n. 55, 58 n. 63, 60 n. 67

Thackeray, Henry St. John 83 n. 10, 84 n. 14, 173 n. 11

Tigchelaar, Eibert 22 n. 36

Tischendorf, Constantin von 142 n. 10

Toorn, Karel van der 19 nn. 28–29, 31, 20 n. 33, 51 nn. 39 and 41

Trebolle Barrera, Julio C. 35 nn. 17–18, 48 n. 26

Tov, Emanuel 17 n. 24, 33 nn. 11–12, 41 nn. 1 and 3, 42 n. 7, 43 n. 8, 47 n. 25, 49 n. 28, 51 nn. 38 and 40, 52 n. 42, 55 n. 53, 57 n. 59, 62 n. 77, 64 nn. 80–81, 69 n. 5, 81 n. 2, 84 n. 15, 86 n. 22, 88 nn. 35–36, 89 nn. 38–39, 90 nn. 43–46, 106 n. 48, 182 n. 44

Trever, John C. 45 n. 17

Trobisch, David 161 n. 1, 169 n. 19

Tuckett, Christopher M. 117 n. 82

Tune, Ernst W. 150 n. 17

Ulrich, Eugene 10 n. 6, 21 n. 34, 29 n. 6, 32–33 n. 11, 40 n. 21, 42 n. 6, 47 n. 26, 49 n. 28, 50 n. 36, 68 n. 4, 69 nn. 5–6, 71 n. 8, 76 n. 17, 84 n. 13, 87 nn. 26–29, 88 nn. 32–34, 89 nn. 40–42

Unnik, Willem C. van 162 n. 3

Urbina, Eduardo 65 n. 84

Vaganay, Léon 106 n. 48

Van Seters, John 10 n. 5, 11 n. 7, 14 n. 15, 18 n. 25, 19 n. 30, 25 n. 1, 28 n. 5, 182 n. 44

VanderKam, James C. 33 n. 11–12, 69 n. 5, 89 n. 39

Vegas Montaner, Luis 48 n. 26

Verheyden, Joseph 119 n. 89

Vielhauer, Philipp 165 n. 15

Vogt, Hermann-Josef 162 n. 3

Wachtel, Klaus 92 n. 2, 93 n. 9, 102 n. 37, 105 n. 46, 124 nn. 3, 5, 125–126 n. 7, 142 n. 11

Wasserman, Tommy 120 n. 92, 144 n. 12

Watson, W. G. E. 82 n. 3

Wegner, Paul D.   86 n. 25, 87 n. 25

Weis, Richard D.   42 n. 7, 61 n. 70

Wellhausen, Julius   14 n. 14

Weren, Wim   147 n. 16

West, Martin L.   62 n. 76, 63 n. 78, 172 n. 6, 180 n. 35

Westcott, Brooke Foss   96 n. 16, 98 n. 23, 109 n. 60, n. 62, 111 n. 68, 112 n. 70, 160 n. 20, 177 n. 28, 178 n. 32, 179 n. 34

Wevers, John W.   74 n. 14, 75 n. 16, 85 nn. 18, 20–21

Whitman, Cedric H.   19 n. 27

Wikgren, Allen   92 n. 4

Williamson, Hugh G. M.   42 n. 7, 44 n. 16, 63 n. 79, 64 n. 82

Wisse, Frederik   116 n. 80, 120 n. 91

Witte, Klaus   146 n. 14

Wolf, Friedrich A.   13 nn. 12–13

Zetzel, James E. G.   13 n. 12

Zsengellér, J.   33 n. 11

Zuntz, Günther   107 n. 53, 108 n. 57, 109 n. 59, n. 61–62, 111 n. 67, 112 nn. 69–70

CPSIA information can be obtained at www.ICGtesting.com
Printed in the USA
BVOW010335160812

297930BV00003B/71/P